Praise for The Impact Guides

The World's Only Travel-Shopping Series

WHAT TRAVEL CRITICS AND PROFESSIONALS SAY ABOUT THE IMPACT GUIDES

"YOU LEARN MORE ABOUT A PLACE you are visiting when Impact is pointing the way." – **The Washington Post**

"THE DEFINITIVE GUIDE to shopping in Asia." – **Arthur Frommer**, The Arthur Frommer Almanac of Travel

"THE BEST travel book I've ever read." – Kathy Osiro, **TravelAge West**

"AN EXCELLENT, EXHAUSTIVE, AND FASCINATING look at shopping in the East . . . it's difficult to imagine a shopping tour without this pocket-size book in hand." – **Travel & Leisure**

"BOOKS IN THE SERIES help travelers recognize quality and gain insight to local customs." – **Travel-Holiday**

"THE BEST GUIDE I've seen on shopping in Asia. If you enjoy the sport, you'll find it hard to put down . . . They tell you not only the where and what of shopping but the important how, and all in enormous but easy-to-read detail." – **Seattle Post-Intelligencer**

"ONE OF THE BEST GUIDEBOOKS of the season – not just shopping strategies, but a Baedeker to getting around . . . definitely a quality work. Highly recommended." – **Arkansas Democrat**

"WILL WANT TO LOOK INTO . . . has shopping strategies and travel tips about making the most of a visit to those areas. The book covers Asia's shopping centers, department stores, emporiums, factory outlets, markets and hotel shopping arcades where visitors can find jewelry, leather goods, woodcarvings, textiles, antiques, cameras, and primitive artifacts." – **Chicago Tribune**

"FULL OF SUGGESTIONS. The art of bartering, including every-day shopping basics are clearly defined, along with places to hang your hat or lift a fork." – **The Washington Post**

"A WONDERFUL GUIDE . . . filled with essential tips as well as a lot of background information . . . a welcome addition on your trip." – **Travel Book Tips**

"WELL ORGANIZED AND COMPREHENSIVE BOOK. A useful companion for anyone planning a shopping spree in Asia." – **International Living**

"OFFERS SOME EXTREMELY VALUABLE INFORMA-TION and advice about what is all too often a spur-of-the-moment aspect of your overseas travel."* – **Trip & Tour**

"A MORE UNUSUAL, PRACTICAL GUIDE than most and is no mere listing of convenience stores abroad . . . contains unusual tips on bargaining in Asia . . . country-specific tips are some of the most valuable chapters of the guidebook, setting it apart from others which may general-ize upon Asia as a whole, or focus upon the well-known Hong Kong shopping pleasures."* – **The Midwest Book Review**

"I LOVED THE BOOK! Why didn't I have this book two months ago! . . . a valuable guide . . . very helpful for the first time traveler in Asia . . . worth packing in the suitcase for a return visit."* – Editor, **Unique & Exotic Travel Reporter**

"VERY USEFUL, PERFECTLY ORGANIZED. Finally a guide that combines Asian shopping opportunities with the tips and know-how to really get the best buys."* – **National Motorist**

"INFORMATION-PACKED PAGES point out where the best shops are located, how to save time when shopping, and where and when to deal . . . You'll be a smarter travel shopper if you follow the advice of this new book."* – **AAA World**

"DETAILED, AND RELEVANT, EVEN ABSORBING in places . . . The authors know their subject thoroughly, and the reader can benefit greatly from their advice and tips. They go a long way to remov-ing any mystery or uneasiness about shopping in Asia by the neophyte."* – **The Small Press Book Review**

WHAT SEASONED TRAVELERS SAY, INCLUDING STORIES THAT CHANGED LIVES

"IMMENSELY USEFUL . . . thanks for sharing the fruits of your incredibly thorough research. You saved me hours of time and put me in touch with the best."* – **C.N.**, DeKalb, Illinois

"FABULOUS! I've just returned from my third shopping trip to Southeast Asia in three years. This book, which is now wrinkled, torn, and looking much abused, has been my bible for the past three years. All your suggestions (pre-trip) and information was so great. When I get ready to go again, my 'bible,' even though tattered and torn, will accom-pany me again! Thanks again for all your wonderful knowledge, and for sharing it!"* – **D.P.**, Havertown, Pennsylvania

"I LOVE IT. I've read a lot of travel books, and of all the books of this nature, this is the best I've ever read. Especially for first timers, the how-to information is invaluable."* – **A.K.**, Portland, Oregon

"THE BEST TRAVEL BOOK I'VE EVER READ. Believe me, I know my travel books!"* – **S.T.**, Washington, DC

"MANY MANY THANKS for your wonderful, useful travel guide! You have done a tremendous job. It is so complete and precise and full of neat info." – **K.H.**, Seattle, Washington

"FABULOUS BOOK! I just came back from Hong Kong, Thailand, and Singapore and found your book invaluable. Every place you recommended I found wonderful quality shopping. Send me another copy for my friend in Singapore who was fascinated with it." – **M.G.**, Escondido, California

"THIS IS MY FIRST FAN LETTER TO A BOOK . . . you made our trip to Indonesia more special than I can ever say. I not only carried it in my backpack everyday, I shared it with everyone I met, including a friend in Hong Kong, who liked it so much he kept it and I had to go out and buy another copy for myself when I got back stateside. The book taught us the customs, and through your teachings on how to bargain, I would even draw crowds to watch the Westerner bargain, and some wonderful chats afterwards, always starting off with 'You good bargainer. Where you from?' It was a wonderful trip and we credit your book for making it so. Thank you from my husband and myself, and everyone else we shared your book with." – **N.H.**, New York, New York

"YOU SAVED ME . . . hurry up with the next book so I can find out what I did wrong in Burma!" – **N.H.**, Chiang Mai, Thailand

"I FURNISHED MY HOME IN FLORIDA using your wonderful books. What countries are you doing next?" – **A.A.**, New York City

"I WANT YOU TO KNOW HOW MUCH I ENJOYED YOUR BOOK. Like many people, I picked up a ton of guide books to China before we took off on our trip in May. However, yours was totally unique, and it was not until we had finished our trip that I fully appreciated everything you covered. It was also the only guidebook I took with us. Your book was the only one that mentioned the Painter's Village in Chongqing. When we arrived in Chongqing early in the morning, our guide told me the village was included in the tour, but several people wanted to skip it and go to the zoo. Fortunately, I was able to lobby the many art lovers on the tour by showing them what you had to say about the village and we did end up visiting it. It was a lovely day and the flowers were in bloom in the gardens surrounding the village. We were greeted warmly and enjoyed visiting some of the artists. I purchased two numbered prints and, although I did not meet the artist, I did get his business card. Once home, the prints were framed and I took a picture of them and wrote to the artist to see what he could tell me about them. Imagine my surprise when several weeks later I received an e-mail from him. His mother and father, both famous artists, lived in the village and his mother had forwarded my letter to their son who now lives in Tokyo. He is a well known illustrator . . . We have been corresponding by e-mail for nearly a year and I have been helping him with his English and in doing his website in English . . . We are looking forward to the day when we can have him visit us in California. Thank you for leading us to one of the highlights of Chongqing for without that experience we would not have found a new and valued friend who has taught us much about China and life under Mao." – **C.S.**, California

"I'VE USED YOUR BOOKS FOR YEARS – *earlier, the book on shopping in Thailand was wonderful and more recently your best of India has been very useful."* – **S.M.**, Prince George, British Columbia, Canada

"I WOULD JUST LIKE TO SAY HOW MUCH I ENJOY YOUR SERIES. *I have been an avid shopper and traveler for many years and it has often been difficult finding even a decent chapter on shopping, let alone an entire book. Your guides are a wonderful contribution to the industry."* – **H.P.**, Honolulu, Hawaii

"GREAT! *I followed your advice in Bangkok and Hong Kong and it was great. Thanks again."* – **B.G.**, Los Angeles, California

"WE ADORE ASIA! *We like it better than any other part of the world . . . We have copies of your earlier editions and they are our "Asian Bibles." We also want to compliment you on doing such a masterful research job, especially on what to buy and where. Thanks to you we have some beautiful and treasured pieces from Asia. We could not have done it without your books."* **L.C.**, Palm Beach, Florida

"WE TOOK YOUR BOOK *(to China) and had to concur with everything you said. We could hardly believe that 80-90% discounts were in order, but we soon found out that they were!! The Friendship Stores were everything you described. Many thanks for the book, it certainly was a help."* – **L.G.**, Adelaide, Australia

"AFTER REVIEWING MANY TRAVEL GUIDES, *I chose this book (China) to buy because it gave me not only insight to the same cities I am about to tour, but the how to's as well. With limited time in each city, I can go directly to the "best of the best" in accommodations, restaurants, sightseeing, entertaining, and shopping. It has also supplied me with advice on how to bargain!"* – an Amazon.com buyer

"WE LOVED THE GUIDE. *It's wonderful (Rio and São Paulo). We don't have anything like this in São Paulo."* – **M.M.**, São Paulo, Brazil

"LOVE YOUR GUIDE *to India. Thanks so much."* – **B.P.**, Minneapolis, Minnesota

THE TREASURES AND PLEASURES
OF VIETNAM AND CAMBODIA

By Drs. Ron and Caryl Krannich

TRAVEL AND INTERNATIONAL BOOKS

Best Resumes and CVs for International Jobs
Directory of Websites for International Jobs
International Jobs Directory
Jobs For People Who Love to Travel
Mayors and Managers in Thailand
Politics of Family Planning Policy in Thailand
Shopping and Traveling in Exotic Asia
Shopping in Exotic Places
Shopping the Exotic South Pacific
Travel Planning on the Internet
Treasures and Pleasures of Australia
Treasures and Pleasures of China
Treasures and Pleasures of Egypt
Treasures and Pleasures of Hong Kong
Treasures and Pleasures of India
Treasures and Pleasures of Indonesia
Treasures and Pleasures of Italy
Treasures and Pleasures of Morocco
Treasures and Pleasures of Mexico
Treasures and Pleasures of Paris and the French Riviera
Treasures and Pleasures of the Philippines
Treasures and Pleasures of Rio and São Paulo
Treasures and Pleasures of Singapore and Bali
Treasures and Pleasures of Singapore and Malaysia
Treasures and Pleasures of Southern Africa
Treasures and Pleasures of Thailand
Treasures and Pleasures of Turkey
Treasures and Pleasures of Vietnam and Cambodia

BUSINESS AND CAREER BOOKS AND SOFTWARE

101 Dynamite Answers to Interview Questions
101 Secrets of Highly Effective Speakers
201 Dynamite Job Search Letters
America's Top Internet Sites
Best Jobs For the 21st Century
Change Your Job, Change Your Life
The Complete Guide to International Jobs and Careers
The Complete Guide to Public Employment
The Directory of Federal Jobs and Employers
Discover the Best Jobs For You!
Dynamite Cover Letters
Dynamite Networking For Dynamite Jobs
Dynamite Resumes
Dynamite Salary Negotiations
Dynamite Tele-Search
The Educator's Guide to Alternative Jobs and Careers
Find a Federal Job Fast!
From Air Force Blue to Corporate Gray
From Army Green to Corporate Gray
From Navy Blue to Corporate Gray
Get a Raise in 7 Days
High Impact Resumes and Letters
Interview For Success
Job-Power Source and *Ultimate Job Source* (software)
Jobs and Careers With Nonprofit Organizations
Military Resumes and Cover Letters
Moving Out of Education
Moving Out of Government
Re-Careering in Turbulent Times
Resumes & Job Search Letters For Transitioning Military Personnel
Savvy Interviewing
Savvy Networker
Savvy Resume Writer

IMPACT GUIDES

THE TREASURES
AND PLEASURES OF

Vietnam
and Cambodia

BEST OF THE BEST IN
TRAVEL AND SHOPPING

RON AND CARYL KRANNICH, PH.DS

IMPACT PUBLICATIONS
MANASSAS PARK, VA

Photos: All cover and text photos were taken by Ron and Caryl Krannich and Tom and Nancy Dungan during 2001.

Library of Congress Cataloguing-in-Publication Data

Krannich, Ronald L.
  The treasures and pleasures of Vietnam and Cambodia:
  best of the best in travel and shopping / Ronald L. Krannich,
  Caryl Rae Krannich
      p. cm. – (Impact guides)
  Includes bibliographical references and index.
  ISBN 1-57023-156-7
      1. Shopping – Vietnam – Guidebooks. 2. Shopping –
  Cambodia – Guidebooks. 3. Vietnam – Guidebooks.
  4. Cambodia – Guidebooks. I. Krannich, Caryl Rae.
  II. Title. III. Series.

  TX337.V5 K73 2001
  380.1'45'00025597–dc21   2001039823

Publisher: For information on Impact Publications, including current and forthcoming publications, authors, press kits, related websites, online bookstore, and submission requirements, visit Impact's website: www.impactpublications.com. For additional information on this and other books in the series, see these related websites: www.ishoparoundtheworld.com and www.contentfortravel.com.

Publicity/Rights: For information on publicity, author interviews, and subsidiary rights, contact the Media Relations Department: Tel. 703-361-7300, Fax 703-335-9486, or email info@impactpub lications.com.

Sales/Distribution: All bookstore sales are handled through Impact's trade distributor: National Book Network, 15200 NBN Way, Blue Ridge Summit, PA 17214, Tel. 1-800-462-6420. All other sales and distribution inquiries should be directed to the publisher: Sales Department, IMPACT PUBLICATIONS, 9104 Manassas Drive, Suite N, Manassas Park, VA 20111-5211, Tel. 703-361-7300, Fax 703-335-9486, or email info@impactpublica tions.com.

Contents

PART II
Great Destinations

Liabilities and Warranties

WHILE THE AUTHORS HAVE ATTEMPTED to provide accurate information, please remember that names, addresses, phone and fax numbers, email addresses, and website URLs do change and shops, restaurants, and hotels do move, go out of business, or change ownership and management. Such changes are a constant fact of life in ever-changing Vietnam and Cambodia. We regret any inconvenience such changes may cause to your travel and shopping plans.

Inclusion of shops, restaurants, hotels, and other hospitality providers in this book in no way implies guarantees nor endorsements by either the authors or publisher. Recommendations are provided solely for your reference. The honesty and reliability of shops can best be ensured by **you** – always ask the right questions, request proper receipts and documents, and observe the many shopping rules outlined in this book as well as on our companion website: www.ishoparoundtheworld.com.

The Treasures and Pleasures of Vietnam and Cambodia provides numerous tips on how you can best experience a trouble-free adventure. As in any unfamiliar place or situation, and regardless of how trustworthy strangers may appear, the watch-words are always the same – *"watch your wallet!"* If it seems too good to be true, it probably is. Any *"unbelievable deals"* should be treated as such. In Vietnam and Cambodia, as elsewhere in the world, there simply is no such thing as a free lunch. Everything has a cost. Just make sure you don't pay dearly by making unnecessary shopping mistakes!

Preface

WELCOME TO ANOTHER IMPACT GUIDE that explores the many unique treasures and pleasures of shopping and traveling in two of Southeast Asia's most fascinating destinations – Vietnam and Cambodia. Join us as we explore these countries' many treasures and pleasures, from great shops and top restaurants to fine hotels, sightseeing, and entertainment. We'll put you in touch with the best of the best these places have to offer visitors. We'll take you to popular tourist destinations, but we won't linger long since *lifestyle shopping* is our travel passion – combining great shopping with terrific dining and sightseeing. If you follow us to the end, you'll discover a whole new dimension to both travel and shopping. Indeed, as the following pages unfold, you'll learn there is a lot more to Vietnam and Cambodia, and travel in general, than taking tours, visiting popular sites, and acquiring an unwelcome weight gain attendant with new on-the-road dining habits.

Exciting Vietnam and Cambodia offer wonderful travel-shopping experiences for those who know what to look for, where to go, and how to properly travel and shop major destinations in these two countries. While these countries are popular places for visiting museums, temples, palaces, beaches, rivers, villages, and obscure historical sites that often characterize Vietnam's and Cambodia's travel images, for us both are important shopping destinations that yield unique art, antiques, textiles, and handicrafts as well as excellent restaurants, hotels, entertainment, and outdoor sports. Their people, products, sights, and sounds have truly enriched our lives.

If you are familiar with our other Impact Guides, you know this will not be another standard travel guide to history, culture, and sightseeing in Vietnam and Cambodia. Our approach to travel is very different. We operate from a particular perspective, and we frequently show our attitude rather than just present you with the sterile "travel facts." While we seek good travel value, we're not budget travelers who are interested in taking you along the low road to Vietnam and Cambodia. We've been there, done that at one stage in our lives, and found it to be an interesting learning experience. If that's the way you want to go, you'll find a several guidebooks on budget travel to Vietnam and Cambodia as well as a whole travel industry geared toward servicing budget travelers and backpackers with everything from cheap guest houses to Internet cafés. At the same time, we're not obsessed with local history, culture, and sightseeing. We get just enough history and sightseeing to make our travels interesting rather than obsessive. Accordingly, we include very little on history and sightseeing, because they are not our main focus; we also assume you have that information covered from other resources. When we discuss history and sightseeing, such as the Chams in Vietnam and Angkor Wat in Cambodia, we do so in abbreviated form, highlighting what we consider to be the essentials. As you'll quickly discover, we're very focused – we're in search of quality shopping and travel. Rather than spend eight hours a day sightseeing, we may only devote two hours to sightseeing and another six hours learning about the local shopping scene. As such, we're very people- and product-oriented. Through shopping, we meet many interesting and talented people and learn a great deal about their country.

What we really enjoy doing, and think we do it well, is shop. For us, shopping makes for great travel adventure and contributes to local development. Indeed, we're street people who love "the chase" and the serendipity that comes with our style

> ❑ Our approach to travel is very different from most guidebooks – we offer a unique travel perspective and we frequently show our attitude.
>
> ❑ We're not obsessed with local history, culture, and sightseeing. We get just enough history and sightseeing to make our travels interesting rather than obsessive.
>
> ❑ Through shopping, we meet many interesting and talented people and learn a great deal about their country.
>
> ❑ We're street people who love "the chase" and the serendipity that comes with our style of travel.

of travel. We especially enjoy discovering quality products; meeting local artists and crafts people; unraveling new travel-shopping rules; making friendships with local business people; staying in fine places; and dining in great restaurants where we often meet talented chefs and visit their fascinating kitchens. In the cases of Vietnam and Cambodia, we seek the best quality art, antiques, textiles, crafts, apparel, and jewelry as well as discover some of the best artists and craftspeople. In so doing, we learn a great deal about present Vietnam and Cambodia and their very talented and entrepreneurial people.

The chapters that follow represent a particular travel perspective. We purposefully decided to write more than just another travel guide with a few pages on shopping. While some travel guides include a brief section on the "whats" and "wheres" of shopping, we saw a need to also explain the "how-tos" of shopping in Vietnam and Cambodia. Such a book would both educate and guide you through these countries' shopping mazes – from finding great art and handicrafts and navigating numerous markets to getting the best deals and arranging for the shipping of large items – as well as put you in contact with the best of the best in restaurants, accommodations, and sightseeing. It would be a combination travel-shopping guide designed for people in search of quality travel experiences.

The perspective we develop throughout this book is based on our belief that traveling should be more than just another adventure in eating, sleeping, sightseeing, and taking pictures of unfamiliar places. Whenever possible, we attempt to bring to life the fact that Vietnam and Cambodia have real people and interesting products that you, the visitor, will find exciting. These are countries with very talented artists, craftspeople, traders, and entrepreneurs. When you leave Vietnam and Cambodia, you will take with you not only some unique experiences and memories but also quality products that you will certainly appreciate for years to come.

We have not hesitated to make qualitative judgments about the best of the best in Vietnam and Cambodia. If we just presented you with travel and shopping information, we would do you a disservice by not sharing our discoveries, both good and bad. While we know that our judgments may not be valid for everyone, we offer them as **reference points** from which you can make your own decisions. Our major emphasis is on quality shopping, dining, accommodations, sightseeing, and entertainment, and in that order. We look for shops which offer excellent quality and styles. If you share our concern for quality shopping, as well as fine restaurants and hotels, you will find many of our recommendations useful to planning and implementing your Vietnam and Cambodian adventures. Best of all, you'll engage in what has become a favorite pastime for many of today's discerning travelers – lifestyle shopping!

Throughout this book we have included "tried and tested" shopping information. We make judgments based upon our experience – not on judgments or sales pitches from others. Our research method was quite simple: we did a great deal of shopping and we looked for quality products. We acquired some fabulous items, and gained valuable knowledge in the process. However, we could not make purchases in every shop nor do we have any guarantee that your experiences will be the same as ours. Shops close, ownership or management changes, and the shop you visit may not be the same as the one we shopped. So use this information as a starting point, but ask questions and make your own judgments before you buy. For related information on shopping in these two countries, including many of our recommended shops, please visit our companion website: www.ishoparoundtheworld.com.

Whatever you do, enjoy Vietnam and Cambodia. While you need not *"shop 'til you drop,"* at least shop these places well and with the confidence that you are getting good quality and value. Don't just limit yourself to small items that will fit into your suitcase or pass up something you love because of shipping concerns. Consider acquiring larger items that can be safely and conveniently shipped back home. Indeed, shipping is something that needs to be *arranged* rather than lamented or avoided.

We wish to thank the many people who contributed to this book. They include shop owners, hotel personnel, and others who took time to educate us about the local shopping, dining, and travel scenes. A special thanks goes to Marcia Selva of Global Spectrum (www.asianpassages.com) for convincing us to do this book and showing us how to do these countries right.

We wish you well as you prepare for Vietnam's and Cambodia's many treasures and pleasures. The book is designed to be used in the streets of these two countries. If you **plan** your journey according to the first three chapters and **navigate** our major destinations based on the next four chapters, you should have an absolutely marvelous time. You'll discover some exciting places, acquire some choice items, and return home with many fond memories of a terrific adventure. If you put this book to use, it will indeed become your best friend – and passport – to the many unique treasures and pleasures of Vietnam and Cambodia. Enjoy!

Ron and Caryl Krannich
krannich@impactpublications.com

THE TREASURES AND PLEASURES OF VIETNAM AND CAMBODIA

Welcome to Surprising Vietnam and Cambodia

ELCOME TO TWO OF ASIA'S MOST DE-lightful, fascinating, and charming countries. They are open for business and travel in a very big way. As the former Vietnamese Ambassador to the United States used to pointedly remind his curious American audience, *"Vietnam is a country – not a war."* The same is true for Cambodia – it's a country in the process of reclaiming its population, culture, and seeming innocence after the horrendous killing years of 1975-1979.

Time has healed many wounds as well as provided much needed perspective on these once very troubled neighbors. It's time to discover the real treasures and pleasures of these beautiful and intriguing countries, whose ever resilient and optimistic people have retained their own unique cultural identities and independence. Both Vietnam and Cambodia welcome visitors with open arms, more so than most other countries we have encountered in recent years. Visit these countries now before they become discovered by millions of tourists who will inevitably crowd their already strained infrastructure and change their rather quaint, romantic, spontaneous, and innocent character forever.

A Surprising New Vietnam

Few places evoke such mixed emotions, as well as exude so many similar positive reactions from visitors, as Vietnam. It's a surprising country where most first-time, including many long-lost, visitors usually comment with enthusiasm that *"It wasn't anything like I expected!"* Some immediately fall in love with Vietnam and want to soon return since they failed to plan enough time to really enjoy this place.

Dashing low expectations and negative stereotypes, today's surprising Vietnam is due in part to the friendliness of the people and in part to the many rapid changes that have significantly altered the economy, infrastructure, and daily lives of the Vietnamese during the past 15 years of deliberate economic reform. Initiated in 1986, the *doi moi* economic reforms have accelerated change during recent years. At least in energetic Hanoi and Saigon, new joint venture high-rise five-star hotels and office buildings – coupled with busy commercial sections jam-packed with traffic, shops, and restaurants – point to a very different Vietnam than just five or 10 years ago. This is a country in the process of intentionally reinventing itself before your very eyes. What you see today will most likely be changed again two or three years from now. Vietnam is on an incredible journey to transform itself into a developed country with all the economic consequences that such changes imply. While it's not quite ready to face the inevitable political consequences that will accompany such changes, they too will come despite efforts to the contrary. What you may well be seeing today is the foundation of a very different regime which will evolve within the next five years. If history is any guide, it will most likely be a resilient and pragmatic regime.

> *Vietnam is a country – not a war. Time has healed many wounds. It's time to visit.*

While Vietnam is still a poor Third World country, it offers many rich and rewarding experiences to visitors. It's an especially rewarding place for those who were initially hesitant to visit Vietnam. In fact, most visitors find Vietnam to be one of the world's best kept travel secrets – great sites, great culture, great people, great food, great hotels, great beaches, great shopping, great prices, and great travel adventures. Its greatest asset is its people. With improved traffic, roads, museums, and tourist infrastructure, Vietnam could well become a great travel destination. In the meantime, it has become a very popular destination for individuals interested in discovering the treasures and pleasures of another unique and charming Southeast Asian country. It's still it bit rough on the edges, but it has come a very long way in just a few years.

SEDUCTION AND NARCISSISM

Vietnam also is a very seductive place that looks and feels easy to navigate. On the one hand, it's an extremely tenacious place, with a proud and fascinating history of resistance against all odds, be it against the Chinese, French, or Americans. A seemingly backwater country with a relatively unorganized population, arrogant outsiders always thought this was an easy place to stake claim – until they learned otherwise. It's a deceptive place populated by a very charming yet determined people. Initially seduced, outsiders soon became frustrated, angry, and drained of energy and resources. In the end, they lost interest and felt fortunate just to get out despite their many losses. Indeed, many of the monuments and museums you'll visit in Vietnam provide evidence of its bloody and proud history of war, resistance, survival, and independence. Combining borderline narcissism with tenacity, this preoccupation with militant history, bloody struggles, heros, and monuments may at times bore you, especially when it's encased in tasteless propaganda museums, but it says a lot about the Vietnamese character which is often obsessed with pride in the past rather than focused on hope for the future. History and culture dominate much of travel in Vietnam – until you discover its people, shopping, and new entrepreneurism!

The fascinating street activity and engaging people make these such interesting places to visit.

For a country that has witnessed a long history of massive death and destruction, one might expect a less than friendly reception to foreign visitors. Not so. Visitors are constantly impressed with the friendliness and optimism, often naive curiosity of the Vietnamese, toward outsiders. Maybe this is what occasionally gets them into trouble. Perhaps this orientation partly reflects the fact that Vietnam's population has nearly doubled in the past 25 years (from 40 million to 80 million) and that only a minority of the population is old enough to have a memory of the last great war of resistance against the Americans.

GETTING OVER ITSELF

Despite its preoccupation with history and ideology, Vietnam in recent years has apparently gotten over itself as it attempts to transform its once dreadful and great leveling communist-socialist economy into one of "capitalism with Vietnamese characteristics," or *doi moi*, reminiscent of China's great leap into the global economy with joint ventures, private ownership, and entrepreneurship. At least in the major urban areas, the result is a vibrant new Vietnam where economics tends to take precedence over what some observers believe is an aging, corrupt, and possibly crumbling communist political system.

From the perspective of many foreign investors, who still must face an incredible number of bureaucratic hassles left over from an often ossified and suspicious communist bureaucracy, Vietnam is gradually opening up to the outside world as it attempts to become part of the global economy. Foreign investment in tourism, from hotels to tour services, has become one of the driving forces for economic reform.

IT'S ABOUT SHOPPING AND CHAOS

Much of Vietnam's recent transformation can be summarized in one word – *shopping*. It's one of our favorite words and travel activities, because it teaches us a lot about the country and its people. In fact, one of the great joys of Vietnam's new-found capitalism is shopping. It's everywhere and it keeps getting bigger, better, and more interesting by the week. Whatever you heard about the end of capitalism in Vietnam simply is not true. It was temporarily silenced in the South by ideologues from the North who didn't have a clue as to how to develop and run an independent and viable economy within a larger global economy. Today even Hanoi shows signs of a new capitalist economy and entrepreneurship.

Always pragmatic, quick learners, relatively well educated, hard workers, and very entrepreneurial – especially in the South – the Vietnamese will impress you with their entrepreneurial spirit. Indeed, from the vibrant street markets, art galleries, and boutiques of Hanoi and Saigon to the lacquer factories, handicraft centers, and ceramic villages in and around these and many other cities, shopping is the symbol of the new and surprising Vietnam.

You'll quickly discover that most shopping in Vietnam is geared toward local residents in search of the latest consumer goods – from television sets and mobile phones to clothes and accessories. But a great deal of shopping also appeals to travelers in search of unique arts and handcrafted items, such as paintings, lacquerware, wood carvings, stone carvings, ceramics, silk, and water puppets. While you may spend a great deal of time getting acquainted with Vietnamese history and culture, which is showcased at every opportunity for visitors, chances are you will be intrigued by its passion for shopping. Welcome to the new Vietnam where making money and shopping seem to be a national passion and pastime.

Vietnam is by no means a shopper's paradise on par with nearby Hong Kong, Thailand, Singapore, or Bali, but it does have a great deal to offer travelers who are interested in participating in the country's old and new economies. Explore and shop its many streets and markets and you'll quickly discover that this is not the Vietnam you had expected to encounter. Eschewing the politics of the old regime, the Vietnamese want to make more money so they can do more shopping and enjoy the ostensible fruits of capitalism. If only Ho Chi Minh could see it now. He would surely lament what the great political and military struggles were all about!

On the other hand, this is a very beautiful and seductive country that seems to thrive on chaos, especially in its crowded urban centers of new economic opportunities. Step into its streets and you may encounter what is arguably the world's most chaotic and dangerous road scenes of motorbikes, bicycles, cars, buses, and trucks all vying, along with pedestrians, for scarce space along its antiquated road system. Rush hour is a noisy experience in pandemonium as honking vehicles and adventuresome pedestrians seem to come at you from all directions. For anyone used to orderliness and some semblance of rules and regulations, this street scene is at best a disorienting experience. Crossing a street is a visual and auditory challenge – this is India without

❑ Vietnam's greatest asset is its people – friendly, charming, and optimistic.

❑ Vietnam is an extremely tenacious place with a proud and fascinating history of resistance against all odds.

❑ History and culture dominate much of travel in Vietnam – until you discover its people, shopping, and new entrepreneurism!

❑ Much of Vietnam's recent transformation can be summarized in one word – *shopping*. Indeed, shopping is the symbol of the new Vietnam.

❑ Crossing a street in Hanoi or Saigon is a visual and auditory challenge – this is India without the cows!

the cars and cows! For some visitors, this chaos leads them to conclude that Vietnam is *"not quite ready for prime time"* in the tourism department. For others, this chaos is what makes Vietnam such an interesting and intriguing place to visit. You'll have to judge for yourself. For us, chaos has always been a way of life throughout relatively unstructured Southeast Asia – except for Singapore and parts of Malaysia. Without the chaos, Vietnam and much of Southeast Asia would lose its delightful and charming character.

GREAT DESTINATIONS

Traveling to Vietnam inevitably puts you in touch with three major areas of this country – Hanoi in the North, Danang/Hoi An in the Central Region, and Saigon (Ho Chi Minh City) in the South. These also are the country's major shopping destinations as well as the places that offer the best accommodations, restaurants, and sightseeing. They are the subjects of the following chapters which focus on the best of the best in travel and shopping in Vietnam.

While there is much more to Vietnam than these three major urban destinations, we choose them because they make a perfect travel-shopping combination for anyone who has one to two weeks available to visit Vietnam. Indeed, these are great "starter" destinations for experiencing the best of Vietnam. They are relatively convenient places to get to and around in, and they yield numerous exciting treasures and pleasures for anyone with limited time but a desire to see and do as much as possible. If you have more time and want to delve more into the history, culture, and ethnicity of Vietnam, we highly recommend expanding your trip to include Sapa in the North, Hui in the Central Region, Dalat and Nha Trang in the South Central and Highlands regions, and the Mekong Delta in the South. While these places do not have much to offer in terms of quality shopping, they are of interest to visitors for other reasons. They also take a lot more travel time and are less convenient than our three prime destinations.

We've also included a separate chapter on Cambodia that covers both Phnom Penh and Siem Reap (Angkor Wat). Since Cambodia is so easily accessible from Vietnam, and it's a fabulous "must visit" destination in Southeast Asia, we highly recommend including it in your trip to Vietnam. We examine these two intriguing places in Cambodia as a four- to seven-day side trip from Vietnam or Thailand. If you're planning to visit Thailand before or after Vietnam, which we also highly recommend (see our companion volume, *The Treasures and Pleasures of Thailand*, and www.ishoparoundtheworld.com), Cambodia should definitely be on your travel agenda since it is so close and convenient to reach from either country.

TALES OF THREE CITIES

If this your first trip to Vietnam, you'll definitely want to visit our three regions and cities – Hanoi, Danang/Hoi An, and Saigon. **Hanoi** in the North remains one of Southeast Asia's most unique cities with tree-lined boulevards, quaint French colonial architecture, and a pleasant outdoor ambience for walking, dining, and shopping. This is also one of Asia's major centers for art, with most of Vietnam's famous painters working from studios in and around the city. From a cultural perspective, Hanoi is one huge art colony with gallery after gallery representing the very best of Vietnamese oil, water color, and lacquer paintings. If you enjoy contemporary and abstract art, especially with many local Vietnamese themes, you'll fall in love with Hanoi – an art connoisseur's paradise. The political and cultural center for Vietnam, Hanoi will undoubtedly become your favorite city in Vietnam. Its population of over 3 million – mostly on foot, bicycles, or motorbikes – crowd the city's many narrow streets. In addition to shopping, which has recently come of age in Hanoi, there's plenty to see and do here, from museums, monuments, parks, and water puppet shows to side trips to villages and beautiful Halong Bay. Some of Vietnam's best hotels and restaurants are found in the center of Hanoi, a convenient location from which to shop and sightsee. Give yourself plenty of time to absorb this delightful city. In fact, you may want to start your Vietnam journey in Hanoi and work your way south to Saigon. We recommend this approach because it's a pleasant and manageable place from which to experience the best of Vietnam. The art alone is worth making

❑ Hanoi is one of Asia's major centers for art.

❑ You may want to start your Vietnam journey in Hanoi and work your way south to Saigon. The art alone is worth making Hanoi your first stop in Vietnam.

❑ Hoi An is a unique art colony, textile center, and architectural community. Make it a full-day excursion.

❑ Saigon is a very vibrant, colorful, and noisy city that offers many of Vietnam's best travel and shopping amenities.

❑ Saigon is to Hanoi what Shanghai is to Beijing – the country's entrepreneurial center and economic powerhouse which occasionally needs to be reigned in by the country's political center.

Hanoi your first stop in Vietnam.

Danang and Hoi An along the Central coast, which also includes China Beach, was the great American staging area during the war of the 1960s and early 1970s. But historically and culturally, this is the area of the ancient Chams who controlled this region from the 4th to the mid-19th centuries and left behind numerous brick and stone structures of particular interest to archeologists and historians at the major Cham site of My Son as well as dozens of other sites along the coast. After visiting the Cham Museum in Danang and perhaps the ruins at My Son, most visitors head for the charming riverside town of Hoi An and to the nearby stone carving center at the base of Marble Mountain to shop, dine, and enjoy the ambience of this fun area. Hoi An is a unique art colony, textile center, and architectural community. Often crowded with visitors, the town is lined with numerous art galleries, tailoring shops, temples, museums, historical homes, and architectural delights to easily spend a full day absorbing its many treasures and pleasures. Very different from the rest of the country, Hoi An may well become one of the highlights of your visit to Vietnam.

> *Saigon is to Vietnam what Shanghai is to China – the country's entrepreneurial center and economic powerhouse that occasionally needs to be reigned in by the northern political center (Hanoi).*

Saigon in the South is big and sprawling, boasting a population of over 7 million. It often gets a comparatively bad reputation because it lacks the ostensible beauty and character of Hanoi. But by any stretch of the imagination, Hanoi is not beautiful – it exudes crumbling Third World elegance and charm, a lumbering big town with a population of 3+ million that especially looks and feels great in the lights of night or along its lake shores in spring. While not as leisurely and charming as Hanoi, nonetheless, Saigon is a very vibrant, colorful, and noisy city that offers many of Vietnam's best travel and shopping amenities. This high-energy city is undergoing dramatic economic changes with numerous new hotels, restaurants, shops, office buildings, bars, and nightclubs crowding for visibility in the downtown section that runs west from the Saigon River along Dong Khoi Street and adjacent thoroughfares. Especially known for their entrepre-

neurism, the Saigonese offer some of the best shopping opportunities in Vietnam for everything from arts and handicrafts to
tailored clothing, jewelry, and pirated videos and CDs. Its city
markets are second to none, especially in the adjacent city of
Colon, which is Saigon's famous Chinatown where capitalism
is very much well and alive despite taking a beating for more
than a decade.

Saigon is one of those cities that can be initially disorienting
and unattractive compared to more laid-back and charming
Hanoi. But after two or three days, Saigon begins to grow on
you as you discover its many hidden treasures and pleasures,
including vibrant markets, temples, churches, cultural performances, art exhibits, and great views of the Saigon River.
Energetic and optimistic, it's a city that requires patience and
perseverance. Rising like a phoenix from its recent disgraced
past, Saigon is becoming increasingly important to the overall
economic development of Vietnam. It is to Hanoi what
Shanghai is to Beijing – the country's entrepreneurial center
and economic powerhouse which occasionally needs to be
reigned in by the country's political center. Undergoing a major
transformation, Saigon will most likely once again become one
of Asia's most important cities for business and tourism. For
tourists, this city has lots to offer, despite its many uninspired,
tasteless, and boring monuments and propaganda museums
emphasizing the fall of Saigon and the defeat of the Americans
during the last great struggle – shopping is much more interesting than this institutional self-aggrandizement. Take the obli-
gatory propaganda tours, but get into the streets where Saigon
really shines with its architecture, shops, restaurants, hotels,
and living chaos of people. Nearby attractions include the
fascinating Cu Chi Tunnels and the whole Mekong delta region.
Plan to spend at least four days here – preferably more. Despite
what others might say negative about Saigon, as compared to
Hanoi, you won't be disappointed if you approach it right.

DISCOVERING CAMBODIA

If you have an extra four to seven days, we highly recommend
a quick side trip to Cambodia. This is one of Southeast Asia's
most beautiful countries, which also boasts both glorious and
disastrous histories. Witnessing one of history's worst geno-
cides, with nearly one-third of the population (1.5 million out
of 7 million) annihilated in 1975-1979 during the reign of the
Khmer Rouge, today Cambodia shows little evidence of this
wretched history other than the many maimed individuals,

turned beggars, wounded by land mines. Phnom Penh once again is back in business with its huge Russian and Central markets and many hotels, restaurants, and art, antique, textile, silver, and handicraft shops. But the real attraction of Cambodia is found in the fabulous temple complex and ruins of Angkor Wat. Located near the sleepy provincial town of Siem Reap, Angkor Wat should be on every Southeast Asian visitor's itinerary. An awesome collection of Hindu temples that once represented the most powerful kingdom in Southeast Asia, this is one of the great wonders of the world. Whatever you do, make sure you have time to visit this incredible awe-inspiring complex. Convenient to reach from both Vietnam and Thailand, Siem Reap boasts an excellent tourist infrastructure, including three five-star hotels and resorts. This side trip from Vietnam may well become the highlight of your Vietnam-centered Southeast Asian adventure.

A UNIQUE PEOPLE PERSPECTIVE

The pages that follow are not your typical treatment of travel to Vietnam and Cambodia. While we recognize the importance of background information for developing a travel-friendly perspective, this book is not big on history, culture, sightseeing, and cheap, sweaty, and inconvenient travel – a type of enduring 1960s and 1970s anthropological and cross-cultural approach to travel that dominates many youth-oriented budget travel guides. We've been there, done that, and now expect more quality travel experiences. Indeed, there are numerous general guidebooks available on Vietnam and Cambodia that basically focus on the same rehashed and seemingly enduring themes – history and culture. Most of these books are heavy on history, monuments, and museums – indeed provide excruciating details – to the near exclusion of contemporary Vietnam and Cambodia and their many talented people. Numerous budget guides, touting the oft repeated *"I'm a traveler not a tourist"* philosophy, outline how to experience inexpensive Vietnam and Cambodia on your own. They provide a generous offering of cheap restaurants, hotels, and trans-

> *We learned long ago that one of the best ways to meet the local people and experience another culture is to shop!*

portation for extreme budget-conscious travelers. If this is your primary interest and style of travel, you will find several guidebooks that offer this approach to Vietnam. However, if this is not your primary travel passion (you get anxious after hours in a museum or at a historic site) and you prefer a different level (class) of travel experience (you're not opposed to five-star hotels and quality restaurants, as well as prefer a car and driver to a crowded bus), you may find such guidebooks less than welcome additions to your luggage.

Like other volumes in the Impact Guides series (see the order form at the end of this volume), this book focuses on quality travel-shopping in Vietnam and neighboring Cambodia. Yes, shopping. Contrary to what some travelers may think, shopping is not a sin. It can and does change lives for the better. We learned long ago that one of the most enjoyable aspects of travel – and one of the best ways to meet people, experience another culture, and contribute to local economies – is to seek out the best shops, markets, factories, and galleries – and shop! In so doing, we explore the fascinating worlds of artisans, craftspeople, and shopkeepers and discover quality products, outstanding buys, and talented, interesting, and friendly people. We also help support the continuing development of local arts and crafts. As many of our enthusiastic readers testify (see the introductory four pages of this book), our approach to travel changes lives. Our approach is all about talented people and what they have to offer discerning visitors in search of such talent.

A TRAVEL-SHOPPING EMPHASIS

Much of *The Treasures and Pleasures of Vietnam and Cambodia* is designed to provide you with the necessary **knowledge and skills** to become an effective travel-shopper. We especially designed the book with three major considerations in mind:

- Focus on quality shopping
- Emphasis on finding unique items
- Inclusion of travel highlights, from top hotels and restaurants to major sightseeing attractions, that especially appeal to discerning travelers.

Throughout this book we attempt to identify the **best quality shopping** in Vietnam. This does not mean we have discovered the cheapest shopping or best bargains, although we have attempted to do so when opportunities for comparative shopping arose within and between communities. Our focus is primarily on shopping for **unique and quality items** that will retain their value in the long run and can be appreciated for years to come. This means many of our recommended shops may initially appear expensive. But they offer top quality and value that you will not find in many other shops. For example, when we discover unique paintings by top artists in Hanoi, we acknowledge the fact that their work is expensive, but it is very beautiful and unique, so much so that you quickly forget their prices after you acquire and continue to admire their outstanding work. At the same time, we identify what we consider to be the best buys for various items, especially lacquerware, stone carvings, ceramics, silk, jewelry, and handicrafts.

We also include many of the top travel amenities and attractions in our selected cities. As with other volumes in the Impact Guides series, many of our readers appreciate quality travel. When they visit a country, they prefer discovering the best a country has to offer in accommodations, restaurants, sightseeing, and entertainment. While they expect good value for their travel dollar, they are not budget travelers in search of the cheapest hotels, restaurants, and transportation. With limited time, careful budgeting, and a good plan, they approach Vietnam as a once-in-a-lifetime travel experience – one that will yield fond memories for many years to come. By focusing on the best of what Vietnam and Cambodia have to offer, we believe you will have a terrific time in these two countries. You'll acquire some great products, meet many wonderful people, and return home with many memories of an exciting travel-shopping adventure.

APPROACHING THE SUBJECT

The chapters that follow take you on a whirlwind travel-shopping adventure of Vietnam, and to a much lesser degree Cambodia, with a decided emphasis on quality shopping, dining, and sightseeing. We literally put a shopping face on these places – one we believe you will thoroughly enjoy as you explore Vietnam's and Cambodia's many other pleasures.

We've given a great deal of attention to constructing a complete **user-friendly book** that focuses on the shopping process, offers extensive details on the "how," "what," and "where" of shopping, and includes a sufficient level of redundancy to be informative, useful, and usable. The chapters, for example, are organized like one would organize and implement a travel and shopping adventure. Each chapter incorporates sufficient details, including names and addresses, to get you started in some of the best shopping areas and shops in each city.

Indexes and table of contents are especially important to us and others who believe a travel book is first and foremost a guide to unfamiliar places. Therefore, our index includes both subjects and shops, with shops printed in bold for ease of reference; the table of contents is elaborated in detail so it, too, can be used as another handy reference index for subjects and products. If, for example, you are interested in "what to buy" or "where to shop" in Hanoi, the best reference will be the table of contents. If you are interested in art galleries in Hanoi, look under "Art" in the index. And if you are interested in learning where you can find good quality ceramics, then look under "Ceramics" in the index. By using the table of contents and index together, you can access most any information from this book.

The remainder of this book is divided into two parts and six additional chapters which look at both the process and content of traveling and shopping in Vietnam and Cambodia. Part I – **"Smart Traveling and Shopping"** – assists you in preparing for your Vietnam and Cambodian adventures by focusing on the how-to's of traveling and shopping. Chapter 2, **"Know Before You Go,"** takes you through the basics of getting to and enjoying your stay in Vietnam and Cambodia. It includes advice on when to go, what to pack, required documents, currency, business hours, international and domestic transportation, tipping, tour groups, useful websites, and local customs. Chapter 3, **"The Shopping Treasures and Rules For Success,"** examines Vietnam's and Cambodia's major shopping strengths, from art and ceramics to tailored clothes and handicrafts. It also includes lots of advice on comparative shopping, shopping tips, bargaining rules, and shipping strategies for shopping at its very best.

The four chapters in Part II – **"Great Destinations"** – examine the how, what, and where of traveling and shopping in and around several of Vietnam's and Cambodia's major destinations: Hanoi, Danang/Hoi An, and Saigon in Vietnam and Phnom Penh and Siem Reap in Cambodia. Here we identify major shopping strengths of each place; detail the how, what, and where of shopping; and share information on some of the best hotels, restaurants, and sightseeing for each community and surrounding area. In the final chapter on Cambodia, we also include introductory information on travel to Cambodia and travel-shopping advice relevant to this country.

OUR RECOMMENDATIONS

We hesitate to recommend specific shops, restaurants, hotels, and sites since we know the pitfalls of doing so. Shops that offered excellent products and service during one of our visits, for example, may change ownership, personnel, and policies from one year to another or they may suddenly move to another location or go out of business. In addition, our shopping preferences may not be the same as your preferences. The same is true for restaurants, hotels, and some tourist sites: they do change.

Since we put shopping up front in our travels to Vietnam and Cambodia, our major concern is to outline your shopping options, show you where to locate the best shopping areas, and share some useful shopping strategies that you can use anywhere in Vietnam and Cambodia, regardless of particular shops or markets we or others may recommend. Armed with this knowledge and some basic shopping skills, you will be better prepared to locate your own shops and determine which ones offer the best products and service in relation to your own shopping and travel goals.

However, we also recognize the "need to know" when shopping in unfamiliar places. Therefore, throughout this book we list the names and locations of various shops we have found to offer good quality products. In some cases we have purchased items in these shops and can also recommend them for service and reliability. But in most cases we surveyed shops to determine the quality of products offered without making purchases. To buy in every shop would be beyond our budget, as well as our home storage capabilities! Whatever you do, treat our names and addresses as **orientation points** from which to identify your own products and shops. If you rely solely on our listings, you will miss out on one of the great adventures in Vietnam and Cambodia – discovering your own special shops that offer unique items and exceptional value and service.

The same holds true for our recommendations for hotels, restaurants, sites, and entertainment. We sought out the best of the best in these major "travel pleasure" areas. You should find most of our recommendations useful in organizing your own special Vietnam and Cambodia adventures.

EXPECT A REWARDING ADVENTURE

Whatever you do, enjoy your Vietnam and Cambodia adventures as you open yourself to a fascinating world of travel-shopping. We're confident you'll discover some very special treasures and pleasures that will also make Vietnam and Cambodia two of your favorite destinations.

So arrange your flights and accommodations, pack your credit cards and traveler's checks, and head for two of Southeast Asia's most delightful destinations. Two to three weeks later you should return home with much more than a set of photos and travel brochures. You will have some wonderful purchases and travel tales that can be enjoyed and relived for a lifetime.

Shopping and traveling in Vietnam and Cambodia only takes time, money, and a sense of adventure. Take the time, be willing to part with some of your money, and open yourself to a whole new world of travel. If you are like us, the treasures and pleasures outlined in this book will introduce you to an exciting world of quality products, friendly people, and interesting places that you might have otherwise missed had you just passed through these countries to eat, sleep, see sites, and take pictures. When you travel our Vietnam and Cambodia, you are not just another tourist. You are a special kind of international traveler who discovers quality and learns about these places through the people and products that continue to define their culture.

PART I

Smart Traveling
and Shopping

2

Know Before You Go

THERE ARE A FEW THINGS YOU SHOULD KNOW about Vietnam and Cambodia before visiting these two intriguing countries. When, for example, is the best time of the year to visit these places? How should you pack? Are you likely to encounter many language problems? Should you join a tour group or travel on your own? What kind of documents do you need? How safe and healthy are these countries? As a shopper, what can you legally export or import? Is Vietnamese art dutiable? Are there any particular websites that can help you plan your trip to this part of Southeast Asia?

Answers to these and many other basic travel questions can help you better prepare for your travel-shopping adventure. They are addressed in this pre-trip planning chapter.

LOCATION AND GEOGRAPHY

Located in lush and tropical mainland Southeast Asia – south of China, east of Thailand, and on the South China Sea – both Vietnam and Cambodia were once part of French colonial Indochina, which also included Laos. Today Vietnam and Cambodia share a 930-kilometer border with each other.

which is similar in size to Malaysia, the Philippines, Japan, Italy, Norway, Poland, or the U.S. state of New Mexico. Its population of 79 million – similar in size to Germany, the Philippines, or the U.S. states of California, Florida, Texas, and New York combined – makes it the thirteenth largest country in the world.

Vietnam is an S-shaped country that is bordered on the mountainous north by China, and on the west by Laos and Cambodia. Its eastern and southern borders consist of more than 3,000 kilometers of shoreline on the South China Sea, which stretches to the nearest island countries of the Philippines and Malaysia some 800+ kilometers away. Running a length of nearly 1,800 kilometers from north to south and a width of 60 to 600 kilometers from east to west, Vietnam is often visualized by locals in agricultural and market terms: a bamboo pole supporting a basket of rice at each end. Its two fertile delta regions – the Red River Delta in the north and the Mekong River Delta in the south – produce the rice that fills those baskets.

❑ Vietnam shares with Cambodia a 930-kilometer border.

❑ Vietnam is similar in geographic size to Italy, with the population equivalent of Germany.

❑ Cambodia is the geographic size of Missouri and the population size of Florida.

❑ For ideal weather, visit during October-December or March-April.

❑ Pack as if you were visiting New Orleans or Atlanta.

Vietnamese geography, history, and culture, as well as its politics and economics, follow three major regions: the **north** with Hanoi, Haiphong, beautiful Halong Bay on the Gulf of Tonkin, the fertile Red River Delta, the border with China and Laos; the **center** with its beautiful sandy beaches, highlands, and plateaus along with the noted cities of Danang, Hoi An, and Hue, and the ruins of the ancient Cham kingdom; and the **south** which borders Cambodia and includes Saigon and the Mekong River Delta.

Cambodia is nearly half the size of Vietnam with a total area of 181,040 square kilometers. It is close in size to Syria, Uruguay, or the U.S. state of Missouri. Its population of 12.6 million is similar in size to that of Guatemala, Cuba, or the U.S. state of Florida. The southeast part of the country, which borders Vietnam and extends to the South China Sea, consists of a large fertile plain that functions as the country's rice growing region. The remainder of the country is heavily forested and includes mountainous areas along the border with Thailand. The Mekong River cuts through a 500-kilometer section of the country, running from Laos in the north to Vietnam in the southeast. The river connects with two other rivers in Phnom Penh, the Bassac and Tonle Sap, which in turn connect with Southeast Asia's largest freshwater lake, Tonle Sap Lake. Phnom Penh also is connected to Saigon via the Mekong River. Siem Reap, a small provincial town that serves as the gateway to the ancient ruins of Angkor Wat, is connected to Phnom Penh via Tonle Sap River and Tonle Sap Lake. The lake, which also functions as a huge reservoir during the monsoon season, is a fascinating natural world phenomenon that expands and contracts each year from 10,400 square kilometers to 2,600 square kilometers. This occurs during the rainy season months of June to October when the mighty waters of the Mekong River back up the tributary Tonle Sap River, which then reverses its course and dumps excess water into Tonle Sap Lake.

CLIMATE AND WHEN TO GO

It's somewhat difficult to get a handle on the weather and the best times to travel in Vietnam and Cambodia because of changing climatic conditions in different areas of these countries. In some respects, any time is a good time to travel in some places in these countries. Being tropical Southeast Asian countries, both Vietnam and Cambodia tend to be hot and humid in the lowland areas. The rainy season occurs between June and September, with major flooding often taking place during July and August. March to May can be very hot. The ideal months for weather are October to December and March to April. However, this is not always the case, especially given regional variations in climate for Vietnam. For example, during the winter months of December and January, the weather can get very cold in the north and central highlands, although it seldom freezes. January and February in the popular hill station of Sapa in the north can be very cold, foggy, and wet – a disappointing time to travel there. During these months you will want to pack a sweater and/or light jacket for a few cool days and many cool evenings, even in Hanoi.

When you get ready to plan your trip, try to avoid the very rainy months of June through August. If that's the only time you can go, chances are you may have good luck with the weather, with rains only occurring a few days or for a few minutes each day. But do check on flooding before you leave. Some parts of Vietnam can have horrendous floods during the rainy season. Also, be prepared by packing rain gear, especially a small collapsible umbrella, which may frequently come in handy. If you forget to do so, you'll have no problem finding adequate rain gear in the markets of Vietnam and Cambodia. Also, check out the many online five- to 10-day weather forecasts provided by CNN, Weather Channel, and other relevant Internet sites:

- **CNN**   cnn.com/weather
- **Weather Channel**   weather.com
- **Intellicast**   intellicast.com
- **USA Today**   usatoday.com/weather
- **World Climate**   weathersite.com
- **Yahoo**   weather.yahoo.com

WHAT TO PACK AND WEAR

Given Vietnam's and Cambodia's tropical climate and informal lifestyle, plan to pack as if you were visiting New Orleans or Atlanta – lightweight cotton clothing is especially important for hot and humid days. If you're visiting the north and central highlands in Vietnam during the winter months, plan to pack a sweater and jacket; it can get cool. You need not pack formal attire since even the best restaurants do not require dresses, suits, or coats or ties. Indeed, don't waste packing space with such unnecessary items, which will probably never get worn on this trip. Smart casual is the best you'll ever have to dress.

Since you will probably do a great deal of walking in the destinations outlined in this book, you are well advised to take the following items with you:

Essentials:

- comfortable walking shoes
- sunglasses

Optional:

- umbrella
- camera
- compass
- swim gear
- hat or cap

Pack your camera and plenty of film for both Vietnam and Cambodia. These are two fabulous destinations for photography. Halong Bay in north Vietnam and Angkor Wat in Cambodia, for example, are two of the world's most photographed sites. But everywhere you go you'll encounter many colorful rural and urban scenes that will quickly eat up your film. Indeed, you may soon discover it's difficult not to take good pictures in these countries. The people are generally very receptive to having their pictures taken.

A compass comes in especially handy since you may frequently become disoriented by streets, maps, and markets which often lack important details. Our compass keeps us on track and helps us get to our destinations.

REQUIRED DOCUMENTS

Most visitors, with the exception of those from a few countries with special bilateral agreements on visa exceptions, will need visas for both Vietnam and Cambodia. In the case of Vietnam, you must have a stamped visa in your passport prior to arrival. You apply for a visa through a Vietnam Embassy or Consulate by completing an application form and sending it along with your passport, two passport photos, and a certified check. Since the cost of a visa varies (US$50 to US$85) from embassy to embassy, and depending on whether you want a single-entry, multiple-entry, tourist, or business visa, it's necessary to call the embassy or consulate about the exact amount of the visa fee before sending your application. If you want your passport and visa returned by mail or special delivery services, be sure to include a self-addressed stamped envelope or a prepaid shipping form with your application. The application process usually takes from four to 10 days to complete. If you are traveling with a tour group, the company may have special arrangements (visa authorization) to acquire a visa upon arrival. Tourist visas are good for 30 days and can be extended in Vietnam.

The easiest way to apply for a visa is to go online and download the visa application form. In the United States, go to the embassy's website for the form and application instructions:

www.vietnamembassy-usa.org/consular/visainfo.php3

For a listing of Vietnam embassies and consulates, go to Vietnam Online:

www.vietnamonline.com/travel/visa.html

Obtaining a visa for Cambodia is much easier and cheaper than in the case of Vietnam. You can get a visa upon arrival at the international airports in Phnom Penh and Siem Reap by completing an application form, including two passport photos, presenting your passport, and paying $25 for a 30-day tourist visa. If you don't want to stand in line with other passengers to complete the forms and get processed – usually a 20- to 40-minute wait – you can get your visa before arriving in Cambodia. Just go to the Cambodian website and download the visa application form and instructions:

www.embassy.org/cambodia/consular

THE PEOPLES

The peoples of Vietnam and Cambodia are a diverse mix of ethnic groups. In Vietnam, nearly 85 percent of the people are Viet, or Kinh, who disproportionately live in Vietnam's two great delta regions – Red River and Mekong River. The remainder of the population includes 54 ethnic and tribal groups. They are well represented in Hanoi's relatively new and informative Vietnam Museum of Ethnology (see chapter on Hanoi). An ethnic Chinese minority continues to play an important role in the commerce of Saigon, as evident in the adjacent city of Cholon, which is Saigon's Chinatown and great wholesale market. Hanoi and Saigon are the country's largest cities with 3 and 7 million people respectively. However only 30 to 40 percent of these people actually live in the urbanized areas of these cities, which tend to encompass large rural areas within the city boundaries.

Cities have a disproportionate number of young people. You'll see few old people.

The Khmers constitute nearly 90 percent of the population in Cambodia. The remainder of the population consists of hill tribes, Vietnamese, Thai, Chinese, and Cham. Approximately 80 percent of the people live in rural areas. Phnom Penh, which literally became a ghost town in 1975 due to forced evacuation of nearly 1 million residents by the murderous Khmer Rouge regime, now has a population of approximately 1 million. It remains the country's most significant urban center.

In the cities of both Vietnam and Cambodia you will most likely find the people to be very young and friendly. Indeed, it striking that so few older people are evident in the cities. The cities seem to be for young people. Once in the countryside, you will see many older people.

LANGUAGE

Language can present difficulties at time. Many young people in the urban areas and who are attached to the tourism and hospitality industries speak some English. In fact, you'll seldom get lost for more than 10 minutes without managing to find someone who can help you through a combination of English and sign language to get you where you want to go. If you are traveling on your own, you may want to occasionally hire an English-speaking guide to assist you in getting around and seeing important sites. They can usually be arranged through travel agencies or at various sites you visit. Their services are usually very inexpensive – perhaps US$2 to US$3 an hour.

The language barrier is not as formidable as it may initially appear. Most personnel at hotel front desks speak some English. Be sure to ask them for assistance with names and addresses. Most will be happy to write out destinations in the local language to give to taxi or cyclo drivers. Many shop owners speak some English, or they will be able to understand you if you use a combination of sign language and sufficient pointing. Restaurant menus in the major cities often include English and French translations. A map and compass will also come in handy so you can resolve many directional problems on your own. Best of all, coping with the language challenge provides some great opportunities to meet many friendly and helpful local people.

❑ Vietnam and Cambodia are fabulous destinations for photography.

❑ Tourist visas must be acquired before arriving in Vietnam; they are good for 30 days and can be extended in Vietnam.

❑ Tourist visas for Cambodia can be acquired upon arrival at the international airports.

❑ You'll seldom get lost for more than 10 minutes without finding someone who speaks some English.

TIME

Vietnam and Cambodia are seven hours ahead of Greenwich Mean Time (GMT). When it's 1pm in London, it's 8pm in Hanoi, Saigon, and Phnom Penh. If you are from New York, these places will be 12 hours ahead – 1pm on Tuesday will be 1am on Wednesday in Vietnam and Cambodia. If you are from North America, expect to experience jet lag due to the significant time change. If you have difficulty figuring out the time differences in reference to your time zone, you may want to visit these two websites:

www.timezoneconverter.com
www.worldtimeserver.com

SAFETY AND SECURITY

Both Vietnam and Cambodia are relatively safe places to visit, if you take basic precautions. Saigon does have a reputation for purse snatchers and pickpockets. In general, we feel relatively safe throughout Vietnam.

You need to approach Cambodia with more caution and less adventure. Remember, this is a very poor country with a recent history of social and political upheaval. Yes, there are still bad guys around who prey on tourists. The good news is that you are most unlikely to encounter them in Phnom Penh, Siem Reap, or the major temples around Angkor Wat. However infrequent, daylight robberies and assaults against tourists have been reported in Phnom Penh. Pickpockets and snatch-and-grab type of incidents from speeding motorcycles do occasionally occur. It's not particularly safe to walk alone at night in Phnom Penh nor explore remote areas on your own. While the government has made good progress in pacifying the country, lawlessness and banditry still exist in many rural areas, and land mines remain a serious problem for anyone wandering off the beaten path without a guide. In addition, bandits are known to operate illegal checkpoints from where they extort money from drivers and passengers on the road to Banteay Srei temple (road runs 30 kilometers north of Siem Reap). For this reason, you may want to stay close to a reputable local guide and driver when venturing outside the secured areas.

The major safety problem is the traffic. Be careful when crossing roads and choosing transportation.

The major safety hazard is the traffic. On average 30 people are killed each day from traffic accidents in Vietnam. Be very careful when crossing streets and roads as well as in choosing a safe mode of transportation. Whatever you do, always focus on safety rather than on charm or price.

Like anywhere you travel, including New York City, you should take normal safety precautions by securing your valuables. It's okay to be somewhat paranoid about your possessions, especially your passport, money, and camera, and yourself. Be very cautious with your purse and wallet – hold them very close and with a firm grip. Keep your valuables, including your money and passport, in safe places, such as your hotel safe or in a money belt. It's always a good idea to carry a photocopy of essential passport information – front info and stamped visa page – as well as traveler's check receipts separate from the originals.

If you need reassurance about travel safety to Vietnam and Cambodia, check out the U.S. State Department's online travel advisories and tips for these countries:

travel.state.gov/travel_warnings.html

You may also want to review their pamphlet, *A Safe Trip Abroad*, which is available online (travel.state.gov), by autofax (202-647-3000), or through the U.S. Government Printing Office (Superintendent of Documents, Washington, DC 20402) and U.S. Embassy in Phnom Penh. It includes several useful safety tips, which many travelers often forget. It's well worth reviewing in preparation for your trip and before you pack your bags!

GETTING THERE

Most visitors arrive in Vietnam or Cambodia by air from Hong Kong or Bangkok. At present, no airlines fly direct from the U.S. or Canada to Vietnam or Cambodia and no U.S. airline flies into either country. So most travelers from North America fly to either Hong Kong or Bangkok and use one of these cities to make a connection for the short flight into Vietnam. Cathay Pacific from Hong Kong and Thai Airways from Bangkok fly to Hanoi or Saigon – often as a code-share with Vietnam Airlines. Thai Airways, Bangkok Airways, and Royal Air Cambodge fly between Bangkok and Phnom Penh or Siem Reap.

On our most recent trip to Vietnam and Cambodia, we chose **Northwest Airlines** for our flights to and from Asia. We found Northwest Airlines' schedules to be the most convenient, the flights very comfortable, the service attentive, and the food well prepared. We have often appreciated the excellent service we find as we travel in Asia. We found the attentive, but not obtrusive, service on Northwest compared very favorably with the legendary service ethic found in that part of the world. The flight attendants went out of their way to make passengers comfortable and well cared for.

Best of all, we found Northwest Airlines' routes – especially from East Coast and Midwest cities – cut flying time off the long journey by using polar routes. But Northwest offers more than just a great routing to Hong Kong and Bangkok – our "jumping off" points to Vietnam and from Cambodia. We enjoyed our Northwest flights and found them to be first rate. We were routed through Memphis on our return trip en route to Reagan National Airport. On the flight out of Memphis, Northwest served the most delicious barbecue we have eaten anywhere!

As America's oldest carrier, Northwest has operated across the Pacific for more than five decades – longer than any other airline. The world's fourth largest airline, with hubs at Detroit, Minneapolis/St. Paul, Memphis, Tokyo and Amsterdam, Northwest has more than 1,400 daily departures serving more than 750 cities in 120 countries on six continents. Based on statistics complied by the U.S. Department of Transportation, Northwest was the most on-time airline among the seven largest network carriers for the period 1990-1999.

If you fly frequently, consider membership in Northwest's WorldPerks^{SM} (frequent flyer) and WorldClubs^{SM} (airport lounges and special services) programs. For more information on the **WorldPerks^{SM}** frequent flyer program which also is partnered with KLM, contact Northwest by phone (1-800-447-3757) or mail: Northwest Airlines Customer Service Center, 601 Oak Street, Chisholm, MN 55719. For information on the **WorldClubs^{SM}** program, contact Northwest by phone (1-800-692-3788), fax (612-726-0988), or mail: Northwest Airlines, Inc., WorldClubs Service Center, 5101 Northwest Drive, Department A5301, St. Paul, MN 55111-3034. Also, be sure to visit Northwest Airline's Web site for detailed information on flights and services: www.nwa.com. You may want to make these contacts before doing your ticketing.

For travelers from America and Europe, the flights to and from Asian destinations are long ones. Thus, you may wish to upgrade your ticket to "World Business Class" for more room and comfort. Northwest's pre-departure services, increased seat space and recline, enhanced meal and wine service, upgraded headsets offering distortion-free sound, and the elegant design of the new World Club facilities – featuring fireplaces, big screen televisions and expanded personal space – may make this option well worth it.

GETTING AROUND WITH EASE

If you have limited time and wish to travel comfortably and safety, we recommend taking taxis and/or hiring a car, driver, and guide. These forms of transportation and assistance are relatively inexpensive in both Vietnam and Cambodia. You also can rent bicycles and motorbikes, ride the three-wheel pedicabs (cyclos), and take buses. However cheap, charming, and culturally correct, these modes of transportation don't pass our test for comfort, convenience, and safety. In most places short taxi rides cost US$.75 to US$1.50, and a car and driver may run US$25 to US$30 a day. A guide may cost another US$25 to US$30 a day. In some places where your driver speaks your language, he also can function as your guide. We outline these transportation and cost alternatives in the individual destination chapters.

INTERNATIONAL GROUP TOURS

Many visitors to Vietnam and Cambodia come with an organized tour group. Several companies offer a wide variety of interesting package tours that may focus on a particular aspect of these countries (ecology, history, veterans, culture, textiles, culinary, shopping, bicycling, trekking, or hill tribe) or they may include Hong Kong, Thailand, Laos, and Burma as part of a general highlights of Southeast Asia tour. Many of these groups offer excellent value and good service. Best of all, they take out the hassles attendant with arranging your own travel details, especially local transportation, hotels, and guides. You'll find such tour groups through your local travel agent, or search for them online by using our favorite search engine for travel planning – google.com. Just enter the keywords "Travel Vietnam" or "Tour Groups Vietnam" and you'll pull up several relevant websites of groups specializing in travel to Vietnam. You may want to check out the ads for Vietnam and Cambodia in *International Travel News*. The names, addresses, and websites (hotlinks) of their advertisers are included in ITN's website: www.intltravelnews.com. We also identify several local travel agencies and tour groups in the individual destination chapters.

We highly recommend one group in particular for either small group tours or individualized programs for both Vietnam and Cambodia:

GLOBAL SPECTRUM
5683 Columbia Pike, Suite 101
Falls Church, VA 22041
Tel. 1-800-419-4446 or 703-671-9619
Fax 703-671-5747
Email: gspectrum@gspectrum.com
Website: www.asianpassages.com

This company is one of the pioneers of travel to Vietnam and Cambodia with several years of experience in Southeast Asia. Operating their own local offices and vehicles in Vietnam, they offer a variety of specialized tours and customized itineraries for individuals and groups. If you are an independent traveler, you can make all ground arrangements through Global Spectrum, which includes a car, driver, and guide. They have an outstanding local staff that delivers a first-class travel product, including many socially-responsible travel programs. Be sure to visit their website for information on their services. You also can register online to receive a copy of their beautifully illustrated 86-page catalog of programs and their newsletter.

LOCAL TRAVEL AGENCIES

While independent travel in Vietnam and Cambodia is possible, it also can be very challenging. If you have limited time, you are well advised to use the professional services of a group such as Global Spectrum. They can customize your itinerary so that you can basically remain an independent traveler who benefits from the services of travel professionals who know these countries well. They can save you a lot of time, money, and headaches, as well as put you in contact with the best of the best in Vietnam and Cambodia. At the same time, you should be able to quickly arrange tours and travel services once you arrive in the country. Numerous tour companies, travel agencies, and travel cafes have offices in the major cities. Most offer regularly scheduled tours as well as customized tours. They can provide cars, drivers, and guides to meet your individual needs. We include several such services in each destination chapter.

ONLINE TRAVEL DEALS

If you use the Internet, you can easily make airline, hotel, and car rental reservations online by using several online booking groups. The four major reservation services are:

www.expedia.com   www.priceline.com
www.travelocity.com   www.hotwire.com

Other popular online reservation services, with many claiming discount pricing, include:

www.air4less.com   www.moments-notice.com
www.airdeals.com   www.onetravel.com

www.air-fare.com
www.bestfares.com
www.biztravel.com
www.cheaptickets.com
www.concierge.com
www.lowestfare.com

www.site59.com
www.smarterliving.com
www.thetrip.com
www.travelhub.com
www.travelscape.com
www.travelzoo.com

However, while these online booking operations may appear to be convenient, we've found many of them can be more expensive than using a travel agent. This is especially true in the case of airline tickets. You'll often get the best airline rates through consolidators, which may be 30 to 40 percent less than the major online ticketing operations. Consolidators usually have small box ads in the Sunday travel sections of the *New York Times*, *Washington Post*, *Los Angeles Times*, and other major newspapers. Some of them, such as International Discount Travel, also provide price quotes on the Internet: www.idt travel.com. Other popular consolidators specializing in discount ticketing include TicketPlanet (1-800-799-8888, www.ticket planet.com), Airtreks.com (1-800-350-0612, www.airtreks. com), Air Brokers International (1-800-883-3273, www.air brokers.com), Airline Consolidator (1-800-468-5385, www.air consolidator.com), and World Travellers' Club (1-800-693-0411). If you're in a gambling mood, try these two "reverse auction" sites that allow you to set the price in the hopes that the company will make your dream price come true: www. priceline.com and www.hotwire.com. Make certain you are aware of any restrictions, such as departure and return dates, before you book.

PASSING U.S. CUSTOMS

It's always good to know your country's Customs regulations before leaving home. If, for example, you are a U.S. citizen planning to travel abroad, the United States Customs Service provides several helpful publications which are available free of charge from your nearest U.S. Customs Office (or write P.O. Box 7407, Washington, DC 20044). Several also are available in the "Traveler Information" section of the U.S. Customs website, www.customs./travel/travel.htm.

- *Know Before You Go* (Publication #512): Outlines facts about exemptions, mailing gifts, duty-free articles, as well as prohibited and restricted articles. Many rather onerous U.S. Customs duties on products from Vietnam were lifted in April 2001 as part of Vietnam's newly evolving political and economic relationship with the United States. Original art purchased in Vietnam should enter the U.S. duty-free, as should items over 100 years old with proper documentation. However, most other items, especially jewelry, will be dutiable.

- *International Mail Imports* answers many questions regarding mailing items from foreign countries back to the U.S. The U.S. Postal Service sends packages to Customs for examination and assessment of duty before they are delivered to the addressee. Some items are free of duty and some are dutiable. The rules have changed on mail imports, so do check on this before you leave the U.S.

- *GSP and the Traveler* itemizes goods from particular countries that can enter the U.S. duty-free. GSP regulations, which are designed to promote the economic development of certain Third World countries, permit many products, especially arts and handicrafts, to enter the United States duty-free, but only if GSP is currently in effect and tied to particular beneficial countries (currently a total of 140 such countries). Unfortunately, because of strained political relations with the United States, Vietnam and Cambodia at present are not GSP-designated countries, which means most items from these two countries are officially dutiable. However, if you are going on to GSP-qualifying countries, such as nearby Thailand, Malaysia, Indonesia, or the Philippines, chances are your purchases from Vietnam and Cambodia may get merged with purchases from these GSP-qualifying countries. Do check on this before you leave the U.S. so you won't be surprised after you make your purchases in these countries.

U.S. citizens may bring into the U.S. $400 worth of goods free of U.S. taxes every 30 days; the next $1,000 is subject to a flat 3 percent tax (effective as of January 1, 2002). Goods beyond $1,400 are assessed duty at varying rates applied to different classes of goods. If you are in Hanoi or Phnom Penh and uncertain about U.S. duties on particular items, which are valued in excess of $1,400, contact the U.S. Embassy.

Currency and Exchange Rates

The Vietnamese unit of currency is the dong (VND). As we went to press in December 2001, the exchange rate between the dong and the U.S. dollar was US$1 to VND15,783. To check on the latest exchange rates for various currencies relating to the dong, visit these two currency converter websites:

www.oanda.com
www.xe.net/ucc

The dong is issued in denominations of 100, 200, 500, 1,000, 2,000, 5,000, 10,000, 20,000, 50,000, and 100,000. You may want to primarily carry 10,000 (red), 20,000 (blue), and 50,000 (green) dong bills for most purchases and a few 5,000 dong bills for small purchases, including cyclo drivers. Many people seem to run out of small change. The smaller denominations tend to be nuisances.

You can exchange your money, as well as conduct other banking business, at the Bank for Foreign Trade of Vietnam (Vietcom Bank). It has several branches. While it's most convenient to exchange money at your hotel front desk, the exchange rate will be less, although not that bad. Some of the best exchange rates are given at small gold shops that convert U.S. dollars. You'll also get the best exchange rates on larger denomination bills, especially US$100 bills.

ATM machines are increasingly appearing in Hanoi and Saigon, although they are not very widespread.

Traveler's checks are accepted at most major hotels and banks. However, banks charge a 1-2 percent fee for using traveler's checks.

Credit cards are increasingly being accepted in Vietnam. However, most shops that accept them will want to add a commission onto the total to offset their credit card and bank processing charges. In addition, there's a good chance your credit card company may be adding an additional 5 percent foreign currency processing fee at your end. This is often a hidden charge many people are unaware of before they travel. Check with your bank to see if they are adding this fee to your credit card purchases abroad.

Cash in the form of U.S. dollars is still king in both Vietnam and Cambodia. In fact, many shops will accept U.S. dollars as readily as they accept the local currency. Some even prefer U.S. dollars, which they can stretch more dong out of than you (there's still a black market in Vietnam and Cambodia). While we do not recommend carrying large amounts of cash, it sure comes in handy when shopping.

In Cambodia the currency unit is known as the riel (R). For information on Cambodia's currency, see the final chapter on Cambodia.

ELECTRICITY AND WATER

Since electrical current is not uniform throughout Vietnam, be cautious when using appliances with specific voltage requirements. Electricity in most cities is 220 volts, 50 cycles alternating currency (AC). Plug configurations for electrical wall outlets vary. The north follows the continental European style, which requires plugs with two round prongs. Many places in the south use the flat-pin type plugs used in the United States. Most major hotels will provide you with plug converters.

Tap water is not safe to drink in Vietnam and Cambodia. Hotels and restaurants usually provide bottled water. You can purchase inexpensive bottled water in many small markets. Be careful about ice in your drinks. Assume the ice is not made from bottled water, which is usually a correct assumption.

HEALTH AND INSURANCE

You should have few if any health problems in Vietnam and Cambodia as long at you take normal eating and drinking precautions. Drink only bottled water and other bottled drinks, avoid ice (except in top restaurants), and stay clear of uncooked street and market vendor foods. If you do encounter a health problem, it will most likely be diarrhea, which can be treated with a few good over-the-counter remedies such as Imodium. You'll find hundreds of pharmacies in the major cities where you can purchase over-the-counter medications as well as receive free medical advice, which may or may not be good. Major hospitals in Hanoi and Saigon have special sections reserved for foreign patients. While they may be able to adequately handle basic or routine medical problems, don't expect them to operate according to U.S. medical standards or handle serious illnesses or injuries adequately. In addition, doctors and hospitals require cash payments before providing medical services. By all means avoid coming in contact with the local blood supply, which is highly suspect. If you have a serious medical condition, plan to be evacuated to the nearest modern medical facility, which will probably be in Hong Kong or Singapore.

You should consider taking out a special insurance policy when traveling to Vietnam and Cambodia to cover situations not covered by your medical, home, auto, and personal insurance back home. For example, many insurance policies do not cover treatment for illnesses or accidents while traveling outside your home country. Check whether your medical insurance will cover treatment abroad, and consider acquiring evacuation insurance in case serious illness or injuries would require that you be evacuated home through special transportation and health care arrangements. Many companies offer this insurance. One of the best kept travel secrets for acquiring inexpensive evacuation insurance is to join DAN (Divers Alert Network). In the U.S., call 1-800-446-2671 (The Peter B. Bennett Center, 6 West Colony Place, Durham, NC 27705; website: www.diversalertnetwork.org). Without this insurance, special evacuation arrangements could cost US$20,000 to US$50,000! Whether or not you are into adventure travel and plan to engage in physically challenging and risky activities, health and evacuation insurance should be on your "must do" list before departing for your international adventure.

❑ You may want to work with a travel professional, such as www.asianpassages.com, to customize an itinerary.

❑ The best exchange rates in Vietnam are often given at small gold shops.

❑ Most shops that accept credit cards will add a commission to your purchase total.

❑ Many shops will accept U.S. dollars as readily as they accept the local currency. Some prefer U.S. dollars.

❑ Consider acquiring evacuation insurance in case serious illness or injuries require being evacuated home – a flight that could cost up to $50,000!

When considering special travel insurance, first check your current insurance policies to understand if you have any coverage when traveling abroad. Also contact a travel agent to find out what he or she recommends for special coverage. The following websites will connect you to several companies that offer special insurance for travelers:

www.worldtravelcenter.com
www.globaltravelinsurance.com
www.travelinsurance.com
www.travelex.com
www.etravelprotection.com
www.travelguard.com
www.travelsecure.com
www.travelprotect.com
www.globalcover.com

DINING

Many visitors find Vietnamese cuisine to be one of the high-lights of visiting this country. Both Hanoi and Saigon boast several good Vietnamese restaurants as well as some serving excellent French and other international cuisines. Often housed in a beautifully decorated and charming old villa and including live traditional music, these restaurants are often delightful forms of evening entertainment. Khmer cuisine found in Cambodia is less well known to many outsiders. But you will find a few very good Khmer restaurants in Saigon, Phnom Penh, and Siem Reap.

While some of the best international restaurants will be found in the major five-star hotels, most of the best Vietnamese restaurants are found outside hotels. With the exception of the signature Khmer restaurant in the Hotel Le Royal in Phnom Penh, the best Khmer restaurants in Cambodia are found outside hotels.

In each destination chapter we identify the best restaurants for dining out in Vietnam and Cambodia. If you enjoy "lifestyle shopping" – combining great shopping with wonderful restau-rants – you'll find these recommendations useful.

ACCOMMODATIONS

Within the past 10 years numerous five-star hotels have been constructed in Hanoi, China Beach, Saigon, Phnom Penh, and Siem Reap in response to the growing number of business people and upscale tourists visiting these places. See the accom-modations section in the destination chapters for information on the "best of the best" accommodations in our featured cities. Many of these properties are managed by major international hotel chains, such as Marriott, Sofitel, Hilton, and Raffles. They have introduced new standards of service as well as many amenities associated with such fine properties – international restaurants, health clubs, swimming pools, and meeting and conference facilities. Because of the current glut of five-star hotels in Vietnam and Cambodia, you can get bargain rates, with some properties offering 40 to 70 percent discounts off the regular published rate. Ironically, some of the best travel values in these countries are on the so-called expensive hotels, which are very inexpensive by international standards. Be sure to check out the various hotel reservation websites we identify in the destination chapters. Many of these sites provide detailed information on the major three-, four-, and five-star properties in each city, including photos of rooms and facilities. Best of all, most offer discounted room rates for online bookings. Sites, such as www.travelnow.com, will even compare the discounted room rates offered by different websites for the same properties.

As the same time, you'll find numerous inexpensive budget hotels and guesthouses, which have long catered to the travel needs of locals and backpackers. Most of these places are found in particular areas that also include inexpensive restaurants, Internet cafes, and travel cafes. If you normally seek out such budget accommodations, you may want to occasionally upgrade to a four- or five-star property that offers a super deal. In fact, in 2001 you could find some properties that might cost US$200 to US$300 a night in Hong Kong actually went for US$50 to $75 a night in Hanoi, Saigon, Phnom Penh, and Siem Reap. How long this situation will continue depends on the local supply-and-demand situation.

BUSINESS HOURS

In Vietnam most **government offices and agencies** are open Monday through Friday from 8am to 4pm or 5pm, but closed from 11:30am to 1 or 1:30pm. Museums tend to open at 7:30am or 8am and close between 11:30am and 1pm and then open again before closing for the day at 4pm or 4:30pm. Many museums are open Tuesday through Sunday. Since Monday is often a day museums are closed, you may want plan non-museum activities for Monday.

Most **shops** open by 9am and close around 9pm, although some shops open earlier and close earlier. Most **markets** are open from 7:30am to 5pm.

Restaurants that serve breakfast usually open very early in the morning, around 6am. Other restaurants stay open all day. Most major restaurants close around 10:30pm.

Bars, nightclubs, and discos seem to set their own hours. Many start getting active around 11pm and close around 3am.

ANTICIPATED AND UNEQUAL COSTS

Vietnam and Cambodia offer good value for your travel dollar. While they are relatively inexpensive destinations, there is one irritating aspect to the cost of travel in Vietnam that reflects the socialist mentality that runs this country; it frankly doesn't sit well with many visitors from abroad who believe in equal treatment regardless of one's nationality. Vietnam has a two-tiered price structure for tourism. As a foreigner, you are expected to pay two to three times more than locals for the privilege of traveling in Vietnam. You may not notice it that much but it happens everywhere you go. Airline tickets, train tickets, museum admissions, and other fees assessed foreigners are much higher than those assessed locals. This may bother you, even though these differential fees still seem inexpensive – you pay a US$2.00 museum admission fee but the local gets in for $.50. On the other hand, one also must sympathize with the pricing situations. Locals would not be able to travel in their country if they had to pay the prices assessed to foreigners. And the price the government charges locals is not enough to maintain many of the sites. The problem here is more the operation of the system, which must create such distortions and inequalities in order to give the appearance of equality. In other words, foreigners are obliged to subsidize services that don't work very well. As a result, you may feel like you are being exploited by a socialist system that preaches equality. This pricing mentality sometimes spills over into other areas, such as shopping: you may be expected to pay more than locals for various products.

Your cost of travel will largely depend on your style of travel. If you are a backpacker, for example, you could easily travel for under US$20 a day within most cities. However, you probably won't be doing much shopping along the way. If, on the other hand, you prefer experiencing the best of the best in Vietnam and Cambodia, you can quickly spend US$200 to US$300 a night on accommodations. But you'll be hard pressed to spend more than US$30 a person (excluding wine) on a meal. You'll most likely get your best travel value by arranging your trip through a travel agency or tour company.

❑ Some of the best travel values are on the so-called expensive hotels.

❑ In Vietnam many museums are closed on Monday.

❑ Vietnam has a two-tiered price structure for tourism. Foreigners are often expected to pay two to three times more than locals for the privilege of traveling in Vietnam.

❑ Tips are greatly appreciated. Money does talk in Vietnam and Cambodia.

❑ Government tourist information is not well organized nor widely available. The most useful information can be found on the Internet.

TIPPING

Vietnam and Cambodia are gradually moving into a tipping culture as international tourism and standards of service transform the tourism industry. While tips are not expected nor demanded at present, they are greatly appreciated, especially given the low wages most people receive. Money does talk in Vietnam and Cambodia, with a tip often incentivizing personnel. Some top restaurants now add a 10 percent service charge. Many of the **major hotels** include a 10 percent service charge on top of the room tax.

Especially in **restaurants** and situations where the service is good, you may want to leave a five or 10 percent tip or some small change to show your appreciation for the service.

Most **tour guides** expect to receive tips. If you are with a group, a tip of US$1 to US$2 a day per person is fine. If you have a personal guide, a tip of US$4 to US$5 a day is acceptable.

Who and how much you tip is up to you. Again, keep in mind that most service personnel are paid very low wages, with many earning around US$50 a month. We normally follow these two general tipping rules:

1. **Carry lots of small change with you for small tips**, especially 1,000 and 5,000 dong banknotes in Vietnam and 500 and 1,000 riel banknotes in Cambodia. We also carry some "beggar money" – several 500 dong banknotes in Vietnam and 200 and 500 riel banknotes in Cambodia.

2. **If you are going to tip, be sure to tip generously to the right people at the right time.** Timing is everything when tipping. Important people should be tipped early on and generously if you want to maximize their services. For example, tip your hotel doorman, porter, and room attendant for initial services received. Let them know you will be appreciating their future service. Don't decide to keep everyone guessing what you plan to give them when you leave. They may turn out to be your best friend for getting things you need, from extra service to information and advice on the city.

For additional advice on tipping practices, visit the following website on proper tipping behavior:

www.tipping.org

TOURIST OFFICES

Government tourist information is not well organized nor widely available in either Vietnam or Cambodia. The Vietnam

Embassy in the United States provides some very general online information about tourism in Vietnam, which includes recommended tour companies, travel tips, transportation, festivals, and linkages to relevant web resources:

www.vietnamembassy-usa.org/travel

Many other websites, which we identify in the next section as well as in the destination chapters, include useful information on tourism in Vietnam and Cambodia.

Once you arrive in-country, don't expect to walk into a government tourism office to receive free brochures, maps, and advice on where to stay and what to do. That's a foreign concept that doesn't operate in these countries. Instead, in Vietnam you will meet government bureaucrats who are trying to run what is usually a private enterprise – tour companies. The government-sponsored tourism agency in Vietnam – Vietnamtourism – operates like a travel agency. It primarily attempts to sell tour services rather than dispense free information to curious travelers. Its provincial counterpart in Saigon – Saigontourist – is more entrepreneurial but also primarily operates as a travel agency in competition with private sector travel agencies. You may have better luck going to a private travel agency or one of the many travel cafes for information on travel in Vietnam. Even your hotel concierge may be more helpful.

To a very large extent, you are on your own in Vietnam and Cambodia with guidebooks and a few commercial maps and brochures you may acquire at bookstores or through travel agencies, tour groups, and hotels. Be sure to visit the many Internet sites we recommend as well as use various search engines to locate travel information about Vietnam and Cambodia on the Internet. Indeed, the Internet will most likely become your most useful source of information on travel in Vietnam.

USEFUL WEBSITES

Several websites provide useful information on Vietnam and Cambodia. In the case of Vietnam, you should start by exploring the following websites:

- **1 Saigon**   1saigon.net
- **Groovy Saigon**   groovysaigon.com
- **Hanoi Travel**   hanoitravel.com

- Saigon Today   saigontoday.net
- Saigon Connect   saigonconnect.com
- SaigonTourist   saigon-tourist.com
- Things Asian   thingsasian.com
- Vietnam Avenue   vietnamavenue.com
- Vietnam Economic
  Times   www.vneconomy.com.vn
- Vietnam Online   vietnamonline.com/travel/
                        hanoi.html
- Vietnam Tourism   vietnamtourism.com
- Vietnam Travel   vietnam-travel.com
- Vietnam.com   vietnam.com
- Where to Go in
  Vietnam   vee-n.com/wtg

A few websites also focus on travel to Cambodia. Start with the first site (Canby Publications) and then go to the others:

- Canby Publications   www.canbypublications.com
- Cambodia Indochina   cambodia.indochina-services.
                         com
- Cambodia Travel   cambodiatravel.com
- Cambodia-Travel   cambodia-travel.ws/links.htm
- Go Cambodia   gocambodia.com/travel
- Visit-Mekong   visit-mekong.com/cambodia

We identify several other websites relevant to hotels in each destination chapter.

For useful online travel guidebook treatments of Vietnam and Cambodia, visit the websites of Fodor's, Lonely Planet, and Rough Guides:

www.fodors.com
www.lonelyplanet.com
www.roughguides.com

For travel-shopping information related to this guidebook as well as several other countries, visit our iShopAroundTheWorld website:

www.ishoparoundtheworld.com

Shopping Treasures and Rules For Success

WHILE SHOPPING IN VIETNAM AND CAM-
bodia may initially look familiar to you, there
are certain things you need to know about these
places that will make your shopping experience
more rewarding. From encountering new people,
discovering unique products, bargaining, and paying for items,
to packing, shipping, and handling customs, you should find
shopping to be one of the highlights of your Vietnam and
Cambodian travel adventure. You'll encounter extremely enjoyable and rewarding shopping cultures that will yield many
cherished treasures to grace your home and wardrobe.

DISCOVER UNIQUE TREASURES

Each destination we examine in subsequent chapters yields its
own unique mix of products and shopping rules. In **Hanoi**, for
example, the overwhelming emphasis is on art. Indeed, art
lovers quickly embrace Hanoi because of its large and talented
art community, which produces some really beautiful works.
Hanoi is the major center for contemporary Vietnamese art and
an important center for Asian art in general. There's a high
probability you will spend some time shopping Hanoi's many

art galleries as well as make a few art purchases in the process of discovering many attractive oil and lacquer paintings. But before making such purchases, you need to know how the art galleries and artists operate when it comes time to make a critical purchase. These are not your typical Western art galleries that represent particular artists. This is a highly competitive and commercial business where a single famous artist may be represented by several galleries on the same street! In addition, prices may appear fixed, but you'll soon discover they are only fixed for people who fail to bargain. Indeed, after doing some comparative shopping for works by the same artist, you should be able to get a 20-percent discount from the initial asking price – but only if you ask. If you persist and the gallery contacts the artists for even more price flexibility, you may be able to get a 30-percent discount. In preparation for such shopping situations in Vietnam, we detail the local shopping culture for art in Hanoi, including bargaining strategies, in Chapter 4. Most of these strategies also are relevant to purchasing art elsewhere in Vietnam. Hanoi also is famous for its silk and embroidery materials, lacquerware, and assorted handicrafts. While by no means a shopper's paradise, Hanoi is a delightful shopping center, which seems to get better and better each month. Indeed, Hanoi continues to amaze many visitors who often vote it to be their favorite city in Vietnam. It's a city of many surprises, including numerous shopping opportunities that add to its aging charm and colorful culture.

Hoi An in central Vietnam seems to be everyone's favorite city and one of the real highlights of any visit to Vietnam. Along with Hanoi, the fishing village, art colony, and tourist magnet of Hoi An is a real charmer. In fact, when asked what really stood out in their visit to Vietnam, many people put Hoi An at the top of their lists of great places to visit and shop. Simply quaint, with aging buildings, fascinating architecture, friendly people, and wonderful ambience, Hoi An is all about shopping for art, silk, tailored garments, handicrafts, and souvenirs. While the art here appears more amateurish than the more professional and expensive art found in Hanoi's and Saigon's top galleries, nonetheless, this is a delightful place to spend a day or two engaged in lifestyle shopping.

Saigon is as energetic and rambunctious as ever, a city that sometimes appears to represent capitalism run amuck. This is a young and vibrant in-your-face city that reminds many seasoned travelers of Bangkok a decade or two ago. It's Vietnam's most entrepreneurial and fashionable city offering numerous and varied shopping opportunities for everything from art, antiques, and home decorative items to jewelry, silk, fashion, lacquerware, handicrafts, souvenirs, and pirated CDs, DVDs, and videos. You can easily spend three days shopping Saigon's many markets and street shops. Saigon also has its own set of shopping rules, which can be added to the many rules we outline for shopping in Hanoi. We detail these in Chapter 5.

Cambodia is still in recovery after several wretched years of debilitating war, genocide, and communism. It has very few well established companies offering quality products to visitors. But you will find some good shopping opportunities for antiques, silver, textiles, gems, and handicrafts. Much of Cambodia's shopping is centered in markets and a few quality street shops and hotel boutiques in Phnom Penh and Siem Reap. The shopping emphasis in Cambodia is on textiles, handicrafts, and gems.

TAKE KEY SHOPPING INFORMATION

Depending on what you plan to buy, you should take all the necessary information you need to make informed shopping decisions. Do your shopping research and documentation *before* you leave home. Shops in Vietnam and Cambodia are not good places to get an expensive education, especially when it comes to purchasing art, antiques, gems, and jewelry. If you are looking for art, antiques, and home furnishings, include with your "wish list" room measurements to help you determine if particular items will fit into your home. Many of the paintings you find in Hanoi and Saigon are done on large canvases that require a great deal of wall space to display them properly. Without floor and wall measurements, you may have to guess whether or not a particular piece of art will work in your home. Consider bringing along photographs of particular rooms you hope to furnish.

❏ Take with you measurements and photographs of rooms that could become candidates for home decorative items.

❏ Be sure to take information on any particular clothes, accessories, or jewelry (sizes, colors, comparative prices) with you to look for or have made when in Vietnam.

❏ Half the fun of shopping is the serendipity of discovering the unique and exotic.

If you plan to shop for clothes and accessories, your homework should include taking an inventory of your closets and identifying particular colors, fabrics, and designs you wish to acquire to complement and enlarge your present wardrobe. Good-quality tailored clothing and handbags can be excellent buys in Vietnam – one-third of what you may pay back home.

Be sure you know what colors work best for your wardrobe and bring photos or models of garments you wish to have copied. Tailoring work in Vietnam can be very good and is usually inexpensive.

DO COMPARATIVE SHOPPING

You should do comparative shopping both at home and within Vietnam and Cambodia in order to get a good idea of what is or is not a good buy. Our rule of thumb is that if a comparable item is avaiable at home, and it is not at least 20 percent cheaper buying it abroad, it's probably not worth the effort of buying it abroad for such a small savings. This is especially true in the case of gemstones and jewelry where it's usually "buyer beware" when dealing with such issues as authenticity, quality, and pricing. After all, back home you most likely will have return privileges, and you may be protected by consumer protection regulations or you can take legal action should such items be misrepresented.

However, many items in these countries are unique, especially in the case of art, antiques, and handicrafts. These are the type of items one has to see, feel, and fall in love with.

The first step in doing comparative shopping starts at home. Determine exactly what you want and need. Make lists. As you compile your lists, spend some time "window shopping" in the local stores, examining catalogs, telephoning for information, and checking Internet shopping sites such as www.novica.com and www.eziba.com. However, many of these places do not include items from Vietnam and Cambodia but they may have comparable items from neighboring countries, such as China, Thailand, Indonesia, and the Philippines. If you find a lacquer bowl made in Vietnam, chances are it will cost five to 10 times more than what you would pay in either Hanoi or Saigon. Lacquerware is definitely a good buy in Vietnam compared to what you will pay abroad. It only requires comparative shopping among various shops in Vietnam, where prices can vary considerably, from US$5 to US$20 for similar items.

Once you arrive in Vietnam and Cambodia, your shopping plans will probably change considerably as you encounter many new items you had not planned to purchase but which attract your interest and buying attention. Indeed, half the fun of shopping while traveling in our featured destinations is the serendipity of discovering the unique and exotic – a beautiful contemporary oil painting, gorgeous silk fabric, lovely lacquer tableware, and an intricately carved stone figure – things you could not have anticipated encountering but which you now see, feel, and judge as possible acquisitions for your home and wardrobe. These are the great shopping moments that require local knowledge about differences in quality and pricing. Many products, such as paintings, lacquerware, embroidery, or jewelry, may be unique one-of-a-kind items that are difficult to compare. You must judge them in terms of their designs, colors, and intrinsic value. Other items, such as gemstones, ready-made clothes, ceramics, and souvenir items will beg comparative shopping because the same or similar quality items are widely available in numerous shops and factories.

You'll have plenty of opportunities to do comparison shopping in Hanoi and Saigon. You are well advised to visit several shops soon after your arrival in order to get some sense of market prices for various items you are likely to frequently encounter, especially art, textiles, lacquerware, and handicrafts. Many of these items can be quickly surveyed in markets.

KEEP TRACK OF RECEIPTS

It's important to keep track of all of your purchases for making an accurate Customs declaration. Be sure to ask for receipts wherever you shop. If a shop doesn't issue receipts, ask them to create a receipt by writing the information on a piece of paper, include the shop's name and address, and sign it.

Since it's so easy to misplace receipts, you might want to organize your receipts using a form similar to the following example.

CUSTOMS DECLARATION RECORD FORM

	Receipt #	Item	Price (VND)	Price (US$)
1.	3211	Hoa painting	2,100,000	$150.00
2.				
3.				
4.				

This can be especially useful when receipts are written in a language you cannot read. Staple a sheet or two of notebook or accountant's paper to the front of a large manila envelope and number down the left side of the page. Draw one or two vertical columns down the right side. Each evening, sort through that day's purchases, write a description including style and color of the purchase on the accompanying receipt, and enter that item on your receipt record. Record the receipt so later you'll know exactly which item belongs to the receipt – especially if the receipt is written in Vietnamese or Khmer! Put the receipts in the manila envelope and pack the purchases away. If you're missing a receipt, make a note beside the appropriate entry.

KEY SHOPPING RULES FOR SUCCESS

We outline 31 important shopping rules relevant to Hanoi and Saigon in the chapters on these major destinations. In general, the following shopping rules are relevant to most places in Vietnam as well in Cambodia. However, be sure to review the rules we outline in the individual destination chapters.

1. **The best quality shopping is found in and near the major five-star hotels.** Quality shops tend to go where the money congregates. While shopping in markets for inexpensive items can be fun, don't expect to find quality items with market vendors.

2. **Remember to seek out the best shops by checking with people "in the know."** The concierges in most five-star hotels know where the best shopping can be found. Some will even have a list of best shops in their city.

3. **Bargain for most items you purchase with the expectation of some success.** Few shops have fixed prices. Most will extend a discount if you ask the simple questions, *"Can we do any better on this price?"* Doing better often means a five- to 10-percent discount and sometimes 20 percent. Few shops will go beyond 20 percent, but you don't know unless you try. In highly touristed Hoi An, for example, we've had discounts go as high as 75 percent!

4. **Expect to pay cash for most items.** These are cash-and-carry countries. Some shops may accept credit cards but most do not. Those that do may want to add a commission fee to the purchase price.

5. **U.S. dollars go a long way when shopping.** U.S. dollars are often preferred to the local currency. You may get a better price by offering to pay in U.S. dollars.

6. **Plan to do your own packing and re-packing.** Most shops will claim to do packing, but chances are you will not be happy with the result. Either closely supervise the packing process by instructing the shop how to pack things securely or do your own packing and re-packing by acquiring packing material, especially bubble wrap and cardboard. Don't trust even the best hotels to do an adequate packing job.

7. **Collect receipts for everything you purchase.** You may need the receipt for Customs or as documentation for contacting the merchant. Make sure you have essential information on the receipt – shop name, address, and telephone and fax numbers.

8. **Take photos of all your purchases.** It's always good to have a visual record of your purchases, and especially with the merchant holding your item. This photo may make a great moment of your shopping adventure as well as serve as documentation for where you purchased the item.

9. **Don't become too zealous in purchasing pirated CDs, DVDs, and videos.** While such items are readily available in the markets of Vietnam and Cambodia, you will be lucky to get good quality copies, which are mass-produced in China. Many of the products have flaws. You often get what you pay for, which in this case is not much.

10. **Decide on how you will ship before making any purchases of large-sized items.** Shipping can be problematic and very expensive. Purchasing a large woven basket for US$50 but then learning you must pay over US$400 to ship it does not make good shopping sense, unless it is especially unique. Many shops will arrange shipping through FedEx, DHL, or UPS, but such shipping is usually very expensive. Consider taking most items with you as part of your carry-on or check-through luggage. Many places can build boxes that can be checked in as part of your regular luggage allowance or taken as excess baggage – often a cheaper alternative to the standard air freight services.

BARGAINING RULES FOR BARGAINS

Unlike many other Asian countries, there is very little bargaining in socialist Vietnam and Cambodia. However, the commercial ethic is well and alive in these countries despite their ostensible communist systems. While stated prices are very close to final prices, this does not mean you should not bargain when shopping in Vietnam and Cambodia. Most merchants will extend a small discount, usually from 10-to 20-percent, if you ask. As we outline in the chapters on Hanoi and Saigon, major art purchases in Vietnam can sometimes result in 20- to 30-percent discounts. But don't expect to get 40-, 50-, or even 60-percent discounts as you might in other Third World countries where bargaining is a standard way of determining prices. Indeed, shopping here is not the same as shopping in China, Thailand, or Indonesia – places where bargaining often results in a 40- to 60-percent discounts, with China sometimes reaching 90 percent!

When bargaining in Vietnam and Cambodia, follow these basic rules:

1. **Do comparative shopping before deciding on what you are willing to pay for an item**. Many shops sell similar items, which may vary in price by as much as 50 percent. Get a good sense of the "going rate" before making final buying decisions – unless it is a unique item and may be gone if you return for it.

2. **Don't get emotional about items in front of salespeople**. The more you let salespeople know you have fallen in love with an item, the more difficulty you will have in bargaining. Try to look disinterested. You want the salesperson to think you need some financial incentive (a discount) in order to make a buying decision.

3. **When asking *"How much is this item?,"* don't show any emotion when you hear the answer**. The stated price should be considered the first asking price. Indicate you are thinking about it, but don't appear emotionally attached to the item. Keep cool, indicating nonverbally that you may be uncertain about buying at this time.

4. **Take your time.** Once you learn the price, count to 20 before responding and then say *"Oh, it's that much?"* Then start looking around at other items in the shop. Take a

few minutes before returning to the item that you asked about. This is not the time to appear overly anxious to buy. The more time the salesperson spends with you, the more likely you will make progress in negotiating the price.

5. **Ask your first bargaining question about the "possibility" of a discount.** Return to the item and examine it again. Take your time and then say something to this effect: *"Is it possible to do any better on the price?"* As you will probably quickly discover, anything is possible in Vietnam and Cambodia. The point of this question is to get the salesperson to volunteer an alternative price. Chances are the response to your question will be a five-percent discount. This is a good starting point because it's likely to be a green light for negotiating another five- to 15-percent discount.

6. **Make a counter offer that is 40 percent of the initial asking price and then keep moving toward an acceptable 20-percent discount.** This offer will most likely be rejected, but it will probably lead to another five-percent discount. If the salesperson says "10 percent," counter by asking for a 30-percent discount. This, too, will most likely be rejected, although in some cases persistence will result in such a discount. Keep going back and forth, giving five percent each time, until you reach an acceptable 20-percent discount.

7. **Slowly leave the shop if you're not getting the discount you want.** Tell the salesperson you'll "think about it" and maybe come back. But make one final offer as you start to step out of the shop. If the response is still unacceptable, say "Thank you" and leave with the idea of looking around some more and possibly returning to negotiate a final price. But don't wait two or three days. By that time someone else may have purchased the item and thus you'll be disappointed for having passed it up because of a few dollars.

8. **Return to the shop either at the very end of the day or the first of the next day.** Timing is important in the final negotiation. The "last customer of the day" or the "first customer of the day" often has a price advantage. It could mean an additional five- to 10-percent discount.

9. **Buy the item regardless of the final outcome of your negotiations.** There's a time to give up and succumb to the inevitable – you're just not going to get your way. Don't feel like you're losing face since your face is going to be gone shortly and no one will know what happened other than you and the salesperson. If you fall in love with an item but you're not making progress on getting a discount, go ahead and buy it anyway. If you don't, you will probably regret having passed it up just because you didn't get the price you wanted. Bargaining can become a very ego-involved activity that can cloud good shopping judgments. In the end, what's really important is acquiring something you love. Your purchase also will come with an interesting bargaining tale.

10. **Bargain for needs, not greed.** Bargaining can be dangerous when it's not put in a larger shopping context. It's easy to get carried away with the bargaining process, especially in busy market settings. Make sure you really want something before starting the bargaining process. If you don't, you may end up acquiring many things you quickly lose interest in because they were "good deals" at the time. Savvy bargainers haggle for things they need and want – not just because they enjoy winning in the bargaining process.

BEWARE OF SCAMS

Although one hopes this will never happen, you may encounter unscrupulous merchants who take advantage of you. Your best line of defense is to be very careful wherever you go and whatever you do in relation to handling money. A few simple precautions will help avoid some of these problems:

- **Do not trust anyone with your money** unless you have proper assurances they are giving you exactly what you agreed upon. Trust is something that should be earned – not automatically given to friendly strangers you may like.

- **Do your homework** so you can determine quality and value as well as anticipate certain types of scams. The most likely scams relate to misrepresenting the value of art, antiques, gemstones, and jewelry. Make sure you're not buying a fake or something of inferior quality.

- **Examine the goods carefully**, assuming something may be or will go wrong. Remember, if it seems too good to be true, it probably is.

- **Watch very carefully how the merchant handles items** from the moment they leave your hands until they get wrapped and into a bag.

- **Request receipts** that list specific items and the prices you paid. Although most shops are willing to "give you a receipt" specifying whatever price you want them to write for purposes of deceiving Customs, be careful in doing so. While you may or may not deceive Customs, your custom-designed receipt may become a double-edged sword, especially if you later need a receipt with the real price to claim your goods or a refund. If the shop is to ship your item to your home address, be sure you have a shipping receipt which also specifies insurance against both loss and damage.

- **Take photos of your purchases.** We strongly recommend taking photos of your major purchases, especially anything that is being entrusted to someone else to be packed and shipped. Better still, take a photo of the seller holding the item, just in case you later need to identify the person with whom you dealt. This photo will give you a visual record of your purchase should you later have problems receiving your shipment. You'll also have a photo to show Customs if they have any questions about the contents of your shipment.

- **Protect yourself against scams by using credit cards** whenever possible – especially for big ticket items which could present problems, even though using them may cost you a little more. Although your credit card company is not obligated to do so, most will ask the merchant for documentation, if you have problems, and if not satisfactorily received, may remove the charge from your bill.

If you are victimized, all is not necessarily lost. You should report the problem immediately to local authorities, the police, your credit card company, or insurance company. While inconvenient and time consuming, nonetheless, in many cases you will eventually get satisfactory results.

Ship With Ease

Shipping can be a problem in Vietnam and Cambodia since many shops are not experienced with international shipping. You should not pass up buying lovely items because you feel reluctant to ship them home. Indeed, some travelers only buy items that will fit into their suitcase because they are not sure how to ship larger items. We seldom let shipping considerations affect our buying decisions. For us, *shipping is one of those things that must be arranged*. You have numerous shipping alternatives, from hiring a professional shipping company to hand-carrying your goods on board the plane. Shipping may or may not be costly, depending on how much you plan to ship and by which means.

Before leaving home, you should identify the best point of entry for goods returning home by air or sea. Once abroad, you generally have five shipping alternatives:

1. Take everything with you.

2. Do your own packing and shipping through the local post office (for small packages only).

3. Have each shop ship your purchases.

4. Arrange to have one shop consolidate all of your purchases into a single shipment.

5. Hire a local shipper to make all arrangements.

Taking everything with you is fine if you don't have much and if you don't mind absorbing excess baggage charges. If you are within your allowable baggage allowance, you can have large items packed to qualify as part of your luggage. If you have more items than what is allowable, ask about the difference between "Excess Baggage" and "Unaccompanied Baggage." Excess baggage is very expensive, while unaccompanied baggage is less expensive, although by no means cheap.

If items are small enough and we don't mind waiting six to eight weeks, we may send them through the local post office by parcel post; depending on the weight, sometimes air mail is relatively inexpensive through local post offices.

Doing your own packing and shipping may be cheaper, but it is a pain and thus no savings in the long run. You waste valuable time waiting in lines and trying to figure out the local rules and regulations concerning permits, packing, materials, sizes, and weights.

On the other hand, many shops, especially art galleries, can ship goods for customers. They often pack the items free and only charge you for the actual postage or freight. If you choose to have a shop ship for you, insist on a receipt specifying they will ship the item. Also, stress the importance of packing the item well to avoid possible damage. If they cannot insure the item against breakage or loss, do not ship through them. Invariably a version of Murphy's Law operates when shipping: *"If it is not insured and has the potential to break or get lost, it will surely break or get lost!"* At this point, seek some alternative means of shipping. If you are shipping only one or two items, it is best to let a reputable shop take care of your shipping.

We did violate this shipping principle in Hanoi by shipping a lacquer painting by Airborne Express. Friends also shipped a box of handicrafts with the same company and at the same time we shipped. We even went to the Airborne Express office with

our items, watched the local official inspect everything, and resealed the package. The packing was more than adequate for this type of air service. As we finalized arrangements, we were alarmed to discover that shipments from Hanoi could not be insured through Airborne Express. Against what we now know should have been better judgment, we went ahead and shipped based upon our inspection and packing job as well as the reputation of Airborne Express. When we arrived home, both boxes had been damaged, either by Airborne Express handlers, U.S. Customs inspectors, or others. Since Airborne Express would not insure the shipment, we had to absorb this loss. Given this experience, our recommendation is two-fold. First, check whether you can insure your shipment against damage and loss. Second, take whatever you can with you. Needless to say, given our ill-fated shipping experience, we are very reluctant to ship anything from Vietnam.

If you have several large purchases – at least one cubic meter – consider using local shippers since it is cheaper and safer to consolidate many separate purchases into one shipment which is well packed and insured. Sea freight charges are usually figured by volume or the container. There is a minimum charge

– usually you will pay for at least one cubic meter whether you are shipping that much or less. Air freight is calculated using both weight and volume, and usually there is no minimum. You pay only for the actual amount you ship. One normally does not air freight large, heavy items, but for a small light shipment, air freight could actually cost you less and you'll get your items much faster. However, many shops in Vietnam prefer shipping everything by air freight rather than sea. Since this can be very expensive, make sure you understand the costs before deciding to purchase a large item. When using air freight, use an established and reliable airline, even though in the end you may not know who will actually transport your shipment. In the case of sea freight, choose a local company which has an excellent reputation among expatriates for shipping goods. Ask your hotel concierge or front desk personnel about reliable shippers. For small shipments, try to have charges computed both ways – for sea and for air freight. Sea shipments incur port charges that can further add to your costs. Port charges at the shipment's point of entry will not normally be included in the price quoted by the local shipping agent. They have no way of knowing what these charges will be. If you have figures for both means of shipping, you can make an informed choice.

We have tried all five shipping alternatives with various results. Indeed, we tend to use these alternatives in combination. For example, we take everything we can with us until we reach the point where the inconvenience and cost of excess baggage requires some other shipping arrangements. We consolidate our shipments with one key shop in a major city early in our trip and have shipments from other cities in that country sent to our shop for consolidation.

When you use a shipper, be sure to examine alternative shipping arrangements and prices. The type of delivery you specify at your end can make a significant difference in the overall shipping price. If you don't specify the type of delivery you want, you may be charged the all-inclusive door-to-door rate. For example, if you choose door-to-door delivery with unpacking services, you will pay a premium to have your shipment clear Customs, moved through the port, transported to your door, and unpacked by local movers. On the other hand, it is cheaper for you to designate port to port. When the shipment arrives, you arrange for a broker to clear the shipment through Customs and arrange for transport to your home. You do your own unpacking and dispose of the trash. It will take a little more of your time to make the arrangements and unpack. If you live near a port of entry, you may clear the shipment at Customs and pick up the shipment yourself.

We simply cannot over-stress the importance of finding and establishing a personal relationship with a good local shipper who will provide you with services which may go beyond your immediate shipping needs. A good local shipping contact will enable you to continue shopping in Vietnam or Cambodia even after returning home.

Great
Destinations

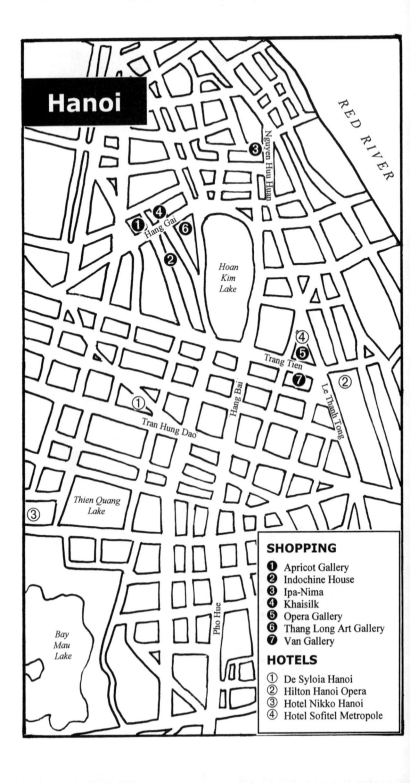

Hanoi

RED RIVER

Nguyen Huu Huan

❸

❶ ❹ Hang Gai
❻

❷

Hoan Kim Lake

④
⑤
Trang Tien

❼

Hang Bai

Le Thanh Tong

②

①

Tran Hung Dao

Thien Quang Lake

③

Pho Hue

Bay Mau Lake

SHOPPING

❶ Apricot Gallery
❷ Indochine House
❸ Ipa-Nima
❹ Khaisilk
❺ Opera Gallery
❻ Thang Long Art Gallery
❼ Van Gallery

HOTELS

① De Syloia Hanoi
② Hilton Hanoi Opera
③ Hotel Nikko Hanoi
④ Hotel Sofitel Metropole

Hanoi

HANOI IS VIETNAM'S CULTURAL AND POLITI-
cal center and one of Southeast Asia's most interesting and seductive cities for travelers. It's the one
city in Vietnam that many visitors fall in love with.
It has the look and feel of the "real Vietnam," more
so than Saigon, which is often viewed as just another big and
chaotic Asian city.

Like much of Vietnam, the realities of Hanoi are not what
one might expect. It definitely feels like it's in a time warp –
think 1950s and 1960s – but reaching out for the 21st century.
Exuding charming yet crumbling Third World chaos, Hanoi is
by stretches of some imaginations a beautiful city. You sense
this immediately as you tour the city, pass by its 18 lakes, visit
its many museums and monuments, attend its water puppet

cultural performances, try its many cafes and restaurants, and shop its numerous art galleries, markets, and streets.

If you're expecting a really beautiful city, as some exuberant writers note, you'll probably be disappointed with what you see. Its superficial beauty quickly wears thin as you discover the city's many Third World characteristics. It's where the arts thrive and where the government readily portrays the country's exaggerated history, arts, culture, and peoples. Considered attractive because of its tree-lined streets, numerous lakes, aging colonial architecture, and charming people, Hanoi is also a city undergoing major transformation as more and more foreign investment results in new high-rise hotels and office buildings as well as an infrastructure of restaurants and shops to cater to Hanoi's new upscale clientele. It will never be the same. A lively, chaotic, and immensely interesting metropolis, Hanoi is not to be missed.

A City of Interesting People

From the moment you arrive at the international airport until the day you leave for other parts of Vietnam, you know this is a very different place from most other cities and countries you may have visited. A sprawling low-rise city of over 3 million people, Hanoi is a charming, friendly, elegant, and worn city which appears to be extremely receptive to visitors. While the city is rich in physical attributes, it's the fascinating street activity and engaging people that really make this city such an fascinating place to visit. Indeed, many visitors find the people to be Hanoi's, as well as Vietnam's, greatest asset. Except for a few persistent beggars and pesky street urchins, who can be irritating after a while, the people are generally friendly and well intentioned. The children are absolutely delightful, often eager to approach strangers and have their pictures taken. Best of all, this is not a place that exhibits many of the negative aspects of tourism, such as touts, hustlers, and rip-off artists who specialize in taking advantage of naive tourists, although scams do occur. In Hanoi, it's the local people who seem to exhibit a certain degree of naivete and innocence that is sweet, charming, and seductive. One hopes

The fascinating street activity and engaging people make this city a very interesting place.

that Hanoi does not lose this special quality as tourism continues to expand.

UNIQUE TREASURES AND PLEASURES

Hanoi offers numerous treasures and pleasures to visitors who know how to approach this city and its surrounding area right. From the moment you step off the airplane and walk down the stairs to the nondescript terminal, you sense this is a bustling city in transition. The small airport, with its aging Russian planes basking on the tarmac, reminds one of a small-town commuter facility which has outlived its usefulness. Indeed, nearby, the partly constructed new concrete and glass terminal stands in anticipation of a significant increase in air travel to Hanoi.

Hanoi is all about mixed images past, present, and future. Despite more than 50 years of indigenous socialism and sacrificial communism, this is a city that still wears its imperial and colonial pasts well, as evidenced in shaded tree-lined streets, fading colonial architecture, the wonderful well-preserved Hotel Sofitel Metropole and Opera House, and the impressive Temple of Literature and Old Pillar Pagoda. It also displays well its post-colonial history of battles fought against foreigners and victories won by its national heros, as displayed in the somber Ho Chi Minh Mausoleum, the larger-than-life Ho Chi Minh Museum, the Hanoi Hilton Prison, and scattered monuments to fallen heros. But this also is a city of impressive art, culture, and religion as evidenced by its always delightful water puppet shows, commercial art galleries, pagodas, the Museum of Fine Arts, and the Museum of Ethnology.

❑ Hanoi wears its imperial and colonial pasts well.

❑ It's increasingly a colorful, vibrant, and entrepreneurial community offering wonderful art, intriguing culture, delightful restaurants, and an amazing amount of shopping.

❑ Visitors are often pleasantly surprised by this city's shopping scene.

❑ History has been both kind and brutal to this city, a sort of hunker-down struggle with both the past and present.

❑ Hanoi's best years most likely lie ahead with tourism playing a significant role.

You can't escape Hanoi's obvious reality – a chaotic yet restrained Third World city in search of a modern future where capitalism might be able to coexist with Vietnamese-style communism, if ever there were such a possible kinship without major political costs. Hanoi surprises many visitors who expect a rather drab and utilitarian city hunkered down to the serious business of governing an always recalcitrant and contentious country. It's increasingly a colorful, vibrant, and entrepreneurial community offering wonderful art, intriguing culture, marvelous restaurants, and an amazing amount of shopping. Indeed, one senses that capitalism is firmly entrenched here, even though it appears to be at a basic cash-and-carry street vendor level. The constant and noisy parade of bicycles and speeding motorcycles puts visitors on notice that this city is on the move. Its people love to eat, drink beer, and shop – and shop, drink beer, and eat. Perhaps this is Hanoi's new destiny, memorable activities you will find most appealing as you explore this city's many treasures and pleasures.

But it's the level and intensity of shopping that often amazes visitors who are not prepared for such a capitalistic activity in what has become one of the last bastions of communism. After all, what's there to buy in Hanoi? Travelers quickly discover there's a great deal of fun shopping in this city – especially street-level bazaar variety where you have an opportunity to meet local people – be it for arts and crafts, pirated music, or consumer goods. Occasionally an exquisite art gallery or exclusive silk shop turns heads as it hints that there is much more to shopping and the Vietnamese economy than what initially meets the eye. From the traditional guild streets of the Old Quarter crammed with consumer goods to elegant galleries along the main streets and in residential areas, visitors are often pleasantly surprised by this city's shopping scene. There are some real treasures here that beg to be discovered by enterprising and adventuresome travel-shoppers. While not quite a shopper's paradise, nonetheless, Hanoi has a great deal to offer visitors who are interested in Vietnam's impressive fine arts scene, craft traditions, and silk garments.

GETTING TO KNOW YOU

Located 100 miles west of the sea, along the banks of the Red River, Hanoi is a flat, sprawling, and chaotic metropolis with a long and tumultuous history. Over 60 miles of dikes protect the city from perennial floods that threaten to engulf it. While occupying a large geographic area, it retains a large-town atmosphere which can be easily explored on foot or by cyclo (three-wheel pedicab).

THE BURDEN AND PROMISE OF HISTORY

History has been both kind and brutal to Hanoi, a sort of hunker-down struggle with both the past and present. Attempts to shed its imperial, colonial, and war-time pasts have been less than successful. Today, Hanoi remains an interesting amalgam of a long and sometimes torturous history, which is well displayed in its many monuments, museums, and neighborhoods. In many respects, Vietnam is a captive of an often obsessive and burdensome history. And Hanoi reminds you of who is in charge of writing a glorious history so future generations can look to the past rather than venture into the future with optimism and enthusiasm. This preoccupation with history becomes even more apparent when you visit more entrepreneurial Saigon in the south where Hanoi has tried to "educate" and tame the locals with lots of value-loaded museums.

Traces of human settlements in this region date to 300 B.C. From 1010 to 1830 this area was known as the Imperial city of Thang Long, "The City of the Soaring Dragon." Influenced by a combination of occupying Chinese forces and indigenous Vietnamese imperial courts, the city became famous for its temples, palaces, lakes, dikes, and artisan and merchant communities (along the city's eastern wall), and Vietnam's first university. In 1831 this area become known as Hanoi, "The City on the Bend in the River." Captured in 1882 by the French, the imperial city Hanoi, the following year, became the capital of the new northern French protectorate of Tonkin. From then until the French defeat in 1954 at the famous battle of Dien Bien Phu, Hanoi took on the character of a small and comfortable French colonial city.

Since 1954, Hanoi has remained the capital of both a divided (pre-1975 North Vietnam) and a united (post-1975) Vietnam. Known for its broad boulevards and French-inspired architecture (government buildings and villas), and reputed to be one of Asia's most beautiful cities for Westerners, Hanoi has retained much of its distinctive French colonial character. Like many visitors who have been charmed by this city, you will most likely find Hanoi to be one of the highlights of your trip to Vietnam. It tends to grow on you after a day or two of exploring its vibrant center.

A CITY IN TRANSITION

Reminiscent of a bygone era, and sometimes referred to as a city of "dilapidated grandeur" or "faded elegance," Hanoi is accented by a mixture of charming and hideous monuments to urban planning, state bureaucracy, and entrepreneurship run amuck. This aging and charming colonial relic is in the midst of transforming this once grand dame of art, culture, and culinary delights into an attractive center for business and tourism.

Today, Hanoi's bustling streets and sidewalks, busy restaurants and shops, and newly constructed hotels and office buildings provide little evidence that as much as 25 percent of this city was physically destroyed, with nearly 75 percent of the population abandoning it for safe havens in the countryside when it became targeted for extensive bombing (Operation Rolling Thunder) by the U.S. from 1965 to 1968 and again in 1972. With great tenacity, the city and its people survived its war-time challenges. As the war with America wound down in 1973 and ended in 1975, the population began migrating back and rebuilding the city. Within 10 years Hanoi's population reached 2.7 million. By 2000 it was over 3 million.

Within the past few years Hanoi has begun to show signs of renewed prosperity attendant with a modest influx of foreign investment and increased tourism. It's a rustic, time-warped, yet talented city that's constantly being discovered by outsiders as offering much more than war-time memories, monuments to Ho Chi Minh, and lakeside pagodas. Often dusty from ongoing construction and at times difficult for someone with asthma, this is definitely a city undergoing a physical transition. Depending on how both the international and local political and economic winds blow, Hanoi could be in for a major make-over in the coming decade as more foreign investment and tourism pour into this area. While not as attractive to foreign investors as more entrepreneurial and energetic Saigon in the south, nonetheless, Hanoi's best years most likely lie ahead with tourism playing a significant role in its future development.

GETTING BRIEFED AND ORIENTED

Located 35 kilometers from the **Noi Bai Airport**, Hanoi is a relatively easy city to understand and navigate as long as you get some basic bearings and orient yourself to exploring this city on foot and/or by cyclo. As soon as you arrive in Hanoi, head for the **Hoan Kiem District** with a basic map of the area. Better still, select a hotel in and around this area so you can conveniently walk to its many shops and restaurants, which are within a five- to 20-minute walk from one another. Unfortunately, the city does not promote itself well to tourists by providing maps or a great deal of useful information on what to see and do. That task seems to be left to commercial guide-books and hotel concierges. Do look for a few publications which are available in hotel kiosks, major bookstores, and a few sidewalk news vendors. Two in particular are well worth acquiring upon arriving in Hanoi:

❑ *Hanoi Pathfinder*: This 16-page combination map, directory, and advertising forum is jam-packed with useful
information on restaurants, art galleries, shopping, hotels,
entertainment, travel agents, and cultural sites. Primarily a
basic listing of names, addresses, and phone numbers. Costs
US$.70 (VND10,000).

❑ *Where to Go in Hanoi:* This biannual 172-page guidebook
offers a wealth of information on Hanoi. Covers hotels,
restaurants, shopping, sports, galleries, sightseeing, local
markets, museums, airlines, travel agencies, government
offices, hospitals, taxis, and much more. Costs US$12.00
(VND170,000). Also check out their useful website: <u>vee-n.
com.wtg</u>.

Two magazines, *Vietnam Economic Times* and *Vietnam Investment
Review*, also publish supplemental guides which cover both
Hanoi and Saigon. The supplement that comes with the
Vietnam Economic Times (VND13,000) is especially useful with
its city maps and listings of prime contacts, travel agencies,
hotels, restaurants, bars, entertainment, shopping, services,
sports, and culture. You also can access a sampling of this guide
online:

<u>www.vneconomy.com.vn</u>

You'll find most of these publications in bookstores and from
sidewalk vendors and stalls. The **Thang Long Bookshop** (53-
55 Trang Tien, Tel. 824-1615), for example, usually carries
these publications along with a few useful English-language
magazines, such as *Vietnam Cultural Window*.

Most major hotels will have a one-page xeroxed copy of a
map covering the central business district where most of
Hanoi's major shops, restaurants, hotels, parks, lakes, architectural masterpieces, and other sites are found. While you
shouldn't expect much – indeed nothing in many cases – do ask
your hotel front desk or concierge for a copy of their in-house
map and any other literature they may have on Hanoi, such as
a list of recommended shops. For example, the guest relations
and concierge staff at the **Hotel Sofitel Metropole** offer a two-
page glossy flier entitled "Hanoi's Best Buys," which includes a
map and list of recommended shops by product category. If
you're staying at this hotel, you'll find the front desk and
concierge services especially useful for identifying top shops,
restaurants, and sites and for arranging tours and private guides
– guest services that often distinguish an exceptional hotel from

just another hotel.

The following websites should prove useful in preparing for your Hanoi travel-shopping adventure:

- **Vietnam Online**   vietnamonline.com/travel/
                              hanoi.html
- **Hanoi Travel**   hanoitravel.com
- **Vietnam Tourism**   vietnamtourism.com
- **Vietnam Travel**   vietnam-travel.com
- **Where to Go in
  Vietnam**   vee-n.com/wtg
- **Things Asian**   thingsasian.com

AT THE BUSY CENTER

The center of the city tends to wrap around **Hoan Kiem Lake**, the city's major landmark for orienting yourself to the site. Immediately to the north of this lake is the Old Quarter; to the southeast is the French Quarter. A pleasant oasis surrounded by willowy trees, young lovers, aging exercise addicts, curious tourists, and the popular tortoise tower and island pagoda, the lake is a delightful respite from Hanoi's incessantly noisy and chaotic streets. It's a great place for rest and relaxation, especially after spending a few hours walking the rather intense nearby streets crammed with shops, markets, people, bicycles, and motorbikes. The banks of the lake are occupied with people from early morning – the T'ai Chi exercise, stretch, and power walker crowds congregate here before 6am – until early evening.

Numerous budget hotels, restaurants, cafes, and shops are found immediately to the north of Hoan Kiem Lake (Old Quarter) as well as radiate for several blocks southeast of the lake (French Quarter). If you select a hotel in this area, most of Hanoi's highlights will be within easy walking distance or a short cyclo or taxi ride. With a map in hand, however inadequate, focus your attention on Hoan Kiem Lake with an eye on the areas north and southeast of the lake. For example, just a few blocks southeast of the lake you'll find three major landmarks, which extend into the French Quarter, for navigating the city's many top shops and restaurants: Opera House, Hilton Hanoi Opera Hotel, and the Hotel Sofitel Metropole. The pleasant streets leading from the southeast corner of the lake to these three structures – especially Tran Tien, Hai Ba Trung, Pho Le Thanh Tong, and Phan Huy Chu – are lined with some of the city's best shops and restaurants. The Hotel Sofitel Metropole itself is well worth a visit for its own in-house shops and restaurants.

The Fascinating Old Quarter

The largest concentration of shops, markets, cafes, restaurants, tour agencies, and budget hotels is found along the bustling old streets immediately to the north of Hoan Kiem Lake. Variously known as the "Old Quarter," "36 Streets," or "Ancient Quarter," this is the city's old merchant quarters, which for centuries was contained by walls and massive gates. It's unlike any other place in Vietnam. A visual feast and auditory challenge, this area comes alive with small shops, congested markets, street vendors, peddlers, and lively street scenes that emanate within a one square kilometer area of narrow streets and lanes. Indeed, this is great bazaar-style street theater where people watching is as much fun and intriguing as shopping and dining. It's a photographer's paradise where many people, who tend to be disproportionately female, actually enjoy having their photos taken – with no intrusive objections nor demands for payment. Flower sellers with bicycles laden with colorful floral collections; women carrying produce in two large baskets balanced on a single shoulder poll; squatting ladies selling items on the sidewalk or alongside the street; bicycles overloaded with ceramic dishes; entrepreneurial street urchins attaching themselves to visitors; cyclo drivers wearing distinctive pea green pith helmets; cheap sidewalk restaurants with patrons squatting on tiny plastic chairs; and honking trucks, buses, taxis, cars, motorbikes, push carts, cyclos, and bicycles are only a few of the many fascinating street scenes that characterize this lively and crowded commercial area.

❑ This is great bazaar-style street theater where people watching is as much fun and intriguing as shopping and dining.

❑ Expect to be approached by several young "certified" orphans selling postcards, books, maps, T-shirts, souvenirs, gum, and other items you neither need or want.

❑ Hang Gai Street is especially noted for its many quality art galleries, silk stores, and handicraft shops.

❑ Adjacent Nha Tho Street is a trendy new street for upscale shops, restaurants, and cafés.

Since you'll stand out as a tourist in this area, expect to be approached by several young "certified" orphans selling postcards, books, maps, T-shirts, souvenirs, gum, and other items you neither need or want, along with friendly flower sellers and shoeshine kids. Some may pester you with their charming innocence, especially the sweet young pleading girls, while others may attach themselves to you for 30 minutes to an hour (they correctly believe in the power of persistence) out of a combination of curiosity and entrepreneurship. Whatever the case, this is not the time nor place to adopt an orphan or street urchin. Be prepared to respond with a rather redundant exit strategy, such as repeating *"Thank you, but not today"* 50 times over a 20-minute period. They will eventually go away, and especially if you buy something from them!

Especially popular with local shoppers in search of specialty items and good bargains, this area is of considerable interest to tourists in search of a cultural experience. While there are many things to buy here, chances are few of the consumer goods will appeal to your shopping tastes. Just walking these streets and absorbing the many sights and sounds of daily commerce is one of the highlights of visiting Hanoi. Reflecting Hanoi's old commercial guild traditions, many of the streets in this area specialize in a single commodity.

Immediately southwest of this area is one of Hanoi's best streets for quality shopping – **Hang Gai**. This street is especially noted for its many art galleries, silk stores, and handicraft shops. You can easily spend hours browsing through the interesting shops that line both sides of this long and densely packed street. A few side streets are lined with attractive shops and restaurants. **Nha Tho Street**, for example, is a trendy new street for upscale shops, restaurants, and cafés. If you do any serious shopping, chances are it will happen in this area.

SOMBER HO CHI MINH TO THE WEST

While the Old Quarter and central Hoan Kiem Lake area are all about people, shopping, cafes, restaurants, hotels, and narrow congested streets, the country's history and culture are encased in several museums and monuments which are located two to three kilometers west of the lake. Quickly reached by car or cyclo, or a leisurely walk through the city, this is the area of the Temple of Literature, Fine Arts Museum, The Citadel, Ho Chi Minh Mausoleum, Ho Chi Minh Museum, One Pillar Pagoda, Presidential Palace, and Ho Chi Minh House, Army Museum, and Cot Co Flag Tower. You can't miss the legacy of Ho Chi Minh, including his well preserved body at the austere and heavily guarded Ho Chi Minh Mausoleum in this area. If you are into local history, which is interesting but often self-serving and overdone, you can easily spend a day exploring this area.

THE FRENCH QUARTER TO THE SOUTH

South and east of pleasant Hoan Kiem Lake and the hectic Old Quarter is the French Quarter. Linked to the southeast corner of the lake by Trang Tien Street, which runs east to the Opera

House, this main street is lined with some of Hanoi's best art galleries, bookstores, and the central post office. This is the area where the French colonists settled and carved out their version of an orderly and coherent French civilization in the midst of a chaotic and irrational Vietnam. Here they developed a city with a distinct French character as reflected in its elegant old buildings and streets. Major landmarks and attractions in this area include the Opera House (now the Museum Theater), Hotel Sofitel Metropole, History Museum, Museum of Vietnamese Revolution, Governor of Tonkin's Residence, Museum of Vietnamese Women, and Hoa Lo Prison (American POW's infamous "Hanoi Hilton").

EXPLORING FARTHER AFIELD

While much of your attention will be focused on the treasures and pleasures of Hanoi, which can be easily covered in three to four days, Hanoi also is an excellent base from which to explore nearby craft villages, the Red River Delta east of the city, and the mountainous northwest. A few craft villages, such as Bat Trang, Van Phuc, and Dong Ky, are found on the outskirts of Hanoi. While ostensibly close to the city, getting to these places may take a couple of hours given the poorly maintained and potholed roads that service these villages.

CRAFT VILLAGES

One of the most interesting places to visit is the huge ceramic village of **Bat Thang**, which is located 13 kilometers southeast of Hanoi. Here you can observe artisans at work producing the many ceramics found in the markets and shops of Hanoi and delicately transported by overladen bicycles along village and city streets. You also can shop at several ceramic shops that cater to both tourists and dealers. The village of **Van Phuc** (8 kilometers southeast of Hanoi) specializes in producing silk. The village of **Dong Ky** (15 kilometers northeast of Hanoi) produces traditional inlaid mother-of-pearl furniture. All three of these villages can be visited in a single day.

HALONG BAY AND HAIPHONG

Most visitors plan a day trip to one of the great symbols of Vietnam, the beautiful limestone outcrops and islands of **Halong Bay**. Similar in many respects to the famous limestone outcrops of Guilin in China and Phangnga in southern Thailand, but in much greater abundance, Halong Bay is one of the most serene and romantic spots in Vietnam – the stuff that draws movie makers to shoot such cinemagraphic triumphs as *Indochine*. Located approximately 150 kilometers east of Hanoi on the Gulf of Tonkin, a slow boat trip on Halong Bay is one of the highlights of any visit to Vietnam. Nearby is North Vietnam's second largest city and its major port and industrial center, Haiphong. Some visitors extend their stays by overnighting in this area. While not as upscale as Hanoi, accommodations are more than adequate here. As might be expected, fresh seafood restaurants abound in Halong Bay and Haiphong.

DIEN BIEN PHU

Two popular mountain trips from Hanoi, Dien Bien Phu and Sapa, require a greater investment of time and effort. **Dien Bien Phu**, the famous battlefield that led to the demise of the French colonial administration in 1954, is located in the northwest highlands approximately 420 kilometers from Hanoi and 35 kilometers from the Laotian border. Reached by air (four flights a week from Hanoi) or road (slow and often bad), Dien Bien Phu is of primary interest to history buffs who enjoy visiting historical battlefields. Except for a small town serving the much anticipated but disappointing tourist trade, there's not much to see and do here other than view this isolated valley that played such an important role in the transformation of Vietnam from a French colony to an independent yet much divided nation.

SAPA

One of the major highlights of visiting the North is a journey to the beautiful, charming, and intriguing Hmong, Dao, Tay, and Giay minority area of **Sapa**. Located near the Chinese border some 350 kilometers northwest of Hanoi, it's a slow 10-hour trip by car, 15-hour trip by bus, or a 13-hour combination train and bus trip (terminus is Lao Cai, 38 kilometers northeast of Sapa). Many visitors prefer taking the overnight train. Perched at an altitude of 1,650 meters, Sapa has served as a popular hill station retreat and resort for more than six decades. From French colonialists to tourists, Sapa has had a reputation similar to Dalat in the South – a wonderful escape from the heat of the lowlands. The scenery is often stunning, with picturesque mountains, terraced rice paddies, and an interesting mix of European alpine and Vietnamese architecture. Although the mountain climate can often be unpredictable, the temperature here is usually very pleasant, with cool evenings, although cold winter days are not uncommon. The area is often covered with a dense fog or mist. The rainy season runs from May to August. The best time to visit this area is September to November (fall) and March to May (spring). If you primarily want to view the scenery and enjoy the quiet of this mountain retreat, visit during the weekdays when the area is largely deserted. If you enjoy market scenes and meeting the local minorities, plan to visit Sapa on the weekend, the time when Sapa becomes transformed into a popular tourist and shopping center. Travel-shoppers especially enjoy the colorful Saturday and Sunday markets (best in the mornings starting around 9am) that bring together many of the area's minorities who offer a wide variety of handcrafted products, from textiles and clothes to hill tribe crafts and souvenirs. Bargaining with the market women and young girls and taking photos of this colorful event are two of the major highlights of visiting Sapa.

THE BASICS

Hanoi is a relatively easy city to understand and navigate. From the moment you arrive and until you depart, this city is filled with many wonderful surprises that spill into its fascinating streets.

ARRIVING

If you arrive by **air**, at present you'll land at the old Hoi Bai airport. A much larger and more modern new airport is being constructed next door. Located 35 kilometers north of the city via a partially completed freeway, the trip into Hanoi takes from 45 minutes to one hour, depending on the traffic and your city destination. Airport to city transportation for foreigners is relatively convenient with minibuses and taxis available at the airport terminal. A minibus ride, which will take you to your hotel, costs about US$4 per person. Taxis booked at the airport taxi stand cost US$15 to US$20 per vehicle. In addition, you may need to pay the toll to cross the bridge, depending on your taxi driver (ask first). If you are approached by someone in the airport terminal asking if you need a taxi, chances are they will charge you two to three times more than the official airport taxi stand. It's best to wait until you leave the arrival hall to check at the taxi stand on the official taxi rate before agreeing to go with one of the freelancers. You also can negotiate with taxi drivers in the nearby parking area.

If you arrive by **train**, the Hanoi Railway Station (Ga

Hanoi) will be located one kilometer southwest of Hoan Kiem Lake at 126 Le Duan Street. Conveniently located near the center of the city, it takes about five to 10 minutes to go by taxi from the train station to most major hotels. Cyclo drivers can cover the distance in 15 to 20 minutes.

If you arrive in Hanoi by **bus**, you're probably an adventuresome budget traveler looking for inexpensive transportation to get from one of the many bus terminals to a hotel. Depending on the distance, a cyclo might be your least expensive option. However, a taxi may only cost about US$3 and be much more convenient.

GETTING AROUND

Traffic in Hanoi is both chaotic and lethal. Accidents and accompanying injuries are frequent for drivers, passengers, and pedestrians. Whatever you do, whether walking or driving, anticipate the unexpected. It's very easy to get hit by a bicycle, motorbike, cyclo, car, truck, or bus if you are not extremely careful about your safety. We do not recommend driving yourself in Hanoi, unless you are experienced in navigating this type of traffic. We especially like the relative safety of taxis and private cars with drivers.

Much of Hanoi can be covered on **foot**, especially if you stay at a hotel near the Old Quarter or French Quarter. If, for example, you stay at the Hotel Sofitel Metropole or Hilton Hanoi Opera, you can easily walk to Hoan Kiem Lake and the Old Quarter within 15 to 20 minutes. However, at times you will want to use public transportation. For both long and short distances, we prefer **taxis** which are very convenient, safe, comfortable, and relatively inexpensive. They are especially convenient when shopping. Just flag them down as they cruise along the street or catch one at a hotel. You'll seldom pay more than US$3.00 for a ride in Hanoi, with many rides costing only US$1.50. Since taxis are metered, you don't need to negotiate the price of this transportation.

Alternatively, the three-wheel pedicabs called **cyclos** are convenient for short distances. Since drivers usually overcharge foreigners by 300 to 500 percent, be sure to bargain hard before getting into a cyclo. Most short rides should cost about US$.50 per cyclo (not per person, with two people being able to squeeze into the larger cyclos in Hanoi). If you pay more than US$1, even for a two-kilometer ride, you're probably paying too much for this ostensibly charming ride. You also can negotiate a daily rate with these drivers who may charge US$5 to US$7 for an eight-hour day.

You also can rent bicycles and motorbikes to get around in Hanoi. Bicycle rentals run about US$1 to US$2 a day. Check with your hotel or at several tourist cafes for such rentals. You also can rent motorbikes from tourist cafes for about US$5 to US$10 per day.

If you are planning to cover many areas of the city or travel beyond Hanoi, consider hiring a **car with driver** for the day. Expect to pay from US$30 to US$40 a day for a car and driver and about US$10 a day more for a minivan. You can arrange for a car and driver through your hotel, travel agency, or travelers' cafe. While you also can rent a self-drive car, getting a car with driver costs about the same and will most likely be more convenient, especially when shopping along congested streets where parking is a problem.

Whatever mode of transportation you choose, make safety your primary concern. The streets of Hanoi are dangerous for everyone involved. While taxis or a car with driver are the most expensive, they also are likely to be your safest forms of transportation.

TOURS AND GUIDES

If you are not part of an organized tour group, you can easily arrange individual tours and guides once you arrive in Hanoi. As noted earlier, we prefer arranging local guides and transportation through our U.S.-based travel operator – Global Spectrum – which operates from Virginia in the United States:

www.asianpassages.com
Tel. 1-800-410-4446

Experienced in working throughout Vietnam, as well as in other parts of Southeast Asia, they regularly arrange personalized itineraries so independent travelers have a great deal of flexibility wherever they go. They also have their own English-speaking local staffs. We highly recommend checking out their group and individual travel services *before* departing for Vietnam. Once in Hanoi, you also can contact them by calling this cell phone number and asking for Global Spectrum: 091-391-84-54.

Tour services can be arranged through a few large government-operated tour services or with several privately-operated travel agencies and tourist or travel cafes. The government-operated tour services include:

❑ **Hanoi Toserco:** 8 To Hien Thanh, Tel. 978-0004. Fax 822-6055. Email: hanotoserco@hn.vnn.vn.

❑ **Hanoi Tourism:** 18 Ly Thuong Kiet, Tel. 826-1627. Fax 825-6418. Email: hanoitourism@hn.vnn.vn. Website: hanoi tourism.com/vn.

❑ **Saigon Tourist:** 55B Phan Chu Trinh, Tel. 825-0923. Fax 825-1174. Website: saigon-tourist.com.

❑ **Vietnamtourism:** 5 Ba Trieu, Tel. 824-4130. Fax 825–7583. Email: vnt.hnbr@fmail.vnn.vn. Website: vietnam tourism.gov.vn. This is the largest state-run tour operator and a major gateway to the tourism industry.

❑ **Vinatour:** 54 Nguyen Du, Tel. 942-4490. Email: vinatour @hn.vnn.vn.

Some of the larger privately-operated travel agencies include the following:

❑ **Ann's Tourist Co. Ltd:** 26 Yet Kieu Street, Tel. 833-2564. Email: anntours@yahoo.com. Website: anntours.com.

❑ **Buffalo Tours:** 11 Hang Muoi, Tel. 828-0702. Email: buffalo@netnam.org.vn. Website: buffalotours.com.

❑ **Exotissimo:** 26 Tran Nhat Duat Street, Tel. 828-2150. Email: exohan@exotissimo.com. Website: exotissimo.com

❑ **Green Bamboo Travel:** 2A Duang Thanh Street, Tel. 828-6504. Email: info@greenbambootravel.com. Website: green bambootravel.com.

❑ **New Indochina Travel Co. Ltd.:** 1A Dang Thai Than, Tel. 933-0599. Email: info@newindochinatravel.com. Website: vietnamtourism.com/NICTravel.

❑ **TF Handspan:** 116 Pho Hang Bac, Tel. 828-1996. Email: tfhandspan@hn.vnn.vn. Website: handspan.com.

Several **tourist cafes** also offer a variety of inexpensive tour services. While many budget travelers, backpackers, and other independent travelers avoid organized tours as indicative of "traveling incorrect," many eventually gravitate to these tourist cafes where they decide it's time to acquire some time-saving inexpensive assistance in touring the area. For example, using a tourist café, you may be able to arrange a tour to Halong Bay for as little as US$10! Many of these places double as small hotels, restaurants, and/or Internet cafes that cater to budget travelers. They especially appeal to tourists who walk in off the street to select from a menu of tours that can range from one to 12 days. Many of these places also can arrange car and motorbike rentals, visa services, airport transportation, and cars with drivers and guides. Independent travelers often meet fellow travelers at these places. A large number of tourist cafes can be found along the congested streets of the Old Quarter in Hoan Kiem District. The original tourist café is the Green Bamboo. The Queen Café, Lonely Planet, and Love Planet are especially popular with expatriates. Most tourist cafes are too small to have their own websites:

❑ **Darling Cafe:** 33 Hang Quat, Tel. 826-9386.

❑ **Green Bamboo:** 28 Trang Thi, Tel. 828-6504. Email: green bambootours@fpt.vn.

❑ **Lonely Planet:** 33 Hang Be, Tel. 825-0974.

❑ **Love Planet Tours:** 25 Hang Bac, Tel. 828-4864. Email: loveplanet@hn.vnn.vn.

❑ **Queen Café Travel:** 65 Hang Bac, Tel. 826-0860. Email: queenaz@fpt.vn.

❑ **Red River Tours:** 73 Hang Bo, Tel. 826-8427. Email: redrivertours@netnam.org.vn.

❑ **Sinh Café:** 56 Hang Be, Tel. 926-0038. Email: opentour@ hn.vnn.vn.

You also can contact your hotel concierge or front desk for assistance in arranging tours. They can recommend travel agencies and tour companies or arrange a hotel car and driver.

INTERNET CONNECTIONS

If you can't travel without an Internet connection, you're in luck in Hanoi. Several Internet cafes offer inexpensive connections. However, connections can be slow and unpredictable. Several tourist cafes include Internet connections with hourly rates that run from US$1 to US$3 per hour. Most are located in the Hoan Kiem District area and especially cater to the budget traveler and backpacker crowd:

❑ **Classyzone Café:** 137 Hang Bac, Tel. 926-0410.

❑ **Emotion Cybernet Café:** 52 Ly Thuong Kiet 60 Tho Nhoam, Tel. 934-1066. Email: emotion@fpt.vn.

❑ **Handspan Travel:** 116 Hang Bac, Tel. 828-1996.

❑ **Lang Viet Café:** 118 Hang Bac, Tel. 926-0410.

❑ **Red River Café:** 73 Hang Bo, Tel. 826-8427. Email: red rivertours@netnam.org.vn.

❑ **VDC:** 18 Nguyen Du, Tel. 826-7209.

❑ **Vinh Phat Co., Ltd.:** 26 Le Thai To, Tel. 828-5799.

SHOPPING HANOI

Two things about Hanoi immediately catch the attention of most visitors – the people and the shopping. There are lots of each. The people tend to be very friendly and receptive to foreigners, and especially when you go shopping and come into contact with many local people and fellow travelers. In a city undergoing major transitions from what was until recently a very drab and austere Vietnamese-style communist city, many visitors are surprised to see and meet so many colorful and friendly people as well as observe so much shopping taking place on the streets of Hanoi. Many visitors simply summarize their experience as follows: *"Amazing place – I never thought it would be like this!"* They find shopping an unexpected treat.

> *Many visitors react to Hanoi by saying "Amazing place – I never thought it would be like this!"*

A NEW SHOPPING CULTURE

But shopping has not quite come of age in Hanoi, at least not in the style you might be accustomed to at home or even elsewhere in Southeast Asia. After all, the country's new capitalism, known as the economic reforms of *doi moi*, are just over 10 years old – not a long time for any new economic system to take root and prosper. Becoming and succeeding as an entrepreneur in Hanoi has not been an easy task, especially given the long shadow of the suspicious government and when you don't have a previous business history nor a reputation for being a shopping mecca for tourists. But compared to 5 or 10 years ago, Hanoi has made remarkable progress. As you will probably notice many times during your sojourns into the streets and shops of Hanoi, the locals seem to catch on to this new capitalism very quickly. Indeed, they are fast learners who seem to have a knack for making money!

IN SEARCH OF QUALITY

While much of Hanoi's shopping is geared toward local consumer goods – from televisions and motorcycles to shoes and furniture, an increasing amount of shopping appeals to foreigners in search of Hanoi's unique treasures. However, don't expect too much when it comes to quality shopping. Hanoi has some wonderful art – indeed, some of the best in all of Asia. But there's a huge quality gap between art and most other products. Many of the other products are often underwhelming, perhaps reflecting the many years of isolation from the rest of the commercial and design world. From handicrafts, souvenirs, and ceramics to clothes and accessories, products found in Hanoi's many shops and markets generally lack great styling and fine finishing touches that many visitors associate with quality products. They may be inexpensive, in abundance, and look appropriate in their Third World setting, but many products do not appeal to up-market Western tastes. In fact, much of what you see in Hanoi's shops will have a decided down-market ethnic look that may appeal more to budget travelers in search of on-the-road provisions – T-shirts, shoes, backpacks, baskets, pirated CDs.

As a result, you'll know quality products when you see them – they definitely stand out from the crowd of mediocre items! And many of these shops may be joint venture operations involving foreigners who have an eye toward Western design and quality craftsmanship. Don't, for example, be surprised to find someone from France, the United Kingdom, Canada, or the U.S. involved with some of the better quality shops. Some are spouses of local Vietnamese who have decided to settle in Hanoi, raise families, and do what they do best – operate businesses that especially appeal to the tastes of expatriates and tourists in Hanoi. You'll also see this pattern in the case of several of Hanoi's best quality restaurants – involvement of expatriates with their Vietnamese spouses.

You can find many nice things in Hanoi – if you know

where to look and what to buy. You'll definitely find many bargains, since most things, except for top quality art, are relatively inexpensive here.

WHERE TO SHOP

Everything seems to spill out into the streets of Hanoi – people, restaurants, cafes, shops, and travel companies. From early morning until late at night, Hanoi is a busy city with a few streets of particular interest to visitors.

This city rises early in the morning. The area around Hoan Kiem Lake, for example, is usually crowded by 6am with people exercising. Since local residents traditionally eat breakfast in restaurants, cafes, and along the sidewalk – often sitting on tiny plastic stools eating the national noodle dish *pho* (sounds like "fur" in English) – by 6:30am thousands of people are on the streets participating in this morning gastronomic ritual. If you're an early riser, you may enjoy the colorful street scenes at this time of day. Between 8am and 9am shops open; many close around 9pm. The major shopping streets are largely confined to the French Quarter and Old Quarter.

FRENCH QUARTER

Within the **French Quarter**, the Hanoi Opera and Sofitel Metropole hotels are the central orientation points from which to explore the main shopping street that runs from the Opera House to Hoan Kiem Lake – **Triang Tien**. Here you'll find several of the city's major art galleries such as **Nam Son** (#41), **Opera Gallery** (#24), **Hanoi Studio** (#13), **Tonkin** (#24), **Hanoi Art Contemporary** (#36), and **Van Gallery** (#25-27). Bookstores, the post office, and several shipping companies (UPS, Federal Express, Airborne Express, and DHL) also are found in this area. South of the Sofitel Metropole Hotel, Hanoi Opera Hotel, and Trang Tioen Street – along Le Thanh Tong Street, Phan Chu Trinh Street, and adjacent streets to the west – are several additional shops as well as some of Hanoi's best restaurants. This is a very pleasant area to walk early in the morning as well as during the evening.

OLD QUARTER

The Old Quarter, or 36 Pho Phuong (36 Guild Streets), is all about shopping and culture. Located immediately to the north end of Hoan Kiem Lake, this one square kilometer maze of streets and lanes is jam-packed with shops spilling over into the sidewalks and streets with goods. Here's where you will find the general household and products market, Dong Xuan Market (Dong Xuan Street), and 36 streets that have a large range of specialty items primarily of interest to local residents, as well as numerous small hotels, tourist services, and Internet cafes. While most streets used to specialize in one particular product, today the product mix here is very broad. Hang Bac Street, for example, the traditional silver street, now has several shops producing distinctive grave stones and plaques, as well as several popular tourist and Internet cafes such as the Queen Café Travel, Handspan Travel, Lang Viet Café, and Classyzone Café. Other streets offer T-shirts, shoes, clothes, handbags, lacquerware, toys, bedding, baskets, cooking utensils, pirated CDs, and appliances – just about everything you can find in a market. Women carrying baskets suspended by split bamboo poles quickly walk down the streets or sit on the pavement selling their fresh fruits and vegetables, while other with flower-laden bicycles peddle by or stop to sell their attractive bouquets. Along the crowded sidewalks, young children entertain them-selves with various forms of play. Other young people approach tourists with a handful of products for sale, from postcards and books to gum and souvenir items – always the same useful things to pester you with. More of a cultural experience than one in quality shopping, the central part of the Old Quarter is a very concentrated form of street theater reminiscent of many crowded Chinatown areas in other parts of the world. It's one big market bazaar strung along many colorful and fascinating streets.

If you're interested in quality shopping, you'll need to head to the southwest section of the Old Quarter where you should concentrate your attention on **Hang Gai Street**, Hanoi's traditional silk street. While you'll still find the city's major silk shops here, the street has diversified considerably with its many quality art galleries and souvenir shops. This is Hanoi's premier shopping street for visitors interested in art, handicrafts, silk, and embroidered items. Here you'll find the city's best art galleries, such as **The Apricot Gallery** (#40B), **Co Do Gallery** (#46), **Thanh Mai Gallery (#64)**, and **Thang Long Gallery** (#15). Its major silk and embroidery shops also are found amidst the art galleries and souvenir shops – **Khai Silk** (#96), **Tan My** (#66), **Tan Thanh Silk** (#102), and **Le Minh Silk** (#79 and #111). A few side streets running south of Hang Gai Street, such as **Nha Tho Street** and **Ly Quoc Su**, also include several shops, restaurants, and cafes worth exploring. This whole area of the Old Quarter can easily take three to five hours to cover, especially if you stop somewhere along the way for lunch (try some of the nice restaurants along Nha Tho Street).

If you have limited time for shopping in Hanoi, you are well advised to head directly for two streets – Trang Tien in the French Quarter and Hang Gai in the Old Quarter. You can easily shop Trang Tien in two hours. Hang Gai Street will take longer – perhaps three to four hours depending on how distracted you become along the way.

SPECIALTY STREETS

If you're looking for particular products, just head for several of Hanoi's streets that offer specialty items and services. Most of these streets can be found in the Old Quarter and French Quarter areas:

▪ Art	Trang Tien, Hang Gai
▪ Baby items	Cau Go
▪ Bags, backpacks, suitcases	Dinh Tien Hoang
▪ Beverages, canned foods	Hang Da
▪ Books, newspapers	Trang Tien
▪ Ceramics	Le Duan, Hang Khoai
▪ Clocks, watches	Hang Ngang, Hang Dao
▪ Embroidery	Hang Gai
▪ Fabrics, cloth	Phung Khac Khoan
▪ Electrical appliances	Hai Ba Trung
▪ Eyeglasses	Luong Van Can
▪ Flowers	Kim Lien, Hang Be
▪ Furniture	Ham Long, Quang Trung
▪ Glass, crystal	Hang Khoai, Ham Long
▪ Hats	Dinh Tien Hoang, Chua Boc
▪ Lacquer	Hang Khay, Hang Gai, Hang Bong
▪ Ready-made clothes	Tran Nhan Tong, Hang Can
▪ Shoes	Hang Dau, Hue
▪ Silk	Hang Gai, Nguyen Thai Hoc
▪ Souvenirs	Hang Gai, Hang Bong
▪ Stationery	Hang Can, Ly Thuong Kiet, Hang Bong
▪ Tableware	Ham Long
▪ Toys	Luong Van Can
▪ Tribal/ethnic artifacts	Hang Be, Hang Gai
▪ Wool products	Dinh Liet

MARKETS

Hanoi boasts over 50 local markets which offer a typical range of market products, from foodstuffs to household goods. While more and more Western-style supermarkets and minimarts open in Hanoi, the city's traditional markets remain very popular with local residents – colorful and lively places jam-packed with products, where tourists enjoy viewing and photographing the fascinating market products and activities. If you decide to buy anything, be sure to bargain for 20 to 30 percent discounts. The major markets are located in the Hoan Kiem District:

❑ **Dong Xuan:** *Dong Xuan Street.* Located in the Old Quarter and reconstructed after a fire destroyed it in 1994, this is the city's largest market. It's a huge three-story market that draws numerous tourists who have fun exploring its many stalls. Specializes in dried foodstuffs, clothes, and footwear.

❑ **Hom Market:** *Pho Hue Street.* One of the city's largest markets. Includes clothing, household goods, a supermarket, and many imported goods.

❑ **Hang Da:** *Hang Da Street.* Located in the Old Quarter, this market includes canned foods, alcohol, and live birds.

❑ **Hang Be Market:** *Hang Be Street.* Located in the Old Quarter, this is the fresh flower, fruit, and vegetable market.

2 I RULES FOR SHOPPING SUCCESS

Shopping in Hanoi follows its own set of rules which we frequently encounter in the streets and shops. Here are 21 we've distilled from our shopping adventures in Hanoi:

1. **The best quality shops are found in and around the major hotels.** In Hanoi this means the Sofitel Metropole and Hilton Opera hotels. If you stay at one of these two hotels, you'll be in the heart of Hanoi's best shopping districts, or at least within short walking distances. Check out their hotel shops, especially the small shopping arcade at the Sofitel Metropole, and shops across the street from the entrances. You'll also find some nice restaurants and cafes nearby, so you can indulge in both dining and shopping!

2. **Expect to do some bargaining but don't expect to receive major discounts.** Many shops will discount 5 to 10 percent if you ask. Some art galleries may discount up to 30 percent if you ask and if they can get the artist to agree to a price change. Determine a price you are willing to pay, make an offer, and be firm. For example, if you find a painting priced at US$1,000, you may say *"I'll give you US$750 for this painting. Is that possible?"* If they agree, you have a deal and should purchase the painting at the price you offered. They may say they cannot sell it at that price, or they may indicate they need to call the artist about your offer. You'll receive the largest discounts in markets from vendors who start out with more highly inflated initial asking prices.

3. **Don't be intimidated by the street urchins who try to sell you things you neither need nor want.** The orphans or kids may be cute, but they can be a real pest after a while. They know one rule to get you to buy – persistence. And they are a very persistent lot, sometimes following you around for an hour. Short of buying their books and postcards or throwing money at them, there's not a nice way of getting rid of them. It's best not to establish eye contact, keep walking, and occasionally repeat the same refrain – *"No, not today. Goodbye."* They will eventually get the message and go away. But if you engage them in a conversation, however positive or negative, they will stick with you like glue! Some 4,600 of these children work the streets of Hanoi. You are bound to encounter them on several occasions. So be prepared to handle what often becomes a real negative of shopping in Hanoi – the human pest.

4. **Plan to use English when shopping in most major shops.** To the disappointment of many Frenchmen traveling in Hanoi, and also in the rest of Vietnam, the mother tongue of colonial France is not widely spoken. If you are French, your English will probably go much further than your French. How soon they forget!

5. **Expect to pay for everything in cash.** Few shops take credit cards or traveler's checks. However, they readily accept U.S. dollars, which are actually preferable to using the local currency. In fact, you can bargain better with U.S. dollars than with inflation-prone dong. Most upscale art galleries will take credit cards, but if you

bargain, a few will offer a better price for dollars or traveler's checks.

6. **Be a very picky and pesky packer.** Few shops know how to pack well. They will tend to disguise an item with paper rather than pack it well for shipping or carrying it in a suitcase. Be prepared to prompt packers as well as re-pack most everything you purchase in Hanoi, including paintings. If you purchase a delicate item, be sure to watch how it is being packed. Don't be afraid to supervise the packing process by telling the packer how to pack according to your expectations. Even major international shippers, such as Airborne Express, may do inadequate packing that may result in items being broken. Air shipments are more expensive from Vietnam than from neighboring countries such as Thailand and may not be covered by insurance.

7. **Shipping is problematic for most shops and many galleries.** Inexperienced in shipping but wanting to make a sale, shops often promise more than they can deliver in the shipping department. If a shop agrees to ship something for you, such as a piece of furniture or a large framed painting, make sure you understand the details of the shipping – the who, where, when, and how much. They may pack the item poorly, send it to the wrong location, or under- or over-estimate the proper costs. If you're trying to ship an antique, expect a problem. Antiques are illegal to export unless they are given special permission by the government. Unless an item is very large and heavy or awkward to hand-carry, you may be better off taking your purchases with you.

8. **Ask to have items delivered to your hotel room.** If you purchase something that is inconvenient to carry around, ask the shop to pack and deliver it to your hotel room. Be sure to get a copy of the receipt so you have proof of purchase. State on the receipt exactly where it needs to be delivered and by what time of day or night. Most hotel concierges and front desks will receive and store such packages.

9. **Be sure to get official receipts for all of your purchases – store name, address, phone number, description of item, and price paid.** You may be asked to show this receipt when you leave Vietnam. This is

especially important in the case of art work which could be confiscated if not properly accounted for with a receipt from the gallery or artist. In part they are checking the age of the painting. If you buy original art, in addition to the receipt, ask for a biographical sheet on the artist. This will indicate the age of the painter and hence the artwork. You will probably enjoy learning more about the artist from this sheet – his birthplace, educational background, and exhibition and award history. In addition, this receipt may come in handy when you pass through Customs in your own country.

10. **Pick up business cards with a mailing address, phone and fax numbers, and email address.** Regardless of whether or not you purchase an item from a shop, if you're interested in what they have to offer, be sure to ask for a card and jot down exactly what the shop has to offer. If you are interested in an item, jot down the best price the seller offered to you as well. As you cover more and more shops, chances are you will forget where you saw particular items, especially if you find one of comparable value and wish to compare prices. Also, you may later regret leaving something behind and want to purchase items from the shop once you return home. Indeed, we do this a lot by email and fax. Without that business card, you may miss out on some future opportunities.

11. **Take pictures of everything you purchase as well as any items you may be interested in purchasing later.** Record the photo information on the back of the shop's business card. We strongly recommend making a visual record of all purchases, especially if you are having items shipped or are uncertain about making a particular purchase. This is especially true if Hanoi is your first stop in Vietnam and you still want to take a look at Hoi An and Saigon before purchasing an item. After visiting these other places, you may decide what you saw in Hanoi is what you want. No problem. You have the photo plus the shop's business card. The photo will come in handy for Customs, for your own reference, and for any future purchases you may make. If you make a long-distance purchase, just email the photo to the shop to let them know what you want. Remember, though, by the time you contact the shop, the item may be gone.

12. **Do comparative shopping before deciding on where to buy and what to pay.** There's a great deal of redundancy in Hanoi's shopping scene. If, for example, you fall in love with a painting in one gallery, chances are a similar painting by the same artist will appear in another gallery. Indeed, few galleries have exclusive arrangements with artists, who are represented simultaneously in several galleries. And prices can vary considerably – as much as 50 percent – for a similar painting, depending on the particular gallery. Many artists, including the very famous, have a tendency to turn out very similar paintings – to the annoyance of many art critics who feel the artists of Hanoi have become too corrupted by tourism and thus have lost much of their creativity once they become famous . . . and rich!

13. **However illegal, pirated CDs and software, as well as knock-off designer-label leather goods, are a good buy in Hanoi.** Pirated CDs and software sell for US$1 to US$2 each. While you may occasionally get a bad CD or defective software, in general these items are great buys. They are especially popular with foreigners who often go wild expanding their music collection inexpensively. Several shops in the Old Quarter offer these products.

14. **Ask shops to hold things for you if you are uncertain about purchasing an item or need to do some comparative shopping.** Most shops will hold items for at least 24 hours. If you don't put a hold an item, chances are it will be sold by the time you return to the shop. Be sure to give the shop your name, hotel, and room number. By putting a hold on an item, you let the shopkeeper know you are looking around and thinking about it. When you return, the price may go down to persuade you to buy. As a courtesy, do let the shop know if you do not plan to purchase the item.

15. **Be very careful when crossing the major shopping streets.** Remember, you have no rights as a pedestrian. You must engage in defensive walking – or running! The traffic in the Old Quarter, especially along Hang Gai Street, is very challenging for jaywalkers. It's best to go down one side of the street and return by the other side. Going back and forth from one interesting looking shop to another will often put your life in other 's hands!

16. **Buying at the production source, such as at the factory shops in the prosperous ceramic village of Bat Trang, does not make good economic sense.** The prices here are invariably higher than in Hanoi. Indeed, you can find the identical items, which have braved the long and tedious bicycle trip along the bumpy road from Bat Trang to Hanoi, for less in the markets and shops of Hanoi. The shops in Bat Trang are designed for unsuspecting tourists who don't know better.

17. **Art is an exceptional buy in Hanoi.** While prices can vary considerably from one gallery to another and from one artist to another, the paintings in oil, watercolor, lacquer, and other mediums are often stunning. Hanoi remains the center of Vietnam's wonderful art community. You can buy paintings from some of the top artists at a fraction of the cost elsewhere in the world. A painting from one of Hanoi's top artists that sells for US$1,000 in Hanoi may cost $5,000 in Paris or New York. If you buy art, purchase only the canvas. While framing is very cheap in Hanoi, it also looks very cheap and airfreighting the painting with frame will be expensive as well.

18. **If you plan to shop outside the Old Quarter and the French Quarter, consider hiring a car and driver to accompany you on your shopping adventure.** You'll find shopping to be most convenient when you know your car is waiting for you and you have a place to put all your loot until the end of the day.

19. **Look for a few interesting shops near the museums and major historical sites.** Most museums and sites have small nondescript souvenir and book shops with limited offerings. Many of the shops are of interest to local tourists. The most interesting shops are found at the Museum of Ethnology, One Pillar Pagoda, and the Temple of Literature.

20. **Expect a very fluid shopping scene in Hanoi in the next few years.** The city is undergoing numerous changes attendant with increased foreign investment and tourism. New shops are constantly opening in response to this new economy and the influx of foreign shoppers. As more and more business people and upscale travelers visit Hanoi, expect to see more shops catering to the

tastes of such visitors. Hanoi is beginning to show signs of a two-tiered shopping scene – cheap bazaar-style shopping of special interest to budget travelers, backpackers, and local residents and upscale shopping for business people and independent travelers in search of unique and quality products, with a special emphasis on collecting the best of the best in fine arts and crafts. The upscale end of shopping should get more interesting in the coming years as Hanoi attracts a new class of travelers in search of its special treasures.

21. **Beware of possible misrepresentation, scams, and misleading information.** Anyone who tries to sell you furniture or antiques and tells you it's okay to ship them abroad is engaged in deceptive practices. Since 1997, wood furniture has been prohibited from leaving the country. Antiques are illegal to export, except in rare cases where special permits must be acquired. Some shops are successful at getting items of questionable age shipped out of the country, but know that you are taking a risk. Since all luggage is x-rayed at the airports, any suspicious looking antiques may be seized, although small items often get through with no questions asked. We are told that the emphasis is on looking out for antique ceramics. Even works of art must receive special permission to leave the country if they are antique. We found that the lacquer painting with frame that we had airfreighted back to the U.S. was given a thorough going-over by a Vietnamese official dispatched to the airfreight office while we waited. However, no one ever asked about the rolled canvases we carried in tubes – both in our luggage and a larger one by hand – when we left the country in Saigon. Have your sales receipt and artist bio handy in case you are asked.

WHAT TO BUY

As indicated from a quick overview of Hanoi's specialty shopping streets, Hanoi offers a wide range of products with a decided local consumer product orientation. Many of its touristy items especially appeal to the city's primary tourist clientele – budget travelers and backpackers who pride themselves on spending as little as possible on the local economy. Their shopping does not significantly impact the main street shops. Nonetheless, they support a very important segment of

the struggling transportation and tourist economy by disproportionately supporting budget hotels, inexpensive restaurants and
cafes, cyclo drivers, bicycle and motorbike rental shops, travel
cafes, Internet stores, and market stalls that populate the
congested streets of the Old Quarter. They do little to support
Hanoi's large art community whose talented artists are represented in more than 200 art galleries.

The following products best represent the shopping scene of
interest to visitors to Hanoi:

ART

There's something very incongruous about art, travel, and
society in Vietnam. On the one hand, you can visit many of
Vietnam's historical sites, understand its history and people,
lament its poverty, participate in its living chaos, and marvel at

its beautiful scenery and friendly people. And then you encounter its striking art in Hanoi. For
many people, it's an amazing
discovery, something you might
find in the best galleries of Paris
and New York. Indeed, Vietnamese art speaks louder than
most other aspects of the country. It's some of the most exciting and compelling art being
produced anywhere in the
world today. Colorful and contemporary, this art transports
you to whole new world that is
simultaneously Vietnamese and international. It's another
aspect of this fascinating country that surprises visitors who
have been focused on other things or who have stereotyped this
country as poor and "underdeveloped." When it comes to art,
Vietnam is very rich. Vietnamese art communicates across
cultures more so than any other art we have encountered in
Asia. This is great stuff worthy of your most serious shopping
consideration.

If there is only one thing you buy in Hanoi – or even
Vietnam as a whole – make sure it's a fine painting by one of
Hanoi's top artists who most likely has exhibited extensively
within Vietnam as well as abroad. Splurge – it's worth it! But
bargain first to ensure good value. If the best costs too much for
your budget, invest in an up-and-coming young artist, or at
least acquire a work of art you fall in love with. Chances are you

will be thrilled with your purchase. Best of all, you'll make a very special connection with Vietnam through your newly acquired "masterpiece" which will last a lifetime. And if you have a chance to meet the artist, your purchase will become even more meaningful.

Hanoi is Vietnam's center for the fine arts and in a very big way. Few cities in the world have as much quality art concentrated in one place. Most of Vietnam's major artists have studios here, and they are well represented in the more than 200 art galleries that enliven the city's shopping scene. Supported primarily by foreign patrons of the arts – business people, expats, and tourists – Hanoi's artists produce some truly stunning works that captivate many visitors to Vietnam who acquire a whole new perspective on this country and its extremely talented people. Indeed, you can quickly get caught up in Hanoi's art scene as you discover many wonderful paintings in oils, watercolors, lacquer, and other mediums. The lacquer paintings are especially unique and attractive. Reflecting a combination of French, Chinese, Cham, and regional folk art traditions, and depicting many Vietnamese social themes in very vivid colors, you can pick up some very remarkable art in Hanoi to grace your home and/or office.

If you buy only one thing in Hanoi, make sure it's a fine painting by one of the top artists. You'll be thrilled with your purchase!

But all is not well within the Vietnamese art community, which quickly came of age and prospered enormously with the *doi moi* (renovation) policy that started in the mid-1980s. From then until the mid-1990s, this newly revived art community prospered enormously under the patronage of big-spending Western buyers. In a sense, Hanoi's new-found capitalism has partly corrupted its art community. Today, art in Hanoi is highly commercialized, with gallery owners and artists understanding that this is first of all a business that enriches them – one of Hanoi's few well-defined pathways to profits. Indeed, many people lament the fact that contemporary Vietnamese art has become too commercialized during the past decade, with artists primarily painting for what was once (mid-1990s) a well-heeled, expanding foreign business community and a growing tourist market. As a result, much of the art you see in Hanoi today looks like formula art – famous artists tend to produce the same paintings over and over (copy themselves!) with only some variation in colors and themes. They paint for only one market – foreigners who are primarily business people and tourists. The commercial building boom of the mid-1990s that absorbed some of this art – hotels, office buildings, restaurants – is over. But as a potential buyer of art, such academic discourses are best left to contentious artists who often like to debate their real mission in life, which is not to make money. As with any art purchase, buy what you like and like what you buy.

When buying art, keep in mind that there is little or no local market for Vietnamese art. With the collapse of neighboring economies in the late 1990s and a worldwide recession in 2001, Hanoi's artists and galleries have been sent an important economic message – life will not be the same given such an international economic downturn. The days of highly inflated art prices and overcharging may have come to an end. Art prices should continue to decline, and many galleries may shut their doors in the face of an evaporating foreign market. Again, when shopping for art, never pay retail. If you do, you're probably paying too much.

Prices and quality of art in Hanoi can vary greatly, from a small US$3 painting to one costing several thousand dollars. From the sublime to the ridiculous, prices are often determined by whatever the buyer is willing to pay rather than by any self-regulating supply-and-demand criteria. There's plenty of supply, indeed, over-supply of works produced by even the top artists who appear to have become excessively commercialized. Inexpensive paintings of young artists can run from US$50 to US$250. The works of better known artists start at US$300 and can go as high as US$45,000. However, art values and prices all depend on local and international economic conditions – whatever the market will bear. In good times, prices go up. In bad times, they come down. While most art galleries may give you the impression that prices are fixed and values are high, in reality prices are very fluid and values can be subject to a great deal of fluctuation. All galleries have a retail price assigned to each work of art, but most galleries also entertain offers, with 10 to 20 percent discounts not uncommon, if you ask. Our advice: **never pay retail for art in Hanoi or elsewhere in Vietnam**. Retail prices are prices set for foreigners who often don't know better. There's too much of the same art being offered at different prices. This is a buyer's market where your dollar is king. All art should be negotiable, often between you and the artist, with the art gallery playing the role of middleman in the transaction. Indeed, we have received 30 percent discounts, but only after the gallery consulted directly with the artist. You might do better, depending on the gallery and artist. After all, this is a very competitive business with too many art galleries and artists chasing after too few customers and dollars.

Unlike the art business in many Western countries, where artists are represented by a single gallery or agent, in Hanoi an artist may display his or her works in 10 different galleries. As a result, galleries do not invest a great deal of money in promoting individual artists, and artists may price their works differently with different galleries. For example, an artist whose paintings in Gallery X may be priced at US$300 may offer nearly identical paintings in Gallery Y for US$500. Why the difference in pricing? Because of the more prestigious name of the gallery and the commission arrangements between the gallery and the artist. Few galleries buy outright the work of artists. Most work on a consignment arrangement. Consequently, if you see a painting priced at US$500, ask the gallery if they will take $300. Chances are they will say *"no."* If you counter by saying *"$350,"* the gallery will probably say *"please wait a moment."* The next step is for the gallery representative to call the artist and ask if he is willing to accept the offer. In many cases, especially if you are only asking for a 20 percent discount, the answer will be *"yes."* If you ask for a 25 or 30 percent discount, the artist may say *"no."* While artists in general tend to be a quirky group, in the end they do understand the market and that the buyer ultimately determines their value by what he or she is willing to pay. Remember, this is a glutted art market in Hanoi. You should never pay the initial asking price.

In most cases you will want to purchase just the painting rather than the fame. While framing is very inexpensive in Hanoi, in most cases the frame encasing a painting is simply dreadful and thus not worth the transportation hassle and cost. You can do much better with a framing shop back home. Unless you really fall in love with a frame, purchase art without frames.

Finding small paintings can be difficult since Vietnamese artists tend to work on large canvases. Be sure you know your wall space as well as the shipping implications of making a major art purchase of a very large painting.

Beware of knock-off paintings. Vietnam has a long tradition of copying the works of masters. In fact, many shops sell knock-offs of famous paintings. Want to purchase the Mona Lisa? It can be yours. You can even watch it being painted! Some people enjoy buying low-cost copies of world-famous art. Usually you will be aware that you are buying a copy. But if you are paying serious money for original art, do so at a reputable gallery that also provides documentation on the artist and painting, as well as gives you a receipt.

Chances are you will fall in love with many of the works of Hanoi's top artists. Several of our favorite artists include:

- Thanh Chuang
- Hoang Phuong Vy
- Dao Hai Phong
- Le Thanh Son
- Le Thiet Cuong
- Nguyen Thanh Binh
- Le Quan
- Bui Huu Hung
- Nguyen Trung Phan
- Dao Thanh Dzuy
- Hong Viet Dung
- Dinh Quan

You'll quickly recognize their works once you visit Hanoi's top art galleries. Better still, visit these galleries online before you visit Hanoi. Most of the top art galleries have websites on which they display the works of their major artists. The following website functions as a gateway to many of these top art galleries:

hanoigallery.com
(hanoigallery.com/HNgall/gall_home.asp)

Most galleries have monthly exhibits which feature particular artists. To start your art shopping right, we recommend starting at the very top – **The Apricot Gallery** (40B Hang Bong Street, Tel. 828-8965, apricot-artvietnam.com). Then go next door to **Co Do Gallery** (46 Hang Bong Street, Tel. 825-8573, codogallery.com). From there, head east along Hang Bong Street, which changes its name to Hang Gai Street, until you get to the **Hanoi Gallery** (101 Hang Gai Street, Tel. 828-6048, vangallery.com.vn), which is part of the Van Gallery in the French Quarter. Farther east along this street you will come to The Apricot Gallery's sister gallery, **Thanh Mai** (64 Hang Gai Street, Tel. 825-1618). Then look across the street to **Thang Long Art Gallery** (15 Hang Gai Street, Tel. 825-0640, thanglonggallery.com).There are many other interesting galleries along this street, but other top galleries are found in the French Quarter along Trang Tien Street. Be sure to visit their group of fine galleries: **Van Gallery** (25-27 Trang Tien, Tel. 825-1532, vangallery.com.vn); **Opera Gallery** (24 Trang Tien,

Tel. 934-4139); **43 Trang Tien** (43 Trang Tien, upstairs, Tel. 824-0038, ceae-artgallery.com); and **Nam Son Art Gallery** (42 Trang Tien, Tel. 825-2993). Prices of some paintings at The Apricot Gallery can exceed US$45,000, although most are less pricey. Prices at other top galleries are less. We found many we liked in the US$500 to US$1,500 range.

Shopping for art on your own in Hanoi is both easy and fun. It's also to your financial advantage to do it on your own, since individuals who offer to take you to the galleries invariably get commissions from galleries on everything you buy. You'll most likely pay full retail, or even 20 percent above retail, and your "guide" will receive at least a 10 percent commission on your purchase from the gallery. He or she will not encourage you to bargain with the gallery, or you will be told it's a "fixed price" gallery. After all, your bargaining will cut into his or her commission. Prices are only fixed for people who come with guides or don't ask for a discount. Our experience is that all galleries can be more or less flexible on prices, if you nicely ask the right question: *"Is it possible to go US$____?"* Anything is possible in Hanoi, especially with struggling artists and galleries, however famous. This is a tough business and you need to be a tough buyer.

Shopping for art in Hanoi is not rocket science. It's great fun and extremely educational. If you visit the top galleries we outline on your own – starting with several informative websites of top galleries – you'll learn a great deal about local art and artists by asking questions and comparing paintings and prices. You'll also meet some very interesting local people. Best of all, you can walk away with some truly fine paintings, at good prices, that may well be the highlight of your visit to Vietnam!

Most of the major galleries are concentrated along two streets – Trang Tien Street in the French Quarter and Hang Gai/Hang Bong Streets in the Old Quarter. Just walk up and down these two streets and you will have covered most of Hanoi's key galleries and discovered its major artists.

However, if you have limited time and prefer hiring an art consultant to assist you in shopping Hanoi's art scene, contact local expat and noted art consultant **Suzanne Lecht** (Tel. 84-4-862-3184, Fax 84-4-862-3185, or email: suzlecht@fpt.vn). She has lived in Vietnam for many years and knows the art scene very well. Like many people in this business, she charges hourly and daily consulting rates and has special relationships with art galleries and artists. She prides herself in having worked with or escorted many famous "big name" clients, including former President Bill Clinton. Many of the art galleries work with her in servicing clients.

SILK AND EMBROIDERY

Hanoi is well noted for its silk and embroidered materials. Unlike the heavy Thai silks, the silks in Vietnam tend to be very supple and thus excellent quality for making blouses and other light-weight garments. Much of the fine embroidery work found in Hanoi is applied to tablecloths, handbags, clothes, and bedding, and is relatively inexpensive.

Hanoi's silk and embroidery shops are concentrated in a short section of Hang Gai Street. You can easily walk from one shop to the other to compare selections and prices. The best shops here are **Tan My** (66 Hang Gai, Tel. 825-1579); **Khai-silk** (96 Hang Gai, Tel. 825-4237; Sofitel Metropole Hotel); **Tan Thanh Silk** (102 Hang Gai, Tel. 928-5056); **Le Minh** (79 and 111 Hang Gai, Tel. 828-8723); **Song** (7 Nha Tho, Tel. 828-9650); and Kenly Silk (102 Hang Gai, Tel. 826-7236).

LACQUERWARE

Lacquerware in the form of black, gold, silver, and red plates, boxes, cups, place mats, screens, furniture, and chopsticks is one of the favorite purchases for many visitors. It's also one of the best buys – if you avoid the lacquerware factory tours and showrooms that seem intent on ripping off unsuspecting tourists and kicking back commissions to tour guides. Since quality, designs, and prices can vary considerably from shop to shop, it's a good idea to do comparative shopping for lacquerware. Lacquer plates that sell for US$3 in the market are likely to cost US$5 dollars in a shop, US$25 in a factory showroom, and US$50 abroad. Many of the lacquer designs are very traditional and ethnic while others are very plain or modern, which display well in Western homes.

Lacquerware can be found in many shops and markets in the Old Quarter, especially along Hang Gai, Hang Khay, and Hang Luoc streets. For good selections and prices, try the shops along Hang Gai Street, especially the downstairs souvenir and handcraft section at **Thang Long Art Gallery** (15 Hang Gai, Tel. 825-0740, thanglonggallery.com). Also try **Craft Window** (99 Nguyen Thai Hoc, Tel. 733-5286); **Nhu Ý Shop** (39 Hang Khay); **Dome Shop** (10 Lane Yen The); **The Art of Lacquer** (65 Nui Truc, Tel. 846-0340); **Minh Tam** (2 Hang Bong, Tel. 828-9907); **Lacquer Factory** (12 Nha Tho, Tel. 828-9616); and **Fine Arts Shop** (66 Ma May, Tel. 828-4999). For export quality lacquerware, visit the **Furniture Gallery** (8B Ta Hien Street, Tel. 934-0825, hiencorp.com).

HANDICRAFTS AND GIFT ITEMS

Numerous shops offer a wide range of handicrafts. Many items are produced by ethnic minorities, the handicapped, and professional artisans. In addition to the ubiquitous lacquerware and ceramics, look for boxes, bags, baskets, sandalwood statuettes, woven masks, Chinese chops, water puppets, wood carvings, silver, rattan and bamboo products, wood hangers, jewelry, stone carvings, and beaded and embroidered purses. The following shops are well stocked with a wide range of handicrafts and gift items: **Craft Link** (43 Van Mieu, Tel. 843-7710, craftlink-vietnam.com); **Craft Window** (99 Nguyen Thai Hoc, Tel. 733-5286); **99 Hang Gai Shop** (99 Hang Gai, Tel. 826-8684); **Vietnamese Traditional Handicraft** (17-19 Dang Dung, Tel. 733-7319); **Quang Minh, Cultural Products of Vietnam's Ethnic Minorities** (40 Hang Be, Tel. 825-1947); **Handicraft Products of Vietnam** (77 Nguyen Thai Hoc); **Lan Huong** (115 Hang Gai, Tel. 828-6585); **Vietnamese House** (92 Hang Bac, Tel. 843-3455); **VietStyle** (5B Yen The, Tel. 733-2784); **The Museum Shop** (Vietnam Museum of Ethnology); and the **Vietnamese Craft-Guild** (1A To Tich, and 47A Ly Quoc Su, Tel. 828-9717, www.vneconomy.com/vn/en/the_guide/art_galleries/vietnamese_craft.htm). For nicely designed export quality rattan and bamboo products, visit the **Furniture Gallery** (8B Ta Hien Street, Tel. 934-0825, hiencorp.com). If you become fascinated with the unique Vietnamese wood- carved water puppets, check out **Craft Link** (43 Van Mieu, Tel. 843-7710) for a good selection of colorful subjects. For transitional sculptures, art accessories, lacquerware, gift items, and reproductions, visit **KAF Art Sculpture** (31B Ba Trieu, Tel. 934-9022, kaf-artsculpture.com). We especially like the attractive hand-carved stone boxes available at the **Van Art Gallery** (21B Ly Quoc Su, Tel. 928-5249).

ANTIQUES, FURNITURE, AND HOME DECOR

Antiques and furniture are touchy shopping subjects because they are illegal to export without special permission. Nonetheless, such items do find their way out of Vietnam, depending on whom you deal with and how they ship above or below the law. At the same time, many so-called antiques are reproductions, or a shop that refers to itself as having antiques actually offers handicrafts, furniture, and home decor items. Suffice it to say that there are very few antiques available for sale and export in Vietnam. The real star in this category is the popular **Furniture Gallery** (8B Ta Hien Street, Tel. 934-0825, hiencorp.com), which actually has antique furniture but for local consumption. Especially oriented toward the export market, this large operation offers tastefully designed bamboo furniture as well as home decor items, from lacquer tableware to bamboo and rattan bags, boxes, trays, and mirror frames. Also worth visiting is the delightful **Indochine House** (13 Nha Tho, Tel. 824-8071) with its tasteful selections. Other home furnishing shops include **Home Decor** (50A Le Dai Hanh, Tel. 976-1177); **Bobois Design** (49 Hai Ba Trung, Tel. 934-4932); **TT Interior** (43 Thuy Khue, Tel. 823-6426); **Can's Rattan** (17 Lane 4 Nguyen Dinh Chieu); and **Maison de L'Asie** (8 Hai Ba Trung). For antique reproductions, visit Tonkin Art Gallery (24 Trang Tien Street, Tel. 824-2017).

CERAMICS

Don't expect much quality in this shopping category nor many attractive designs that appeal to Western tastes. Indeed, this stuff is not ready for prime export time. In the form of plates, cups, bowls, vases, trays, most ceramics found in Hanoi are produced in very traditional ethnic designs and drab colors, which may or may not work with your home decor. The largest selection of ceramics is found in the ceramic and porcelain town of Bat Trang, located about 13 kilometers southeast of downtown Hanoi. Most ceramics in the shops of Hanoi originate in this village. From a cultural and curiosity perspective on how people live and work, it's worth a trip to see how these items are produced, packed, and shipped to Hanoi – usually piled high in baskets strapped to bicycles. However, prices in Bat Thrang's factory shops and so-called wholesale outlets are often higher than in Hanoi simply because it's a popular tourist stop where unwitting foreigners are willing to pay above-market prices because they think they are getting a deal. Be sure to bargain hard for any purchases you make in Bat Trang. Within Hanoi, several shops in the Old Quarter sell ceramics. Try **Minh Than** (62 Hang Be, Tel. 926-0046); **Quang**'s Ceramics Gallery (22 Hang Luoc, Tel. 828-3440); **Fine Arts Shop** (66 Ma May, Tel. 828-4999). For ceramic designs and quality that especially appeal to Westerners, visit **Indochine House** (13 Nha Tho, Tel. 824-8071) and the **Fine Arts Exhibition Hall** (7 Hai Ba Trung, Tel. 934-6695).

CLOTHES, TAILORING, AND ACCESSORIES

Numerous shops in Hanoi offer a wide range of ready-made and tailored clothes and accessories. Ready-made sizes tend to be on the small size, although top silk shops offer a good range of sizes for shirts and blouses. The best silk shops, such as Khai-silk and Tan My, offer tailoring services in addition to their ready-made choices. The beautiful and graceful Ao Dai, the traditional dress worn daily by girls and women, is available in several dress shops such as **My Hao** (82 Cau Go, Tel. 825-66078), **Ngan An** (7 Tran Phu, Tel. 843-8397), and **La Hang** (34 Yet Kieu, Tel. 826-1089). Several handicraft shops, such as **Craft Link** and **Quang Minh**, also offer a wide range of ethnic minority clothes which are best purchased for decorative purposes. They also offer beaded and embroidered handbags. For uniquely designed handbags with a French flair, try **Ipa-Nima** (30B Nguyen Huu Huan, Tel. 934-3982). Good quality and fashionable knock-off bags (Gucci, Chanel, Louis Vuitton, Fendi, Versace) can be found at **Jade Bags** (9A Phan Chu Trinh Street, Hoan Kiem District, Tel. 825-1964). For tailoring, try **Cao Minh** (47 Tran Hung Dao, Tel. 825-1278), **Phu Hung** (14-16 Trang Tien, Tel. 825-9644), and **Jade-Lingerie** (219 Hang Bong).

If you're planning to visit the Danang/Hoi An area after Hanoi, you may want to wait and have tailoring work done in Hoi An. It's the tailoring mecca of Vietnam, where you can get nicely tailored clothes at unbelievable prices – US$15 for a dress and US$30 for a suit!

SOUVENIRS

If you want to go native in Vietnam – look like a war veteran, farmer, or market lady – you're in luck. Head for the main market area in the Old Quarter where you can purchase lots of Vietnamese-theme T-shirts, pea green pith helmets, and woven conical hats worn by women. If you look like a tourist, many of these items, along with postcards and other souvenirs, will quickly find you as you are frequently approached by young street urchins trying to sell you an armfull of truly forgettable souvenirs!

PIRATED CDS, SOFTWARE, AND VIDEOS

Hanoi, along with many other areas of Vietnam, is a pirate's haven for CDs, software, and videos. Illegal to bring into the U.S., most of these pirated items are produced in China under poor quality control conditions. You'll have no problem finding these items along Hang Bbai, Hang Gai, and Hang Bong streets in the Old Quarter. Most CDs and software sell for US$1 to US$2. The only problem is that the quality may be poor, especially when your CD skips a lot. If you buy a CD, be sure to play it first or ask if you can bring it back if it doesn't work (assuming you can play it before leaving Hanoi). You may want to pass on the videos – your VCR back home may not be able to play the videos.

KNOCK-OFF NAME-BRAND GOODS

Hong Kong, Taiwan, and Singapore continue to feed the Asian markets with name-brand knock-off goods, from clothes and footwear to watches, handbags, and accessories. Similar to pirated CDs, software, and videos, the market for fake designer goods is well and alive in the markets and shops of Hanoi. Those nice-looking but cheap (US$15) Nike, Adidas, and Reebok shoes overflowing in the footwear shops along Hang Dau and Hue streets are not the real thing. How long they will last before falling apart is another question.

If you are interested in good quality leather purses, briefcases, wallets, shirts, gloves, pens, and sunglasses – fit for an executive or fashion maven – stop by a small shop near the Hilton Opera Hotel called **Jade Bags** (9A Phan Chu Trinh, Hoan Kiem District, Tel. 825-1964). Their two rooms are jam-packed with the latest knock-off arrivals from Singapore under the brand names of Hermes, Versace, Chanel, Gucci, Louis Vuitton, Fendi, and Mont Blanc.

Like pirated CDs, software, and videos, name-brand knock-off products are illegal to bring into the U.S. However, there's a high probability they will get through Customs with no problem. If it becomes a problem, Customs will either confiscate the goods or charge you duty on the actual cost of the real items – Ouch!

NAME-BRAND AND DESIGNER GOODS

Authentic designer shops have opened in Hanoi near the Sofitel Metropole Hotel on Ngo Quyen Street: **Gucci**, **Louis Vuitton**, and **Nina Ricci**. **Adidas** also has a real store at 83 Hang Gai.

BOOKSTORES

Several bookstores carry a good selection of English-language books, magazines, newspapers, and maps. These three bookstores should take care of your needs: **Thang Long Bookshop** (55 Trang Tien, Tel. 824-1615); **Tien Phong Book Store** (175 Nguyen Thai Hoc, Tel. 733-6235); and **Dong Tay 1 Bookshop** (466 Nguyen Chi Thank, Tel. 773-1436).

BEST OF THE BEST

If you have limited time in Hanoi, you may want to concentrate your shopping on what we believe are the top shops in Hanoi. These shops offer some of the best quality products for discerning travel-shoppers. While several of these shops may initially appear expensive, they generally offer good value for their quality selections.

ART

❑ **The Apricot Gallery:** *40B Hang Bong Street, Tel. 828-8965. Website: apricot-artvietnam.com.* This is Hanoi's, and Vietnam's, premier commercial art gallery – perhaps too commercial for serious art connoisseurs. Housed in an attractive two-story building, The Apricot Gallery displays only the top Vietnamese artists who command top prices. The paintings on display here are gorgeous, with many huge oils enhanced with terrific lighting. Prices can go as high as US$45,000 or more, so expect to pay well for this quality. You can get some very nice pieces for around US$1,500. Very helpful English-speaking staff who is happy to explain about the paintings and artists. After visiting this gallery, you may find many other galleries look less than adequate. Be sure to visit their website for information on their artists, upcoming exhibitions, and gallery news. You can view the paintings of their artists online before visiting the gallery.

❑ **Co Do Gallery:** *46 Hang Bong Street, Tel/Fax 825-8573. Website: codogallery.com.* Located next to The Apricot Gallery, this large three-story gallery is jam-packed with the works of many top Vietnamese artists as well as several young painters and artists from remote areas of the country. In addition to oil and lacquer paintings, the gallery offers ceramics and installation art. Regularly hosts exhibitions. Be sure to explore several rooms at the rear of this building as well as on the upper floors. This place can become dis-orienting because of the different levels and rooms. There are some real treasures here that are not well displayed.

❑ **Hanoi Gallery:** *101 Hang Gai Street, Tel. 828-6048. Website: vangallery.com.vn.* This is the sister gallery to the Van Gallery in the French Quarter. An attractive gallery offering several quality paintings as well as stone carved boxes.

❑ **Thanh Mai:** *64 Hang Gai Street, Tel. 825-1618.* This is the sister gallery to the nearby Apricot Gallery. Offers a much wider and less expensive selection of paintings by lesser known artists. Be sure to go into the back room, which serves as a large gallery where you can view many of the best paintings.

❑ **Thang Long Art Gallery:** *15 Hang Gai Street, Tel. 825-0640. Website: thanglonggallery.com.* A combination handi-craft/souvenir shop and art gallery, this could well be your one-stop shop for acquiring arts and crafts. The downstairs area includes a good selection of attractive lacquerware. The stairwell and two upstairs rooms house a good selection of paintings from several of Hanoi's famous artists. Includes many large paintings.

❑ **Trang An Gallery:** *15 Hang Buom Street, Tel. 826-9480.* Operated by artist Nguyen Xuan Tiep, this fine gallery primarily works with young and midcareer artists. Fre-quently puts on excellent art shows. One of the few profes-sional galleries involved in promoting the development of Vietnamese art at home and abroad.

❑ **Van Gallery:** *25-27 Trang Tien, Tel. 825-1532. Website: vangallery.com.vn.* This well appointed two-story gallery offers a wonderful selection of paintings by leading artists whom you'll immediately recognize from visits to other top galleries. Includes many large oils as well as lacquer paint-ings on the second floor.

❑ **Opera Gallery:** *24 Trang Tien, Tel. 934-4139.* One of the city's newest galleries, it offers a good selection of relatively inexpensive paintings by young artists. There's always some-thing here that are different from other galleries. Includes some nice small paintings among the typically large canvases that grace most gallery walls. A very friendly and knowledge-able gallery managed by Ms. Ha.

❑ **43 Trang Tien:** *43 Trang Tien, upstairs, Tel. 824-0038. Website: ceae-artgallery.com.* Also known as the **Centre for Exhibition & Art Exchange**, this state-owned art center promotes Vietnamese art through numerous exhibitions. It currently works with nearly 250 artists and sponsors over 200 exhibitions/shows each year. Includes two floors of paintings. Souvenir shop operates on the first floor. Visit their informative website for a good overview of what they do and offer in the world of art. Includes online information for purchasing paintings.

❑ **Nam Son Art Gallery:** *42 Trang Tien, Tel. 825-2993.* Offers a nice range of excellent quality canvas and lacquer paintings by some top artists as well as several up-and-coming young artists. Includes a good selection of art books featuring many of Hanoi's top artists. Good prices and helpful service.

❑ **Mai Gallery:** *3B Phan Huy Chu Street, Tel. 825-1225.* This small two-story gallery is somewhat difficult to find – on a side street and down a narrow walkway near some popular noodle stands. A very well respected professional art gallery known for its serious work in promoting art. Run by Ms. Mai, the daughter of poet and art critic Duong Tuong. Represents and promotes the works of 10 to 15 young painters who work on canvas and lacquer. Frequently puts on shows at major hotels, such as the Sofitel Metropole.

❑ **Fine Arts Exhibition Hall:** *7 Hai Ba Trung, Tel. 934-6695. Website: hanoigallery.com/hanoiEH.* Located off the beaten art gallery path, a few blocks south of Trang Tien Street, this large gallery represents the paintings and ceramics of many up-and-coming young artists. Good quality and nice selections displayed in a central open gallery. Keeps great hours – 8am to 9pm.

❑ **Salon Natasha:** *30 Hang Bong, Tel. 826-1387. Website: art salonnatasha.com.* One of Hanoi's most interesting and unusual galleries. If you're into avant garde art, this is the center for it in Hanoi. Operated by Vietnamese artist Vu Dan Tan and his gracious Russian-born, English-speaking wife Natasha, this combination bohemian gallery/shop/home functions as the center for Hanoi's experimental, non-commercial art movement. The room is filled with all kinds of "interesting" objects hanging from the walls and ceiling.

❑ **Song Hong Gallery**: *71A Nguyen Du, Tel. 822-9064*. Another one of Hanoi's professional art galleries. Operated by Mr. Thach who frequently sponsors exhibitions. Includes four rooms of paintings by some of Hanoi's leading artists, such as Hoa, Nguyen Than Binh, and Cuong.

❑ **Mai Hien - Anh Khanh Studio**: *99 Nguyen Thai Hoc, Tel. 846-9614*.This is a real trip! Somewhat difficult to find – located behind and upstairs from the Craft Window. This is the home studio and gallery of a creative husband and wife art team. Artist Bui Mai Hien works in lacquer whereas Anh Khanh works on canvas and with oils. Watch your head as you climb through the narrow stairs and passageways of this interesting studio to survey the many colorful paintings.

❑ **Van Art Gallery**: *21B Ly Quoc Su, Tel. 928-5249*. Offers an interesting collection of paintings as well as attractive hand-carved stone boxes produced by the owner who is a de-signer/carver. The stone boxes are one of the more unique and reasonably priced handcrafted items available in Hanoi. Pack the boxes well – they can break if not packed properly.

If these are not enough to get you off and running on a fabulous art shopping tour, here are several additional art galleries well worth exploring:

❑ **A Dong Art Gallery**: *17 Hang Gai (Tel. 828-6694); 6 Bao Khanh (Tel. 838-8837); and 61 Trang Tien (Tel. 934-6960)*. Offers a good range of easily affordable paintings. The new Hang Gai gallery carries a few nicely priced Hao paintings.

❑ **Art Gallery 7 Hang Khay**: *7 Hang Khay, Tel. 825-2294*. On the east side of Hoan Kiem Lake and housed in an historic old building.

❑ **Co Xanh Gallery**: *51 Hong Gai, Tel. 826-7116*.

❑ **Friend Gallery**: *11 Hang Da, Tel. 828-6900*.

❑ **Gallery Toserco**: *36 Le Thai To, Tel. 934-7192*.

❑ **Gide**: *5 Dang Thai Than, Tel. 933-1169*. Across from Hilton Opera Hotel and includes a café.

❑ **Hanoi Art Contemporary Gallery**: *36 Trang Tien, Tel. 934-7192*.

❑ **Hanoi Studio:** *13 Trang Tien, Tel. 934-4433.* Very attractive small gallery displaying the works of several nontraditional artists.

❑ **New Gallery:** *115 Kim Ma, Tel. 846-0868.*

❑ **Indochine House:** *13 Nha Tho, Tel. 824-8071.* After browsing through the ceramics and furniture on the first floor, head for the art gallery on the second floor.

❑ **Tonkin Art Gallery:** *24 Trang Tien, Tel. 824-2017.* Includes reproduction antiques in the midst of many attractive paintings.

SILK AND EMBROIDERY

❑ **Tan My:** *66 Hang Gai, Tel. 825-1579. Email: <u>tanmyhuong</u> <u>@fpt</u>.* This is Hanoi's oldest (28 years) and best embroidery shop which employs nearly 500 workers. It's a favorite stop for many independent travelers and tour groups. Offers some wonderful selections of tablecloths (US$15-50), bed linens (go upstairs), children's clothes, beaded purses, and accessories. Also includes embroidered art with scenes of life in Vietnam, landscapes, and floral arrangements. One of Hanoi's more stylish shops. Very knowledgeable and helpful staff that also speaks good English. You're bound to find some unique and lovely items here.

❑ **Khaisilk:** *96 Hang Gai, Tel. 825-4237; Hotel Sofitel Metropole, 56 Ly Thai To, Tel. 826-3968; and Hotel Nikko Hanoi, 84 Tran Nhan Tong, Tel. 822-3885.* This is Vietnam's most famous silk shop offering a wide range of attractive silk fabrics, garments, and accessories for both women and men. The worn Hang Gai shop is in need of major renovation – does not do justice to owner/designer Hoang Khai's talents that are best displayed at his Sofitel Metropole Hotel boutique and exquisite shop in Saigon. Fashionable designs but not quite prime time international.

❑ **Le Minh:** *79 - 111 Hang Gai, Tel. 828-8723.* This small traditional silk and tailoring shop is a favorite of many visitors, including several celebrities. Offers good quality silk and excellent tailoring services. Not a particularly stylish shop. Includes a good selection of fabrics, jackets, scarves, and neckties.

Other shops offering a nice range of silk garments, fabrics, and embroidered items include:

❑ **Hoa Silk:** *86 Hang Gai, Tel. 826-6148.* Includes ready-made clothes, fabrics, and neckties.

❑ **Kenly Silk:** *108 Hang Gai, Tel. 826-7236.* Offers a good selection of silk fabrics, ready-made clothes, and accessories.

❑ **Song:** *7 Nha Tho, Tel. 828-9650.* Includes a good selection of upscale ready-made clothes, embroidered items, and home wares.

❑ **Tan Thank Silk/Hadong Silk:** *102 Hang Gai, Tel. 928-5056.*

❑ **Thao Silk:** *73 Hang Gai, Tel. 828-1680.* Relatively new shop offering clothes, fabrics, scarves, neckties, and purses.

LACQUERWARE

❑ **Thang Long Art Gallery:** *15 Hang Gai, Tel. 825-0740, thanglonggallery.com.* First floor of this popular art gallery (paintings and gallery setting upstairs) is devoted to lacquerware, especially bowls, cups, plates, and serving pieces. The designs and colors are very attractive and stylish. A good one-stop shop for acquiring nice lacquerware.

❑ **Furniture Gallery**: *8B Ta Hien Street, Tel. 934-0825, hien corp.com.* Offers export quality lacquerware, especially bowls and trays. Popular with wholesalers interested in exporting these and other products abroad.

❑ **The Art of Lacquer:** *65 Nui Truc, Tel. 846-0340.* Offers an attractive selection of lacquerware and wood and bamboo handcrafted items.

Other shops offering selections of lacquerware include:

❑ **Craft Window:** *99 Nguyen Thai Hoc, Tel. 733-5286.*

❑ **Dome Shop:** *10 Lane Yen The, Tel. 843-6036.*

❑ **Fine Arts Shop:** *66 Ma May, Tel. 828-4999.*

❑ **Lacquer Factory:** *12 Nha Tho, Tel. 828-9616.*

❑ **Lacquer Minh Tam**: *2 Hang Bong, Tel. 828-9907.*

❑ **Nhu Y Shop**: *39 Hang Khay.*

HANDICRAFTS AND GIFT ITEMS

❑ **Craft Link**: *43 Van Mieu, Tel. 843-7710. Website: craftlink-vietnam.com.* Located across the street from the Temple of Literature, this well-established nonprofit organization works directly with traditional artisans and women in ethnic minority communities in designing and marketing a wide range of handcrafted products and training local artisans. Their goal is to alleviate poverty and develop communities. Traditional handcrafted items include bamboo bowls, Bat Trang ceramics, carved wooden textile hangers, lacquerware, water puppets, and beaded and embroidered purses. Ethnic minority products include Dao and Hmong, Black Thai, and Nung embroidery, applique, Christmas ornaments, cushion covers, blankets, baskets, and hemp purses.

❑ **Craft Window**: *99 Nguyen Thai Hoc, Tel. 733-5286.* This small shop is jam-packed with handcrafted items from traditional artisans and ethnic minorities. Offers a nice collection of baskets, textiles, lacquerware, purses, and water puppets.

❑ **Quang Minh, Cultural Products of Vietnam's Ethnic Minorities**: *40 Hang Be, Tel. 825-1947.* This small dusty shop includes several items from ethnic minority communities – baskets, textiles, clothes, and ceramics. Offers some excellent large woven baskets at very good prices.

❑ **KAF Traditional Sculptures and Art Accessories**: *31B Ba Trieu Street, Tel. 934-9022. Website: kaf-artsculpture.com.* Specializes in producing Buddha statues, lacquerware, bronze reproductions, traditional arts and crafts, and accessory pieces for interior decoration. Also involved in the construction and restoration of old temples and pagodas.

Other shops offering some interesting selections of Vietnamese handicrafts include:

❑ **99 Hang Gai Shop**: *99 Hang Gai, Tel. 826-8684.* Offers traditional handicrafts and artifacts. Look for ceramics, lacquerware, woven masks, silk, and sculptures.

❑ **Appealing Gifts:** *121 Chua Boc, Tel. 563-3991.*

❑ **Art Antique Shop/Thien Long Co.:** *3 Hang Can, Tel. 826-6109.*

❑ **Dome Shop:** *10 Lane Yen The, Tel. 843-6036.*

❑ **Fine Arts Shop:** *66 Ma May and 9 Luong Ngoc Quyen, Tel. 828-4999.* Small corner shop, with two addresses, offers numerous attractive ceramics, lacquerware, and souvenirs at excellent prices.

❑ **Furniture Gallery:** *B Ta Hien Street, Tel. 934-0825. Website: hiencorp.com).* Export-quality rattan and bamboo products for home decor.

❑ **Handicraft Products of Vietnam:** *77 Nguyen Thai Hoc.*

❑ **Hoa Sen:** *1 Nha Tho, Tel. 826-9073.* Specializes in traditional handicrafts and water puppets.

❑ **Lan Huong:** *115 Hang Gai, Tel. 828-6585.* Products of ethnic minorities – textiles, baskets, and primitive carvings.

❑ **Minh Thanh:** *62 Hang Be, Tel. 926-0046.* Attractive ethnic ceramics, paintings, and silver.

❑ **The Museum Shop:** *On the grounds of the Vietnam Museum of Ethnology, Nguyen Van Huyen Street, Tel. 756-1754.* Small but nice selection of water puppets, books, textiles, and lacquer boxes.

❑ **Pho Co Art Gallery:** *82 Hang Gai, Tel. 826-0220.* Offers an attractive collection of carved stone boxes, lacquerware, and paintings.

❑ **Vietnamese Craft-Guild:** *1A To Tich, and 47A Ly Quoc Su, Tel. 828-9717. Website: www.vneconomy.com/vn/en/the_guide/art_galleries/vietnamese_craft.htm).*

❑ **Vietnamese House:** *92 Hang Bac, Tel. 843-3455.* Offers fine art, gems, ceramics, bamboo items, handicrafts, and antiques.

❑ **Vietnamese Traditional Handicraft:** *17-19 Dang Dung, Tel. 733-7319.* Offers handcrafted products from 18 villages.

❑ **VietStyle:** *5B Yen The, Tel. 733-2784.* Offers handmade Buddha statues and figures, mirrors, frames, and lacquerware.

❑ **Van Art Gallery**: *21B Ly Quoc Su, Tel. 928-5249.* Unique hand-carved stone boxes.

ANTIQUES, FURNITURE, HOME DECOR

❑ **Indochine House:** *13 Nha Tho, Tel. 824-8071.* This tastefully designed two-story shop, operated by British expat Justin Wheatcroft, sells both new and old furniture. Will also custom-make furniture. Has lots of ceramics. The second floor includes a nice small art gallery.

❑ **Furniture Gallery:** *B Ta Hien Street, Tel. 934-0825. Website: hiencorp.com).* Includes some antique furniture among its warehouse of newly produced export-quality rattan and bamboo furniture. Offers several attractive home decorative and accessory pieces.

Several other shops offer furniture and home decorative accessory pieces:

❑ **A Design:** *20 Thuy Khue, Tel. 847-3045.*

❑ **Bobois Design:** *49 Hai Ba Trung, Tel. 934-4932.*

❑ **Can's Rattan:** *17 Lane 4 Nguyen Dinh Chieu.*

❑ **Home Decor:** *50A Le Dai Hanh, Tel. 976-1177.*

❑ **Maison de L'Asie:** *8 Hai Ba Trung.*

❑ **TT Interior:** *43 Thuy Khue, Tel. 823-6426.*

CLOTHES AND ACCESSORIES

❑ **Khaisilk:** see above under "Silk and Embroidery."

❑ **Song:** *57 Nha Tho, Tel. 828-9650.* Offers upscale ready-made casual wear, accessories, and linens.

❑ **Ipa-Nima:** *30B Nguyen Huu Huan, Tel. 934-3982.* This small shop, in the midst of the famous neighborhood of headstone carvers, offers uniquely designed and fashionable beaded handbags and shoes by Hong Kong lawyer-turned-designer Christina Yu who has operated from Hanoi for more than 10 years. Produces very fancy, whimsical, quirky, trendy, one-of-a-kind creations that may be more art than fashion. You may see her signature handbags clutched by a few local patrons in Hanoi's trendy cafes and restaurants.

❑ **My Hao:** *82 Cau Go, Tel. 825-6607.* One of Hanoi's oldest shops for making the traditional Ao Dai dress worn daily by most Vietnamese girls and women.

Some of Hanoi's best tailors include the following:

❑ **Cao Minh:** *30-32 Le Thai To, Tel. 825-1287.*

❑ **Phu Hung:** *14-16 Trang Tien, Tel. 825-9644.*

❑ **Jade-Lingerie:** *219 Hang Bong.*

ACCOMMODATIONS

The accommodations scene in Hanoi is more than adequate for travelers. Whether five-star or budget hotels, or somewhere in between, Hanoi has plenty of rooms to accommodate the preferences of most travelers. During the past decade, but especially beginning in the mid-1990s, several new five-star hotels were built to handle the growing foreign business community and much anticipated increase in tourism. The downturn in Asian economies in the late 1990s left many of these hotels with less than stellar occupancy rates. As a result, some of your best hotel buys in Hanoi will be with the five-star hotels which offer special rates.

For information on hotels in Hanoi, including reservations and special online discounts of up to 75 percent off the rack rate, check out the following hotel websites:

- **Hanoi Hotels Travel Guide** — hanoi-hotels.net
- **Asia Hotels** — asia-hotels.com/hl/Hanoi-vietnam.asp
- **AsiaTravelTips.com** — asiatraveltips.com/Hotels inHanoi.htm
- **Vietnam Hotels** — vietnamhotels.net
- **Vietnamese Hotels** — vietnamesehotels.net/hanoi
- **AsiaTravel.com** — asiatravel.com/vietnam.html

- **All-Vietnam-Hotels** all-vietnam-hotels.com/
vietnam-hotels.com

Most major hotels also have their own websites through which you can view rooms, survey facilities and services, check room rates, and book online. Be sure to compare their online rates with the discounted rates offered by the other hotel websites. They may be higher.

The following hotels represent the best of the best in accommodations in Hanoi. While they are relatively expensive compared to the cost of budget accommodations in Hanoi, compared to hotels elsewhere in the world they are real bargains.

The visitor will find fewer international luxury standard hotels in Hanoi than in Saigon. But there are a few fine hotels available and no doubt more will open between our visit and the time you read this. Our personal favorites in Hanoi are the well located Hotel Sofitel Métropole Hanoi and the Hilton Hanoi Opera. The Hotel Sofitel Métropole combines the charm of a colonial hotel with a renovation of international standard so that it provides all the amenities the traveler expects from a five-star hotel. Add to this a truly superb location and a well-trained staff dedicated to providing the services expected by the international traveler and in our book you have a winner. We prefer the ambience of the rooms in the original hotel – now the Métropole wing. The Hilton Hanoi Opera is located very near to the Hotel Sofitel Métropole and shares its ideal location within easy walking distance of the old city center and the majority of shopping venues. The Hilton is a totally new hotel and offers comfortable rooms, a very nice marble and tile bathroom with a separate shower enclosure, and either views of the city or the Opera House.

❑ **Hotel Sofitel Métropole Hanoi:** *15 Ngo Quyen Street, Hanoi, Vietnam, Tel. (844) 826-6919, Fax (844) 826-6920. Email: sofitel@sofitelhanoi.vnn.vn. Website: sofitel-hanoi-vietnam. com*. Vietnam's first officially accredited five-star property, the Hotel Sofitel Métropole Hanoi is an award-winning French colonial-style hotel situated in the heart of Hanoi within easy walking distance of major businesses, government ministries, and upmarket shopping areas. One of the region's few remaining hotels of its era (opened in 1901), its quality renovation in 1992 and the opening of a new wing in 1996 have made it into one of Hanoi's top hotels, being voted "Best Business Hotel in Hanoi" for four years in a row, 1997-2000, by *Asia Money* magazine. We were also well impressed by this hotel that combines Old-World charm with a top-notch renovation. The 244 guestrooms and suites, comprised of the original Metropole wing and the new Opera wing, provide guests with all the convenience and amenities expected of a five-star hotel combined with the charm of an historical property. The mini-bar includes tea and coffee making facilities, and the soundproof windows keep out the noise of the busy streets below. *Le Beaulieu* is an elegant restaurant offering the best in French cuisine, and brunch on Sunday is a tradition among Hanoi residents. For Vietnamese cuisine, visit *Spices Garden* where authentic tastes of Hanoi are enjoyed in an elegant setting. *Le Club Bar* serves a continental breakfast, lunch buffet, afternoon tea, and evening snacks. The *Bamboo Bar* provides a relaxing poolside spot to enjoy light snacks or a refreshing cocktail. The *Met Pub* serves snacks, as well as lunch and dinner buffets. Guests who wish to learn more about Vietnamese cuisine firsthand may attend the Métropole's cooking school. Accompanied by the chef of the *Spices Garden*, participants learn about Vietnamese ingredients in a local market. Back in the Métropole kitchen everyone has the chance to actively take part in the cooking demonstration. After the class, lunch is served in the *Spices Garden* restaurant where participants sample the dishes prepared during the demonstration. Business Center; Clark Hatch Fitness Center; Conference and Banquet Facilities.

❑ **Hilton Hanoi Opera:** *1 Le Thanh Tong Street, Hoan Kiem District, Hanoi, Vietnam, Tel. (844) 933-0500, Fax (844) 933-0530. Email: hanhitwpr@hilton.com.* Opened in 1999, the five-star Hilton Hanoi Opera, next to the restored Opera House, is ideally located in the heart of the business district and within easy walking distance to major office buildings, government ministries, and upmarket shopping areas. After only 18 months of operation, the Hilton Hanoi Opera was voted "Best Business Hotel in Vietnam 2000" by *Business Asia* magazine and Bloomberg television. The 269 guestrooms are attractively furnished and decorated with local textiles and paintings. Guestrooms have a large armoire with the television and mini-bar along with tea and coffee making facilities tucked discreetly inside. Double glazed windows keep the street noise outside. The bathrooms of granite and tile feature separate shower and bathtub units. Rooms look out on the city or on the Opera House. *Chez Manon*, a 150-seat contemporary brasserie, specializes in international selections – especially grill and rotisserie items – as well as local Vietnamese cuisine. *Café Opera* presents fresh pastry and bakery items that can be casually enjoyed in the lobby lounge or for take-away. A unique offering is the *Café Opera Bakery* "happy hour"– from 5:30pm until closing all items are half price! *Turtle's Poem,* voted Hanoi's number one Cantonese restaurant, offers an array of a la carte drinks or the famous dim sum consisting of a varied selection of bite size delicacies. Five private dining rooms are available. The *Lobby Lounge* serves light snacks and beverages and the *Bar des Artistes* is a cozy bar designed to become a bistro at lunch time. Business Center; Fitness and Health Center; Conference and Banquet Facilities.

❑ **Hanoi Daewoo Hotel:** *360 Kim Ma Street, Ba Dinh District, Hanoi, Vietnam, Tel. (844) 831-5000, Fax (844) 831-5010, Reservations, (844) 831-5555. Email: hotel@daewoohn.com.vn.* A member of the Leading Hotels of the World, the Hanoi Daewoo is a five-star hotel which, as a part of the Daeha Business Center, is adjacent to a luxury apartment tower and an office tower. Situated in the heart of a newly developing business hub and diplomatic quarter, hotel guests may take a shuttle or taxi to visit the old quarter of Hanoi encompassing the main business and shopping district. The 411 guestrooms and suites offer all the amenities expected of an international luxury property. The hotel owns an extensive collection of Vietnamese modern paintings which grace the public areas and guestrooms. The Daewoo also operates an art gallery in conjunction with an Hanoi gallery, as well as an arcade with several small shops. The *Café Promenade*, an international coffee shop, serves breakfast, lunch, and dinner buffets. *Edo*, a Japanese restaurant, has a teppanyaki table and sushi bar. *Silk Road* serves Chinese cuisine while *La Paix* caters to patrons preferring Italian continental food. The *Palm Court* lobby lounge, *Pool Side Bar*, and *Lake View* provide options for light snacks and beverages. *Club Q*, a nightclub and discotheque, has five karaoke rooms. Business Center; Health and Fitness Center; Conference and Banquet Facilities.

❑ **Hotel Nikko Hanoi:** *84 Tran Nhan Tong Street, Hanoi, Vietnam, Tel. (844) 822-3555, Fax (844) 822-3555 or toll-free from U.S. or Canada (800) 645-5687. Email: sales@hotel nikkohanoi.com.vn. Website: www.nikkohotels.com.* Located in the city center surrounded by lakes and parks, the Hotel Nikko Hanoi is convenient to business and shopping locations. The 260 guestrooms and suites are spacious and nicely decorated with light colored woods and neutral colored fabrics.

Expected amenities are in place plus an unexpected bonus – an in-room fitness machine. Additional services and amenities are provided for Nikko Floor guests. *La Brasserie* serves international cuisine and offers guests a choice of buffet or an a la carte menu. Try *Tao-Li* for Chinese cuisine or *Benkay* if you prefer Japanese specialties. *Portraits Bar* (the name originates from the artistic black and white photographs of Vietnamese people that adorn the walls) serves beverages and light snacks. Business Center; Health/Fitness Center; Conference and Banquet Facilities.

You'll find other good quality five-star accommodations in Hanoi, including the relative new boutique De Syloia Hanoi Hotel:

❏ **De Syloia Hanoi Hotel:** *7A Tran Hung Dao Street, Hoan Kiem District, Tel. (844) 824-5346, Fax (844) 824-1083. Website: www.desyloia.com. Email: desyloia@hn.vnn.vn.*

❏ **Horison Hotel:** *40 Cat Lin Street, Tel. (844) 733-0808, Fax (844) 733-0888. Website: swiss-belhotel.com/hanoi. Email: hhh_sale@netnam.org.vn.*

❏ **Melia Hanoi Hotel:** *448 Ly Thuong Kiet, Tel. (844) 934-3343, Fax (844) 934-3344. Email: melia.hanoi@solmelia.com.*

❏ **Meritus Westlake Hotel:** *1 Thanh Nien Road, Tel. (844) 823-8888, Fax (844) 8293888. Email: marcom.mwh@meritushotels.com.vn.*

If you are interested in more budget-oriented accommodations, survey the many options found on several hotel websites, such as Asia-Hotels.com.

RESTAURANTS

Hanoi is a city of sidewalk cafes and restaurants, which seem to appear everywhere, along the streets and down narrow lanes. Dining here makes for both great street theater and wonderful entertainment. Outdoor dining starts in earnest around 6:30am as thousands of local residents head for their favorite neighborhood café or restaurant for breakfast. Usually consisting of a cheap bowl of noodles (*pho*), breakfast is often eaten on small plastic chairs that line the crowded sidewalks. This dining ritual seems to continue throughout the day.

This also is a city of big draught beer (*Bia hoi*) drinkers, especially starting late in the afternoon when men leave work and meet their friends for a *Bia hoi*. Beer is one of the most popular drinks in Vietnam, and it is consumed with vigor by men in Hanoi. Cheap, robust, tasty, and widely available, beer plays an important role in Hanoi's many cafes and restaurants.

Hanoi also has an appetite for dogs – literally eating them. Indeed, you'll see several places selling live dogs which eventually end up in specialty dishes. Several restaurants north of the city specialize in dog meat. If you see a sign at the front of a restaurant that says *thit cho* or *thit cay*, the restaurant specializes in dog dishes. Most animal lovers really hate Hanoi for this "uncivilized" dining tradition.

Hanoi offers an excellent selection of Vietnamese and international restaurants. Indeed, one of the highlights of visiting Hanoi is dining. We generally recommend avoiding the many tempting local restaurants because of potential health problems ranging from diarrhea to hepatitis A. Hanoi's top restaurants remain relatively inexpensive by most international standards. Indeed, it is often difficult to spend more than US$25 on a meal for two. Since many of the top restaurants are small and very popular, we recommend making reservations for dinner, especially if you plan to dine after 8pm.

Restaurants and cafés have increasingly become important forums for entertainment and social recognition. For many local expats and socially mobile Vietnamese, dining out at trendy and quality places, such as Indochine, Au Lac Café, Emperors Restaurant, Press Club, and Cha Ca La Vong, means being seen at the right places and with the right people.

While Hanoi's restaurant scene is constantly changing, with more and more Italian and French restaurants opening with expat chefs, the following restaurants come highly recommended as some of the best in Hanoi. They are places where the food, ambience, and entertainment are exceptional. However, don't expect efficient service. Dining in Hanoi, as elsewhere in Vietnam, takes time and can try your patience. But take it easy. Your just reward will be found in many outstanding dishes served in these fine restaurants.

VIETNAMESE

❑ **Indochine:** *16 Nam Ngu, Hoan Kiem, Tel. 942-4097.* Considered by many expats and visitors to be Hanoi's best Vietnamese restaurant. Indeed, you almost want to take this one home with you so you can return again and again. This well appointed restaurant is divided into separate buildings with two-story dining rooms. The expansive menu includes many wonderful Vietnamese specialties. Try the excellent chicken and banana leaf salad. Attentive waiters dressed in traditional costumes provide excellent service. A delightful female string trio plays both traditional and modern tunes. Great ambience. Reminiscent of old colonial Hanoi. A truly memorable dining and entertainment experience.

❑ **Nam Phuong:** *19 Phan Chu Trinh, Tel. 824-0926.* Located within easy walking distance of both the Hilton Opera and Sofitel Metropole hotels, this cozy restaurant offers a wide selection of excellent Vietnamese dishes. Try the spring rolls – the best we found in Vietnam – soft shell crabs, and pork in coconut sauce as well as several dishes recommended by your waitress or waiter as house specialties. Wonderful ambience accompanied by a female string trio playing many traditional Vietnamese tunes. Excellent service.

❑ **Seasons:** *95B Quan Thanh, Tel. 843-5444.* This small but cozy restaurant has lots of colonial ambience. Offers both indoor and outdoor dining along a busy, and sometimes noisy, side street. Inside dining is accompanied by two musicians playing the piano and violin. Try the prawns in coconut sauce. Excellent service. Reservations recommended.

❑ **Emperor Restaurant:** *18B Le Thanh Ton, Tel. 826-8801.* This well appointed restaurant, with a beautiful wooden pavilion in its garden, is especially popular with expats and business people who entertain guests. Serves classic Vietnamese dishes in a restored French villa. Try the delicious *banh beo* (rice crepes with minced shrimp).

❑ **Le Tonkin:** *14 Ngo Van So, Tel. 943-3457.* If you've dined at Indochine, you'll notice many similarities. After all, Le Tonkin is owned by the person who operates Indochine. Excellent food and service. The special set menu, which includes 10 courses, only costs US$10. Nice ambience in this restored garden French villa.

❑ **Bun Cha:** *1 Hang Manh, Tel. 828-6803.* This crowded five-story restaurant, in one of the most densely populated sections of the city, is a luncheon favorite for many locals and expatriates . Specializes in *bun cha* (grilled pork patty) and noodles.

ITALIAN

❑ **Il Grillo:** *116 Ba Trieu, Tel. 822-7720.* The intimate setting for this classical Italian restaurant makes it a favorite of many expatriates.

❑ **Mediterraneo:** *23 Nha Tho Street, Tel. 826-6288.* This delightful relaxing open-fronted Italian eatery is the perfect stop for lunch while shopping in and around Hang Gai and Nha Tho streets. Offers an expansive menu of pizzas, pastas, spaghetti, ravioli, and other Italian specialties. Uses a wood-fired pizza oven.

FRENCH

❑ **Le Beaulieu:** *Hotel Sofitel Metropole, 15 Ngo Quyen, Tel. 826-6919.* This elegant restaurant serves some of Hanoi's best French dishes in an expansive dining room. Sunday brunch is especially popular with local residents.

❑ **Hoa Sua:** *81 Tho Nhuom, Tel. 942-4448.* This combination French and Vietnamese restaurant also serves as a training school for disadvantaged youth. Excellent food served in pleasant indoor and outdoor settings. Serves a popular Sunday brunch. Their adjacent bakery offers a wonderful selection of French pastries. A very good value restaurant.

MEDITERRANEAN

❑ **Press Club:** *59A Ly Thai To, Tel. 934-0888.* Located behind the Sofitele Metropole Hotel, this elegant fine dining restaurant serves excellent dishes along with a good selection of wines. Includes a bistro and cigar bar. Popular at lunch time.

WESTERN

❑ **Red Onion Bistro:** *49 Hai Ba Trung, Tel. 934-2342.* Located in the Hanoi Towers apartment complex, this comfortable expat restaurant and fusion bistro offers a wide selection of dishes, including excellent hamburgers. Pleasant atmosphere with nice views of the city below.

❑ **Al Fresco's:** *23 Hai Ba Trung, Tel. 826-7782.* This Australian-operated restaurant is popular for its mix of excellent international dishes, from ribs to pizza.

ASIAN

❑ **Spices Garden:** *Hotel Sofitel Metropole, 15 Ngo Quyen, Tel. 826-6919.* This intimate hotel restaurant offers an excellent sampling of Asian cuisines, especially Vietnamese, Thai, Chinese, and Indian. Serves a luncheon buffet and also sponsors a cooking school.

❑ **Khazana:** *41B Ly Thai To, Tel. 824-1166.* This popular Northern Indian restaurant serves excellent dishes in an opulent setting. Try the tandoor dishes.

SEAFOOD

❑ **San Ho:** *58 Ly Thuong Kiet, Tel. 822-2184.* This combination French and Vietnamese restaurant is especially popular with French expatriates. Its luxurious setting and talented kitchen turns out some of Hanoi's best seafood dishes. Serves a popular Sunday brunch.

❑ **Cha Ca La Vong:** *14 Cha Co, Tel. 825-3929.* Located in the heart of the Old Quarter, this popular Vietnamese seafood restaurant is famous for its specialty fish dish – *cha ca* – which is marinated in dill, cooked in a sizzling hot pot at your table, and served with noodles, mint, peanuts, and fish sauce. Dine upstairs.

CAFES AND BISTROS

❑ **Au Lac Cafe:** *57 Ly Thai To, Tel. 825-7807.* Located across the street from the Sofitel Metropole Hotel, this wonderful outdoor café and bar offers one of Hanoi's most expansive menus of sandwiches, dishes, and drinks. Pleasant ambience, excellent service, and delicious food – the perfect place for lunch, dinner, or just a cup of coffee.

❑ **Brothers Café:** *26 Nguyen Thai Hoc, Tel. 733-3866.* Serves excellent lunch (US$5) and dinner buffets of Vietnamese dishes as well as popular noodle dishes, soups, and dumplings.

❑ **Moca Café:** *14-16 Nha Tho, Tel. 825-6334.* This trendy café serves a good variety of inexpensive Western and Vietnamese dishes. Popular with both expats and Vietnamese.

❏ **Hot Rock Café:** *11A1 Giang Vo, Tel. 844-5661.* Expansive menu but especially noted for its pizza and sizzling beef steak and chicken dishes.

BAKERIES

❏ **Hoa Sua:** *81 Tho Nhuom, Tel. 942-4448.* See above notes under French restaurants.

❏ **Opera Bakery:** *Hilton Opera Hotel.* Offers an excellent selection of breads, pastries, and cakes. The only bakery to offer a "bakery happy hour" – all breads and pastries are sold at half-price after 5:30pm. A great place to put together an inexpensive breakfast!

VIETNAMESE NOODLE SOUP (PHO)

❏ **Mai Anh:** *32 Le Van Huu, Tel. 943-8492.* This is one of Hanoi's best restaurants for the ubiquitous national noodle dish, *pho.* Stop here for lunch, order this dish, and enhance its basic bland flavor by experimenting with the accompaniment of spicy condiments. There's nothing fancy about this place – lots of long tables lined with benches. Go to the second floor where you'll have more privacy and a good view of the busy street below.

SEEING THE SITES

In addition to enjoying the city's rich variety of shopping, restaurants, accommodations, transportation, and people-watching, Hanoi also is a city of pleasant lakes and interesting museums, temples, pagodas, and entertainment. Be sure to set aside enough time to take in several of Hanoi's major travel pleasures which are popular with most visitors to Hanoi. Many may underwhelm you – *"Is that all there is?"* – but a few are of special interest. History buffs will find lots of things to see, which are primarily found in several state-sponsored museums that praise the glory of Vietnam and its war-time leaders. Many of these museums are heavily attended by groups of local tourists who come in from the countryside to experience Hanoi firsthand. Again, more people-watching opportunities await you in many places throughout Hanoi.

MAUSOLEUM

❑ **President Ho Chi Minh Mausoleum.** *Ba Dinh Square. Open daily, except Mondays and Fridays, 8-11am.* This is one of those must-do-when-in-Hanoi activities – see the man who remains Vietnam's great revolutionary and inspiring hero. He lies here in splendid repose as thousands of individuals pass by his glass-encased body out of a combination of curiosity and respect. Your timing has to be right to experience this popular attraction. Well preserved and appearing almost ethereal for public viewing, Ho Chi Minh's embalmed corpse lies in rest at the center of this solemn, austere, and cool marble mausoleum. But each year he is sent to Moscow for yearly maintenance and touch-up. His trip usually occurs during the month of October or November. Foreign visitors must sign in, leave their cameras and bags at a checkpoint, and line up for entering single file into the mausoleum. The guards strictly enforce dress and decorum rules – no shorts, tank tops, or talking. Nearby are the Ho Chi Minh Museum, Ho Chi Minh's Residence, and One Pillar Pagoda, which are usually combined with a visit to the mausoleum.

MUSEUMS

❑ **Vietnam Museum of Ethnology:** *Nguyen Van Huyen, Tel. 836-0352. Open daily except Mondays, 8am-5:30pm. Entry fee: VND10,000.* Often overlooked, this museum is located approximately six kilometers west of the downtown area. Opened in 1997, this is one of the best museums in Vietnam. It is designed to showcase the cultures of the nation's 54 ethnic minority groups – their artifacts, dress, and music. And it does so very well with two floors of informative displays of different ethnic groups at work and play. The demonstration on making the popular conical hats is especially interesting. Includes numerous well organized and presented displays, reconstructions, photographs, and videos. The museum also functions as a research institute for studying Vietnam's interesting minority groups. A small but nice handicraft shop – **The Museum Shop** – is located near the entrance to the museum grounds. It includes a small but interesting collection of water puppets, books, textiles, and lacquer boxes that make good souvenirs or gifts.

❑ **Vietnam Fine Arts Museum:** *66 Nguyen Thai Hoc, Tel. 823-3084. Open daily except Mondays, 9:15am-5pm. Entry fee:*

VND10,000. If you're interested in paintings and sculptures, be sure to visit this informative museum. Housed in an old three-story colonial building which once served as a boarding school for French girls, this museum chronicles art, architecture, and sculpture from the Stone Age until today. Includes many paintings of Vietnam's old masters but little on contemporary Vietnamese art. That art is better represented in the pricey galleries along Hanoi's two main art streets. The first floor exhibits interesting folk art and wonderful lacquer paintings. Includes a small souvenir shop and café on the second floor.

❏ **Ho Chi Minh Museum:** *3 Ngoc Ha, Tel. 823-0896. Open daily except Mondays and Fridays, 8-11am and 1:30-4pm. Entry fee: VND5,000.* This lotus-shaped building houses the only museum in the country devoted to a single individual. Includes lots of war relics, photos, and correspondence relating to the role of Ho Chi Minh in Vietnam's many struggles with foreigners. Visitors often quickly leave this museum muttering "propaganda," "bizarre," or at best "interesting." Indeed, this museum gives new meaning to the term "propaganda." Even Uncle Ho might be embarrassed by such displays. If you decide to visit, don't feel obligated to linger too long. There are more interesting and educational things to do with your time in Hanoi.

❏ **Ho Chi Minh's Residence and the Presidential Palace:** *Huong Vuong Road. Open daily, 7:30-11am and 1:30-4pm. Entry fee: VND3,000.* Finally, peace and quiet, even though this site may be a bit crowded with local tourists and school children. Located in the lovely gardens in the rear of the imposing mustard-yellow Presidential Palace, this small and simple house on stilts served as President Ho Chi Minh's residence from 1958 until his death in 1969 (he refused to live in the Presidential Palace). Crowds meander around the outside of the house, through the gardens, and around the delightful large pond with cascading water streams. The whole area emphasizes the simple and austere life of Vietnam's major hero. This is the stuff of myths and legends. You can purchase a booklet on the compound at the entrance for VND20,000 – *The Living Quarter and Working Place of President Ho Chi Minh.*

❏ **History Museum:** *1 Pham Ngu Lao, Tel. 825-2853. Open daily except Mondays, 8-11:30am and 1:30-4:30pm. Entry fee: VND10,000.* This museum should tell lots of great stories about more than 3,000 years of Vietnamese history. It tells a few stories but not particularly informative ones for English-speaking visitors. The first floor covers history from Paleolithic times until pre-15th century. The second floor primarily emphasizes history from the 15th century until independence in August 1945. Includes some very interesting bronze drums not found in most Southeast Asian museum.

❑ **Revolutionary Museum:** *25 Tong Dan, Tel. 825-4151. Open daily 8am - 4:15pm.* If you're interested in how the government portrays its struggle against French colonialism and imperialism, this museum tells its story. Displays numerous documents, newspapers, and photos documenting the many struggles that led to independence and reunification. Not quite up to Army Museum standards.

❑ **Army Museum:** *28A Dien Bien Phu, Tel. 823-4264. Open daily except Mondays and Fridays, 8-11:30am and 1-5pm. Entry fee: VND10,000.* You can't miss this one with the imposing statue of Lenin out front. This is one of the better museums for portraying the role of the People's Army in both liberating and defending the nation from the 1930s until today. Includes lots of photos, videos, and dioramas. Covers such important battles and milestones as Dien Bien Phu, the Ho Chi Minh Trail, and the fall of Saigon in 1975. The **Cot Co Flag Tower**, which is 30 meters tall and provides a good overview of the city, is also located in this compound.

❑ **Hoa Lo Prison Museum:** *1 Hoa Lo. Open Tuesday to Sunday, 8:30-11am and 1:30-4pm.* Also known as the infamous "Hanoi Hilton" for Americans, this is just one representative slice of the old city prison – a wall and a few rooms and cells that constitute a museum – that witnessed many tortures and executions of political dissidents at the hands of the French colonial administration. Primarily documents the cruelty of the French. Makes an important point about struggle and sacrifice in pre-1954 Vietnamese history. This was also the "home" for many American POWs, including Senator John McCain and Ambassador "Pete" Peterson, the first U.S. ambassador to Vietnam since the American withdrawal in 1975. The prison/museum now abuts a high-rise commercial complex, the Hanoi Towers, which ironically is a monument to the victory of capitalism that is now shaping Hanoi's central business district.

TEMPLE, PAGODA, AND CHURCH

❑ **Temple of Literature (Van Mieu):** *Van Mieu. Open daily, 7:30am - 6pm (summer) and 8am -5pm (winter). Free entry.* This lovely setting houses one of the finest examples of traditional Vietnamese architecture, a Confucian temple dating from 1070, as well as Vietnam's first university which was built in honor of Confucious. Includes five interesting courtyards, 82 stone tablets mounted on stone tortoises, temple buildings, and a newly constructed wood dormitory. The compound also includes a shop which offers a wide range of handcrafted items – paintings, lacquer boxes, water puppets, silver boxes, jewelry, clothes, scarves, and dolls.

❑ **One Pillar Pagoda:** *Chua Mot Cot.* Located near the Ho Chi Minh Mausoleum, Presidential Palace, and Ho Chi Minh Museum, this unusual small pagoda is build on top of a single pillar. It sometimes serves as a symbol of Vietnam. Destroyed by the French in 1954, it was rebuilt and now sits on top of a concrete pillar that rises from a small pond. A very popular site for local tourists. Also look nearby for **Dien Huu Pagoda** (Ong Ich Kiem) with its courtyard filled with bonsais and side rooms with Buddhas. Nearby shops offer books, cards, clothes, hats, and other souvenirs.

❑ **Tran Quoc Pagoda:** *Thanh Nien. Entry fee: VND5,000. Open daily, 8am - 4:30pm.* This is Hanoi's oldest (6th century) temple, which also remains a practicing Buddhism monastery. Very popular with local tourists.

❑ **Ngoc Son Pagoda:** *Dinh Tien Hoang. Entry fee: VND12,000.* Located on an island in Hoan Kiem Lake, this picturesque temple is one of the most popular in Hanoi for visitors.

❑ **Saint Joseph's Cathedral:** *Nha Tho Street.* Also known as the Hanoi Cathedral. Constructed in 1886, the church is similar in design to Notre Dame Cathedral in Paris. However charming, it has seen better days – rather worn and crumbling – but still a symbol of Christianity in Hanoi.

EVENING ENTERTAINMENT

While Hanoi is not as lively in the evening as Saigon, nonetheless there is plenty to see and do from dining at trendy restaurants and cafes, which often include musical entertainment, to catching a water puppet show or visiting a bar. Dining still ranks at the top for evening entertainment. Since dinner and café crawling can be three-hour affairs, from 8pm to 11pm, an evening of dining out becomes an evening of entertainment. Since many shops stay open until 9pm, walking around the major shopping areas and lakes in the evening is another form of enjoyment.

WATER PUPPET THEATER

❑ **Thang Long Water Puppet Theater:** *57B Dinh Tien Hoang, Tel. 824-5117. Performances take place daily at 6:30pm and 8pm.* VND20,000 for second-class seats and VND40,000 for first-class seats (includes free audiocassette of music). This is an adult play, especially for its technical execution, even though you might think it's theater for children. A "must see" cultural activity when in Hanoi, the water puppet theater is uniquely northern Vietnamese. Standing waist deep in the water behind a screen, a troupe of eight or more talented performers manipulate through a series of bamboo poles, pulleys, and levers colorful lacquered wood-carved marionettes as they tell folk stories involving love, war, and other challenges. This theater is home to the most famous water puppet troupe in Vietnam, which has performed all over the world. Includes a very colorful set accompanied by a live band and singers who sit to the left of the set. Since all of the show is in Vietnamese and no attempt is made to translate what's going on, the story lines are difficult to follow for anyone who does not understand Vietnamese. Nonetheless, it's a fascinating show which becomes even more interesting once the performers come out from behind the set for their curtain call. Be sure to reserve your tickets earlier in the day since the 300-seat theater is often full. Performance times may vary, but the 8pm show is usually standard except for Monday. After seeing the show, you will probably have a renewed appreciation for the many water puppets you see in the handicraft and souvenir shops, especially those found at Craft Link.

BARS AND NIGHTCLUBS

From karaoke bars and pubs to jazz bars and nightclubs, Hanoi has a budding nightlife of sorts. Many budget travelers hang out at the many travel cafes which often double as a café, bar, and meeting place. The following places are especially popular with expats and travelers in the evenings:

❑ **Press Club:** *59A Ly Thai To, Tel. 934-0888.* Popular Friday night happy hour on the rooftop garden for expats. Also try the classy **Library Bar** in the Press Club.

❑ **Bamboo Bar:** *Hotel Sofitel Metropole, 15 Ngo Quyen, Tel. 826-6919, ext. 8042.* Offers drinks and snacks in a pleasant poolside setting.

❑ **Met Pub:** *Hotel Sofitel Metropole, 15 Ngo Quyen, Tel. 826-3968.* Offers a good selection of drinks and pub food.

❑ **Bar des Artistes:** *Hilton Opera Hotel, 1 Le Thanh Tong, Tel. 933-0500.* Popular with French expats.

❑ **Lakeview Sky Lounge:** *Daewood Hotel, Tel. 831-5000, ext. 3216.* Serves BBQ and drinks in a pleasant rooftop setting on the 18th floor. One of the best views of the city.

❑ **Spotted Cow:** *23C Hai Ba Trung, Tel. 824-1028.* Popular expat hangout offering lots of beer and jazz.

SHOPPING BEYOND HANOI

Plan to leave at least a couple of days to explore a few areas outside Hanoi. Most are within a one- to four-hour drive and thus make good day trips.

CRAFT VILLAGES

❑ **Bat Thrang:** While ostensibly close to the city – only 13 kilometers southeast of the city center – it may take an hour to get to because of congested city traffic and the pot- holed dirt road that leads into the large village or small town of 14,000 people. Bat Thrang is Hanoi's famous ceramic production center where you can visit several small factories producing a wide variety of ceramics. It's a very friendly town where the children are always delightful and the street scene very photogenic. Several factories also have their own shops which nicely display their wares. As you will quickly discover by comparing prices with shops in Hanoi, prices are not always better at the production source. A popular stop for tour groups, the factories and shops in Bat Thrang have adjusted their prices for the monied crowds. We personally have difficulty finding anything here that speaks to us, especially given the many traditional designs and less than attractive colors. Many of these places could use some outside design talent to orient more of their producer to what could be a more lucrative market – Western buyers. In the meantime, you may find something here that speaks to you. If not, a visit to this interesting town is still well worth the trip. Since the streets can be extremely muddy when it rains – most are torn up because of the heavy ceramic hauling through the town – be prepared for lots of mud if you arrive here within a day or two of a downpour. You'll hear the name "Bat Thrang" frequently when you shop in Hanoi, and even in Saigon.

❑ **Binh Da:** Located 23 kilometers southwest of Hanoi, this is Hanoi's famous firecracker-making village. An interesting place to see where they are made – as well as demonstrated – including the underwater firecrackers used in the water puppet shows,. This is not something you will want to buy and put in your suitcase!

❑ **Dong Ky:** Located 18 kilometers northeast of Hanoi, this village is noted for its production of inlaid mother-of-pearl furniture.

❑ **Van Phuc:** Located 14 kilometers southwest of Hanoi, this is a popular silk-weaving village. Here you can watch the silk production process as well as purchase silk fabric by the meter.

THE ROAD TO HALONG BAY

Most visitors to Hanoi set aside at least one day to visit beautiful and romantic Halong Bay which is located about 150 kilometers east of the city. It takes about three hours by car or one hour by helicopter to reach Halong Bay from Hanoi. Assuming you will be going by car, be sure to stop at one of the shopping highlights along the way:

❑ **Hong Ngoc Humanity Center:** *Sao Do Town, Hai Duong, Tel. 882-911, Fax 883-868, or Email: hongngochd@hn.vnn.vn. Website: Hongngochumanitycenter.com.* This large production center and craftshop primary help employ and train people with disabilities – those who are deaf (60 percent) or physically handicapped (30 percent). Approximately 10 percent of the young workers are orphans. Drawn from four provinces in northern Vietnam, over 200 craftspeople work here producing many lovely products that are on display and for sale in the expansive workshop and store. You can watch the people at work producing delicate embroidered pictures from postcards. Indeed, the center is happy to accept commissions – just bring your own photo and have it copied as embroidery into a framed work of art. The shop also offers a good selection of clothes, oil paintings, lacquerware, carvings, ceramics, scarves, shoes, purses, tablecloths, and pillow covers. This also is one of the few places we encountered that offered gemstones and jewelry, primarily rubies and topaz. While prices may appear to be fixed, you are welcome to ask for a discount, especially on gems and jewelry – offer 70 percent of the asking price and then work toward agreement. Be sure to visit the center's website to preview their various products. If you are interested in commissioning an embroidered picture, contact the center by email. Indeed, it might be a real shopping treat to arrange for such a picture by email and pick up the finished product (allow one month) when you visit this area. Several salespeople speak excellent English and are very knowledgeable about the artisans and products. They also are very savvy at sales and marketing. This center could become one of your shopping highlights in Vietnam.

Enjoy a relaxing boat ride around Halong Bay. It will be one of the highlights of your visit to Vietnam. If you want to prepare for this area, rent the popular French film *Indochine* which was filmed here. Hopefully you'll have as good weather as the film makers!

SAPA

As we noted earlier, Sapa is more than a day trip from Hanoi. Indeed, think of Sapa as a three- to four-day trip – one day to get there, one day to get back, and a least one or two days to enjoy the hills, people, and ambience of Sapa. The beautiful mountain setting, coupled with the rich ethnic minorities in the area, make Sapa a very special place and one of the highlights for many visitors to Vietnam. Assuming you want to have a chance to meet the local people and shop, plan to arrive for the weekend markets, which take place on Saturday and Sunday. The mornings are usually the best time to visit the market. Here, tribal women and young girls sell their products, from clothes and textiles to jewelry and souvenirs. Be sure to bargain for everything – it's expected.

5

Hoi An and Central Vietnam

ANANG, CHINA BEACH, HUE, AND THE DMZ (Demilitarized Zone) have had special meaning to millions of people who followed the American War in Vietnam during the 1960s and 1970s or those who have subsequently studied the important role of these places in the history of Vietnam. Strategically located, coastal and sweltering Danang was the great staging area for American military forces who entered and exited Vietnam through the huge air and naval bases constructed in Danang.

China Beach, with its expansive beaches, served as the key R&R destination for American troops as well as became the subject of the popular television series *China Beach* in the U.S. during the 1980s. And Hue, with its surprising Tet Offensive in 1968, played a key role with U.S. involvement in Vietnam.

But as Vietnam often reminds visitors in so many ways, this is a unique country with a long history, distinct culture, and many talented people rather than just a recent set of war memories. For us, the central coastal region is also one of Vietnam's most interesting travel-shopping destinations. Nowhere is this more evident than in the small ancient town of Hoi An that lies just 30 kilometers south of Danang. Surprising to many visitors, it's a major shopping center with a unique historical and cultural twist. Indeed, it gives new meaning to the term "lifestyle shopping." If you're traveling to both Hanoi and Saigon, be sure to stop here along the way. You'll be pleasantly surprised by this little gem of a town that will transport you back to a bygone era.

> *The central region is one of Vietnam's most interesting travel-shopping destinations.*

SURPRISING CENTRAL VIETNAM

From ancient history to shopping, diverse and relaxing central Vietnam has a great deal to offer visitors. Many travelers who enjoy history, culture, and sightseeing primarily come to central Vietnam to explore the old Imperial City of Hue and walk through the intriguing ancient ruins of the Cham Kingdom at My Son.

Other visitors focus their attention on three major destinations just south of Danang – Marble Mountains, China Beach, and Hoi An. Taken together, these three places offer beachfront relaxation and some very interesting shopping experiences.

All of these destinations are within easy driving distance from the international airport at Danang. The problem becomes knowing where to stay for exploring the diverse attractions of this area. Not surprisingly, many visitors find Hue, and Danang in particular, disappointing. Hue is a bit out of the way and Danang, Vietnam's fourth largest city, with over 1 million people, is a big, ugly, and chaotic industrial and port city best noted for its interesting Cham Museum. These cities have few attractive places to stay and not a great deal to offer outside of visiting some interesting historic sites.

Our recommendation: head south to where all the fun is at China Beach and Hoi An. You'll find nice accommodations and a great deal to do in these two nearby locations. China Beach is all about enjoying the beach and resort facilities. Hoi An is all about shopping, history, and small-town ambience. In the end, Hoi An is the real star of this area, a place you'll probably wish you had decided to spend more time exploring its many streets, shops, restaurants, architecture, and sites. It has become the favorite city of many travelers to Vietnam, regardless of whether they like to shop or not. Indeed, even the most die-hard "I-hate-shopping" travelers find infectious Hoi An hard to resist – they even end up shopping either in the colorful market or in the tempting galleries and shops lining the pedestrian-only streets. Hoi An is a travel-shopper's paradise. If you miss Hoi An, you'll miss a very special place in Vietnam.

THE BASICS

SPEND THE RIGHT TIME WISELY

There's enough to see and do in this area to occupy at least three days of sightseeing, shopping, and relaxation. Two days are fine if your primary destinations are Hoi An, Marble Mountains, and China Beach. If you also want to include Hue and Danang, four days would be fine for seeing the major attractions. If you especially enjoy beaches and resorts, take whatever time you need for sand, sun, surf, and relaxation. Inviting China Beach is well worth a few days of your time before heading for the chaos, noise, and bright lights of Saigon or Hanoi. A week in this area is not necessary unless you plan to spend a lot of time on the beach.

❏ Many visitors find Hue and Danang disappointing.

❏ China Beach is all about enjoying the beach and resort facilities.

❏ Hoi An is all about shopping, history, and small-town ambience.

❏ Marble Mountains is a stone carver's paradise.

ARRIVING

Daily flights from Hanoi to Danang or from Saigon to Danang take just over one hour. The relatively small airport, which is only two kilometers from Danang, has car rental services and taxis available. The train also passes through Danang as well as connects to nearby Hue (a three-hour trip).

You also can fly into Hue from either Hanoi or Saigon (daily flights), but Danang is much more centrally located for visiting several places in this region. Danang is especially convenient for reaching Hoi An and China Beach.

GETTING AROUND

Unless you've already arranged to be met upon arrival by a tour group or travel agency representative, you can easily arrange for a car and driver at the airport. Expect to pay about US$30-35 a day. Taxis also are readily available in Danang. Drivers will be happy to arrange an hourly, half-day, or full-day rate should you wish to use them as your car and driver.

Since there are lots of things to see and do in this 140-kilometer area stretching from Hue in the north to Hoi An in the south, a car and driver will be the most convenient way of getting around. You can rent motorbikes and take buses and minibuses, but nothing beats the convenience of a car and driver. Once arriving in Hoi An, you may want to do what many other visitors do to enjoy the streets of this quaint town – rent a bicycle from one of the hotels or cafes, which should cost about US$1 a day.

TOURS AND GUIDES

Assuming you will arrive in **Danang**, you can contact several tour groups in the city to assist you in visiting the area:

❏ **Global Spectrum:** 46/3 Nguyen Thanh Han, Tel. 829-669.

❏ **Danang Travel Information Center:** 3-5 Dong Da Street, 823-431.

❏ **Vietnam Tourist Company:** 274 Phan Chu Trinh, Tel. 825-891.

❏ **Danang Tourist and Service Company:** 76 Hung Vuong, Tel. 823-993.

You'll also find several travel offices in **Hoi An**, especially along Le Loi and Tran Hung Dao streets, that can assist you with all your travel needs. The **Hoi An Tourist Office** (6 Tran Hung Dao Street, Tel. 861-363), provides information and services. Your hotel also should arrange such assistance.

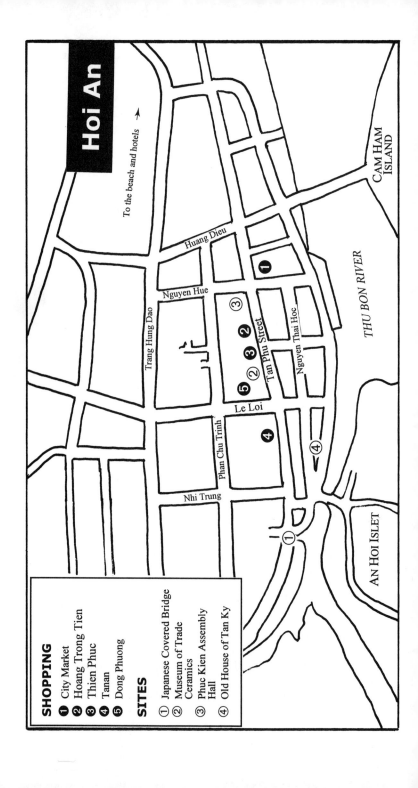

CONNECTING TO THE AREA

The following websites provide some useful information on the area:

- **China Beach** — furamavietnam.com
- **Danang City** — www.danang.gov.vn
- **Hoi An** — geocities.com/Vienna/7148
- **Hue** — namviet.net/hue.html
- **Things Asian** — thingsasian.com

WEATHER

The weather in this area is frequently unpredictable and awful. It's often steamy hot, rainy, or shrouded in fog. What initially appears to be a beautiful day may turn out to be depressingly overcast.

HOI AN

Located only 30 kilometers south of Danang, Hoi An, which also is known as the old port of Faifo, is one of those small jewels many travelers yearn to discover from time to time. While it's easy to over-hype this place, on the other hand, it may be just the type of place you've been looking for in your travels. One of Southeast Asia's oldest ports, Hoi An was an important trading center as early as the 15th century. Chinese and Japanese traders, along with the Dutch, French, Portuguese, English, and Americans, played important commercial roles here as well as significantly influenced the design and architecture of the two. Its trading role declined in the late 19th century with the silting of the Thu Bon River, which hampered navigation to the city.

CHARMING HOI AN

Hoi An is truly a charming old town with narrow winding streets, distinctive Chinese and Japanese architecture, interesting temples, a picturesque waterfront, and bustling markets, shops, and restaurants. In 1999 the town was declared a World Heritage site by UNESCO (unesco.org/whc/sites/948.htm) in recognition of its distinctive architecture and fusion of many cultures.

For many visitors, Hoi An is a shopper's paradise with lots of street-level character. This town made a simple decision that has really transformed its character and has turned it into such an appealing destination – no vehicles on the major streets which also house the town's best shops, restaurants, and architectural masterpieces. The old section of the town is restricted to pedestrians only – a real treat after dodging the many noisy motorbikes and vehicles in the streets of other cities that can quickly wear you down. You can leisurely stroll up and down the streets visiting shop after shop selling everything from inexpensive ready-made clothes and handicrafts to art and tailored garments. Indeed, this town is justly famous for its tailoring skills and paintings. You can have a blouse, dress, shirt, or suit made here in 24 hours at unbelievable prices. Many artists produce inexpensive paintings that grace the charming shophouse walls of galleries that line the streets of Hoi An. While most of it looks like "starter art" – done by artists just starting out on what eventually may be a career that takes them to the studios and galleries of Hanoi – Hoi An's art also is relatively inexpensive compared to what you find in Hanoi and Saigon. Indeed, many of Hanoi's artists got started in Hoi An. If you're lucky, you might purchase the work of a someday-will-become-famous Hoi An artist.

❑ This is a charming old town with narrow winding streets, distinctive Chinese and Japanese architecture, interesting temples, a picturesque waterfront, and bustling markets, shops, and restaurants.

❑ Much of the art looks like inexpensive "starter art" – done by new artists just getting started.

❑ Hoi An begs to be walked and savored. The old section is relatively small and can be covered in an hour – without distractions.

❑ Expect to bargain for everything in tourist-savvy Hoi An – 20-75% discounts!

APPROACHING THE TOWN

Hoi An is for strolling. While the town is spread out for about two kilometers along the Thu Bon River, the main old port section, which includes many well-preserved old houses, a temple, a museum, shops, restaurants, and boats, consists of three main east-west streets that run parallel to each other: Tran Phu, Thai Hoc, and Bach Dang. Bordered on the west by the famous Japanese Covered Bridge and on the east by Hoang

Dieu Street that connects to the Cam Nam Bridge, the area encompassed here begs to be walked and savored. Best of all, this is a vehicle-free area where pedestrians can peacefully stroll down the streets, visit sites, and absorb all the sights and sounds from the various shop houses. It's a relatively small area which you could cover within an hour, but since it has so many distractions along the way, you will probably spend two to three hours covering this area.

As a visitor, you must purchase a ticket to enter this part of town as well as to visit several of the major attractions. Tickets cost VND50,000 per person and can be purchased at the main tourist office on the corner of Nguyen Hue and Phan Chu Trinh streets. You'll receive a small map which outlines the various streets and points of interest. From there, walk directly south for one block. Immediately to your left, and adjacent to one another, will be Quen Cong's Temple and the Hoi An Museum of History and Culture. In the next block, on your left, will be the big colorful **Central Market** (65 Nguyen Duy Hieu Street) with its vendors spilling out onto the street with baskets full of fruits and vegetables. From here, turn right and start walking along Hoi An's main shopping artery, **Tran Phu Street**. Along the way you will encounter several tailoring shops, clothing stores, art galleries and studios, and arts, crafts, and souvenir shops, as well as the **Phuc Kien Assembly Hall**, **Museum of Trade Ceramics**, **Old House of Quan Thang**, and the **Cantonese Assembly Hall**. If you turn right at the intersection of Tran Phu and Le Loi streets (just after the Museum of Trade Ceramics), you'll find numerous fabric and tailoring shops along **Le Loi Street** which also becomes **Nguyen Truong To Street** at the intersection with Phan Dinh Phung/Tran Hung Dao Street. If you continue west along Tran Phu Street, you come to the famous **Japanese Covered Bridge** at the end. **Nguyen Thai Hoc Street** includes several interesting old buildings, including the famous **Old House of Tan Ky**. **Bach Dang Street** fronts on the colorful river with its many boats. You can rent a small boat, with driver, to take you up and down this quaint riverfront.

BEST SHOPPING BETS

Shopping in Hoi An can be lots of fun. The two main shopping streets also intersect with each other:

- **Tan Phu Street:** Runs east to west starting at the Central Market and ending at the Japanese Covered Bridge. Encompasses a diverse mix of art galleries and studios, antique shops, ceramic and stone carving stores, souvenir and craft shops, tailors and seamstresses, and clothing stores.

■ **Le Loi:** Goes south to north starting at the waterfront and crossing Phan Dinh Phung/Tran Hung Dao as it continues north as Nguyen Truang To Street. Includes several tailor shops, seamstresses, and fabric stores.

While many shopkeepers do not speak English, nonetheless, you should be able signal your intentions with cash or someone will come along and help you in English. Personnel in many of the tailor shops speak English, which is essential for communicating your design preferences. Expect to bargain for everything in Hoi An, receiving discounts ranging anywhere from 20 percent to 75 percent. This includes bargaining directly with artists in their studios. Remember, shops in this town live on the tourist trade and thus merchants are used to inflating prices for tourists who are often willing pay the first asking price.

Four of our favorite art shops along Tran Phu Street include:

❑ **Hoang Trong Tien:** *101 Tran Phu, Tel. 862-199. Email: quocthai.ha@dng.vnn.vn.* Very nice oil paintings produced in the studio of this artist.

❑ **Ha Ly:** *122 Tran Phu, Tel. 863-574.* Local artist who also has a shop at 141 Phan Chu Trinh.

❑ **Thien Phuc:** *126 Tran Phu, Tel. 862-280.* Nice selection of paintings, especially by artist Hoang An.

❑ **Tanan:** *142 Tran Phu, Tel. 861-307.* Specializes in producing wood carved panels, figures, boxes, and furniture; you can see the carvers at work in this shop as well as arrange to have customized carvings done to your specifications.

Numerous tailoring shops, many of which will quickly produce simple garments, are found in small stalls within the **City Market** (mainly same-day seamstresses) as well as along Tran Phu Street and adjacent Le Loi and Nguyen Truong To streets. If you have the time (a day or two for more sophisticated work for dresses, jackets, and suits), you may want to have garments made at one of these places. Most of the shops produce similar quality garments and do so quickly – often same-day service. Don't expect anything elaborate or to approximate top tailoring skills you might find in Hong Kong, Bangkok, or even Hanoi,

Saigon, and Danang. Keep your design preferences simple and go with model garments appearing in the shop – at least you know they can produce what you see rather than what you dream of getting. The following tailoring shops come highly recommended by many travelers who have had "good luck" on the cutting boards:

❑ **Dong Phuong:** *15b Le Loi, Tel. 861-422.* Quickly produces a wide range of garments. Nice fabric selections and good service.

❑ **Phuong Huy II:** *21B Tran Phu.* Small shop but talented in producing formal wear.

❑ **Thu Thao:** *32D Than Phu.* Located just across from the Central Market.

❑ **Thu Thuy:** *60 Le Loi Street.* Uses Vietnamese and Chinese silks and cottons.

❑ **Tien:** *54 Nguyen Truong To. Tel. 863-900.* Produces nicely tailored silk and cotton garments. Speaks English and French.

If you are in the market for antiques, suffice it to say that there are no old antiques in Hoi An – just "new" antiques made yesterday. If you are tempted to buy what is purported to be an antique ceramic piece – like what you see in the Museum of Trade Ceramics along Tran Phu Street – overcome this temptation by offering a "new" antique price which will probably accurately reflect the true value of what invariably will be a reproduction piece.

ENJOYING YOUR STAY

In addition to shopping, most activities in Hoi An center around sightseeing, dining, boat riding, and bicycling.

SIGHTSEEING

Most sightseeing focuses on the various museums, temples, houses, architectural structures, and waterfront outlined on the map you receive when you pay your VND50,000 entrance fee to the old city. These include:

- Cantonese Assembly Hall
- Hoi An Museum of History and Culture
- Japanese Covered Bridge
- Museum of Sa Huynh Culture
- Museum of Trade Ceramics
- Old House of Phung Hung
- Old House of Quan Thang
- Old House of Tan Ky
- Phuc Kien Assembly Hall
- Quan Cong's Temple
- Tran Family's Chapel
- Trieu Chau Assembly Hall

While most of these sites are interesting, you may choose not to visit all of them unless you are a real local history buff.

Keep in mind that all of these sites can be conveniently reached on foot within the small pedestrian-only section of the old town. You may need a guide to explain everything in English or pick up a travel guide book that's big on history for doing a self-guided tour. Outside this central shopping area, you may want to rent a bicycle for touring the town – the most popular way of seeing Hoi An. Most hotels and some cafés will rent bicycles for around US$1 a day.

You may also want to take a boat ride along the river as well as to the nearby islands. Just go to the dock along Bach Dam Street (just south of the Central Market) to arrange for a boat trip. The Hoi An Tourism office can also help you make such arrangements.

RESTAURANTS

Hoi An has several good small restaurants and cafes. We especially like the **Song Do Restaurant** at the **Hoi An River-side Resort** on Cua Dai Road. In addition to serving excellent Vietnamese and Chinese dishes, the view of the river and rice fields from the second floor dining area is wonderful. You can easily wile away the afternoon or evening at this delightful restaurant which also has attentive service. Other good restaurant choices include **Café des Amis** (52 Bach Dang Street, Tel. 861-616); **Ving Hung Restaurant** (1 Nguyen Hue Street, Tel. 862-203); **Faifoo** (104 Tran Phu Street, Tel. 861-548); **My Lac** (106 Tran Phu Street, Tel. 861-591); and **Restaurant Thanh** (76 Bach Dang Street, Tel. 861-366).

OVERNIGHT

Since you can easily cover Hoi An in a few hours, you may decide a half-day trip here is plenty. On the other hand, you may want stay overnight. If you do, one of the best places to stay is the relatively new riverside resort, **Hoi An Riverside Resort**, which is located about one kilometer from the downtown section along Cua Dai Road (see Accommodations section).

MARBLE MOUNTAINS AND FACTORIES

Located about 10 kilometers south of Danang, Marble Mountains consist of five marble hills ("Mountains of the Five Elements") which attract visitors because of their mysterious caves and expansive views of the surrounding area as well as the fascinating stone carving village of Non Nuoc at the foot of the mountain. The largest hill, **Thuy Son**, includes several caves with Buddhist sanctuaries filled with altars and burning incense. You'll have to pay an entrance fee of US$4 at the base of the mountain in order to gain admittance to this area. The walk up the steep hill is accompanied by numerous vendors along the 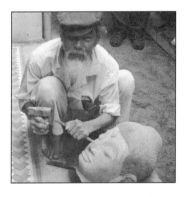 way selling souvenirs and drinks. The main cave, Huyen Khong, includes both Buddhist and Confucian shrines. During the American War, this cave served as a field hospital for the Viet Cong. The cave is dark, damp, and smoky, often dripping with water seeping in from the ceiling. This is good time to use your flashlight or to be accompanied by one of the local kids who volunteer to take you into the caves with their flashlight. Since these children are not permitted to take tips, you are expected to buy a souvenir from them in lieu of tipping.

At the southern base of Thuy Son is a small yet noisy stone carving village of **Non Nuoc** (Ngu Hanh Son District). This village basically consists of one long street, **Huyen Tran Cong Chua**, which is lined with over 100 stone carving factories and shops that work in white, gray, and rose marble as well as some sandstone. They make just about anything you can conceive of

– tables, chairs, fountains, lions, elephants, fish, human figures, heads, boxes – you name it, they will make it. They make from very small souvenir pieces to huge sculptures for gardens, homes, and offices, especially giant elephants and lions that can stand eight feet tall and 10 feet long. Indeed, if you're interested in having something sculpted in marble or sandstone, just bring your photos and negotiate a price with a factory. Most factories will make to order. They also can arrange to have your creations shipped abroad (they usually leave by sea freight from the docks of neighboring Danang).

> *Most factories will make to order – be sure to bring your photos.*

While there are numerous stone carving factories and shops along this road, most tend to produce similar items with a decided ethnic look – Vietnamese and Chinese. Unfortunately, much of the current stock looks borderline tacky or reflects an acquired taste for which you may have little interest. Nonetheless, the stone carvers here are very talented. They can make anything as long you provide them with a photo or model, including copies of ancient Greek and Italian sculptures or contemporary French masterpieces. If you can do that, chances are you will acquire some beautiful stone carvings at very good prices.

We found the following factories and shops offered good selections as well as have reputations for reliable shipping. However, if you go to these and other shops with a tour guide, they will most likely give your guide a commission on everything you buy. Your best pricing is done without a guide. These four places should give you a good start on shopping for stone carvings at Marble Mountains:

❑ **Nyuyen Hung:** *85 Huyan Tran Cong Chua Street, Tel. 836-310.*

❑ **Tien Hieu 2:** *42 Huyen Tran Cong Chua Street, Tel. 847-272.*

❑ **Xuat Anh:** *16-28 Huyen Tran Cong Chua Street, Tel. 836-349.*

❑ **Nguyen Long Buu:** *55 Huyen Tran Cong Chua Street, Tel. 836-279.*

DANANG AND THE CHAMS

While Danang is the country's fourth largest city, with over 1 million people, it's also much avoided by most tour groups and independent travelers. The city has yet to attract visitors much beyond its airport and the Cham Museum. However, should you decide to visit or stay in Danang, you will find a few shopping opportunities, especially for silk and tailored garments. The major shopping section, including cafes and restaurants, is near the **central market**. The major silk and tailoring shops are found along **Phan Chu Trinh Street**. Cafes and bars tend to be concentrated around Hung Vuong and Phan Chu Thinh streets. While you can get tailoring done in Hoi An, tailoring is reputed to be of much better quality in more business-oriented Danang than in touristy Hoi An. Buy your fabric and head for one of the many tailor shops near the central market.

If you want to get a good historical perspective on central Vietnam, we highly recommend stopping at the **Cham Museum** in Danang. Located at the intersection of Tran Phu and Le Dinh Duong streets, the museum is open daily from 8-11am and 1-5pm; admission is VND20,000. You can easily visit this interesting museum on your way from the airport to Marble Mountains, China Beach, and Hoi An. As you'll quickly discover, this whole area was once ruled for over 1,000 years (4th to the 13th centuries) by the Indianized (Hindu) Kingdom of Champa, which created some great sandstone sculptures and impressive red brick tower temples. What remains of this art (much of it disappeared with the ending of the American War in 1975), is found at the small Cham Museum in Danang and a few other sites in the area.

Many of the red brick tower temples of the Chams are scattered throughout the coastal area of central Vietnam in various stages of restoration and neglect. The best preserved area, which is also the most popular tourist attraction for viewing the largest complex of Cham monuments, is **My Son**. Located about 60 kilometers southwest of Danang or 25 kilometers from Hoi An, this area includes 71 monuments. Unfortunately, many of these monuments were destroyed during the American War – My Son functioned as the field headquarters for the Viet Cong, who were systematically bombed by the Americans. Since the area at one time was heavily mined, you are well advised not to wander off the well-trodden path since not all mines have been accounted for. Today, like Hoi An, My Song in 1999 was designated as a

World Heritage site by UNESCO. Today, it is being very slowly restored.

My Son is a relatively easy area to get to, but once there you must either walk or take a jeep up a very difficult road – especially if it is muddy – for approximately two kilometers to reach the entrance of the temple complex. While it is not clear when you purchase your entrance ticket, your admission fee (US$5) covers the cost of the jeep shuttle to the site. However long the queue, do use the jeep when it rains. The muddy road with its deep water-logged ruts is nearly impossible to walk, and the walk is very long, hot, and humid – not our idea of a good time!

CHINA BEACH

Today, China Beach is primarily a big inviting beach with a wonderful five-star resort – the Furama Resort Danang (see Accommodations) – which is one of Vietnam's best resorts. Here you can enjoy golf (driving range), tennis, archery, kite-flying, badminton, beach volley ball, and mountain biking as well as a full range of water sports before indulging in the resort's bars and restaurants. The resort also operates a shuttle bus service for its guests to Danang, Marble Mountains, and Hoi An.

The resort operates two small, but very good quality shops which are adjacent to each other. The **Art Gallery** in particular offers a nice range of quality gems and jewelry. Look for good values on rubies, topaz, sapphires, jade, and pearls. This shop also includes a rare collection of remaining sculptures produced by the famous Hue sculptress Madame Thi (Diem Phung Thi) as well as several paintings of the quality you might associate with the major art galleries in Hanoi and Saigon rather than the tourist art of Hoi An. Even if you don't stay at the resort, a stop at its shops may be well worth the trip, especially if you are looking for unique quality items.

HUE

Located along the Perfume River some 108 kilometers north of Danang and 689 kilometers south of Hanoi, Hue was once Vietnam's great Imperial city (1802-1945). Emperor Gia Long, who established the Nguyen dynasty in 1802, became the first of 13 consecutive Nguyen emperors to rule Vietnam until 1945. He and other emperors created a city of great self-indulgent splendor. Over the years Hue has experienced a great deal of devastation due to wars and conflicts. Most recently it was the scene of the great Tet Offensive of 1968 in which much of the city was "destroyed in order to be saved." If you are interested in these phases of Vietnamese history, you'll want to include Hue in your travel plans.

Hue is basically a history lesson filled with a famous palace, tower, pagoda, and several royal tombs. Visitors normally visit the **Citadel**, a 1½ square mile area surrounded by a 65-foot wide moat. The Citadel contains the **Imperial City** with its palace, library, museum, and Forbidden Purple City.

Hue is not a place for shopping. While it has an interesting central market (**Dong Ba Market** on the west bank of the Perfume River near Trang Tien Bridge), there's not a lot of interesting things to buy here. In the shopping department, Hue is primarily noted for making colorful conical hats (will custom-make for visitors), rice paper, silk paintings, and sesame seed candy. That's it. It's time to head off to Saigon where you're in for some great travel-shopping experiences!

ACCOMMODATIONS

While you can find many places to stay in Danang, Hue, and Hoi An, two places stand out as special – one in China Beach and one in Hoi An.

❑ **Furama Resort Danang:** *68 Ho Xuan Huong Street, Bac My An, Danang City, Vietnam, Tel. (84511) 847-333, Fax (84 511) 847-666. Website: www.furamavietnam.com. Email: furama dn@hn.vnn.vn*. A deluxe five-star international resort over-looking China Beach and just a 15-minute drive south of the international airport and city center. The 198 guestrooms in six categories ranging from garden superior to ocean suite are spacious, nicely appointed, and provide all the amenities expected – including tea and coffee making facilities – in a beautiful and tranquil setting. The marble bathroom is spacious as well, and every guestroom and suite features a private balcony or terrace with a view of the ocean, the tropical garden or the freshwater swimming lagoon. *Café Indochine* reflects the French colonial era in its brasserie-style setting with an open kitchen offering a variety of interna-tional cuisines. The *Ocean Terrace* serves a Mediterranean inspired menu in an oceanfront setting. *Hai Van Lounge* and the *Lagoon Bar* serve beverages and light snacks. The facili-ties are top-notch, the setting beautifully tropical, and the management exceptional, which translates into superior service from all the staff. Business Center; Health/Fitness Center; Recreational Facilities, including the Diana Diving Base; Conference and Banquet Facilities.

❏ **Victoria Hoi An Resort:** *Hoi An Beach, Quang Nam Province, Tel. (84510) 927-040, Fax (84510) 927-041. Website: www. victoriahotels-asia.com. Email: victoriaha@dng.vnn.vn.* Located five kilometers outside Hoi An, along a white sand beach, this resort opened in April 2001. Its 100 attractive rooms are set in an area resembling a fisherman's village with small streets and water ponds, clay-tiled roofs, and round Chinese cloth lanterns. Its intimate restaurant overlooks the sea and offers international, local, and sea food in indoor or al fresco dining. Includes a pool, spa, Jacuzzi, two tennis courts, billiards room, business center, conference facilities, tour service, souvenir shop, library, private jetty, and free shuttle via an old antique Renault to town.

❏ **Hoi An Riverside Resort:** *Cua Dai Road, Hoi An Town, Quang Nam Province, S. R. Vietnam, Tel. (84510) 864-800, Fax (84510) 864-900. Email: hoianriver@dng.vnn.vn.* A charming resort overlooking the Do River and rice fields and near the preserved communal houses, pagodas, and art shops of the 15th century town of Hoi An and about 30 minutes from Danang International Airport. Surrounded by landscaped gardens this 4-star resort offers both Western style and Vietnamese/Japanese style guestrooms. *Song Do Restaurant* and *Faifo Bar* overlooking the river, offer traditional Vietnamese cuisine as well as European and other Asian cuisines. Meeting Rooms and Banquet Facilities.

6

Saigon
(Ho Chi Minh City)

L OCATED IN THE FERTILE MEKONG DELTA AND
sprawling along the west bank of the Saigon River, this
is a big, bustling, and chaotic low-rise metropolis with
tree-lined streets overrun by motorbikes, cyclos, pedestrians, and young people. Officially referred to as Ho
Chi Minh City by the central government in Hanoi and by
those who wish to remain politically correct – but better known
as Saigon to local residents – this is an exciting and vibrant city
of over 7 million people. It offers visitors a wonderful selection
of fine hotels, restaurants, and shops as well as many interesting
sightseeing and entertainment opportunities. Spend four to six
days here and you'll be impressed with a rapidly developing
Vietnam and the new capitalism that in recent years has been
fueling this country's hybrid economy. Saigon may not be as

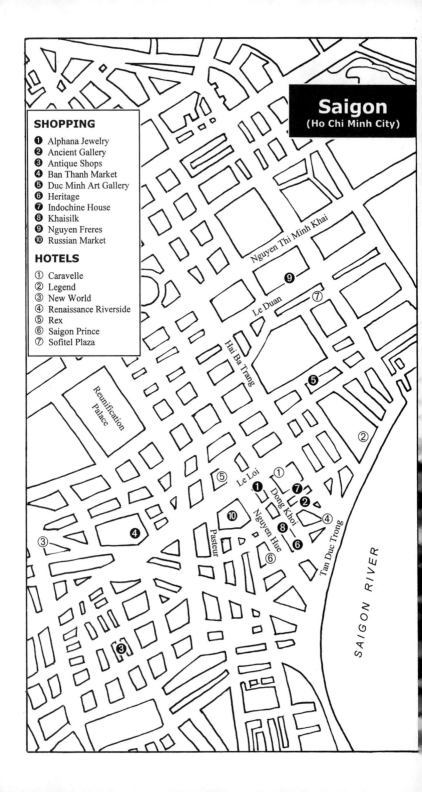

Saigon
(Ho Chi Minh City)

SHOPPING

❶ Alphana Jewelry
❷ Ancient Gallery
❸ Antique Shops
❹ Ban Thanh Market
❺ Duc Minh Art Gallery
❻ Heritage
❼ Indochine House
❽ Khaisilk
❾ Nguyen Freres
❿ Russian Market

HOTELS

① Caravelle
② Legend
③ New World
④ Renaissance Riverside
⑤ Rex
⑥ Saigon Prince
⑦ Sofitel Plaza

Nguyen Thi Minh Khai

Le Duan

Hai Ba Trang

Reunification
Palace

Le Loi

Dong Khoi

Nguyen Hue

Pasteur

Tan Duc Trong

SAIGON RIVER

quaint and charming as Hanoi, but it has a certain dynamism that speaks well for its future. Much of that dynamism centers on shopping. Take to Saigon's streets and you'll quickly discover a remarkable New Vietnam that is headed somewhere, however uncertain.

SURPRISING SAIGON

Saigon is an anomaly of sorts – the ostensible loser that actually became the winner. While it lost major political and military battles in 1975 – as clearly depicted in the propaganda museums in Hanoi and Saigon – by the 1990s Saigon had won the economic war that continues to transform Vietnam in more ways than Hanoi could ever imagine. Just drive along the streets of Saigon and pull into one of those museums in a Mercedes or Toyota van and think about the real winners. In the end, those museums represent the human costs of trying to be a political win-

Saigon has reasserted its role as the economic catalyst for Vietnam.

ner. But survey the streets of Saigon and the message comes through loud and clear: this is a city, and a country, with a great future. Saigon will most likely lead the way. As recent events already indicate, these economic changes will probably change the way Hanoi does its political business in the future.

Returning to its past patterns of exuberant capitalism, Saigon has now reasserted its dominant economic role through its renewed ties with foreign investors and influx of business people and tourists. If you want to invest in Vietnam, do so in Saigon where its talented people, entrepreneurism, and cosmopolitan culture are supportive of new initiatives. Saigon's renewed economic role is not surprising since the South has always been more economically assertive and entrepreneurial than the more deliberate, conservative, political, and bureaucratic North. Saigon's large entrepreneurial Chinese population, coupled with many talented people forced to work in the private sector because of their family ties with the discredited South Vietnamese regime, has helped move Saigon's economy in the direction of increased consumerism. Add to this many overseas Vietnamese investing in Vietnam via Saigon, and you have a powerful formula for creating a new economically assertive Saigon.

While hopeful, nonetheless, Saigon's fragile new economy is subject to the political winds that blow from Hanoi as well as the vicissitudes of an unpredictable and wacky global economy, which occasionally gets mired in recessions. Since the economic downturn in Southeast Asia beginning in 1997, Saigon's once promising new economy has been limping into an uncertain future.

Saigon has quickly reasserted its role as the economic catalyst for Vietnam. You see this in its dramatically changing skyline and in its bustling streets, from relatively new high-rise hotels and office buildings to increased traffic congestion. New hotels, shops, restaurants, and trendy cafes and bars open to capture much of the economic growth that gravitates to Saigon and into the pockets of its many optimistic young people who have never had to struggle like their parents or grandparents. Saigon represents a new generation and a new economy. It also portends what economic direction Vietnam will be taking in the coming decade.

Capitalism seems to come easy to this city, as if it never really left this place during its interlude with force-fed socialism and communism brought to local residents by the victorious post-1975 forces in Hanoi. Ostensibly re-educated but apparently poor learners, the Saigonese are back to what works best for them – making money. The real winners now seem to be found in the streets of Saigon – a new generation of young people in pursuit of Saigon's new-found treasures and pleasures.

❑ Take to Saigon's streets and you'll quickly discover a remarkable New Vietnam.

❑ Saigon is an anomaly of sorts – a real political loser in 1975 that managed to become the real economic winner two decades later.

❑ Saigon represents a new generation and a new economy. Its ever-changing skyline tells an exciting story about where this country is heading.

❑ Capitalism seems to come easy to this city, as if it never really left. History is treating this city well.

❑ Ostensibly re-educated but apparently poor learners, the Saigonese are back to what works best for them – making money.

More so than any other place in Vietnam, Saigon is a shopper's paradise. Stroll down Dong Khoi Street, Saigon's main shopping avenue, and you'll be impressed with the numerous boutiques, art galleries, souvenir shops, cafes, and restaurants that draw crowds of window shoppers and enthusiastic buyers along this tree-lined street. Slip down a few side streets, such as Mac Thi Buoi and Dong Du, and you'll discover newly opened upscale art galleries and home furnishings shops. Head for the central Ben Thanh Market, Russian Market, and the Ban Tay Market in Chinatown (Cholon) and you'll encounter a riot of colorful shopping activity and bargains galore for those who know how to really bargain. Explore Saigon's many antique, furniture, and bric-a-brac shops along Le Cong Kieu Street, or head for a few outstanding neighborhood art galleries and shops, and you'll see why this is Vietnam's premier shopping destination.

While Hanoi is a charming city with interesting shopping opportunities, Saigon has more shoppers to support its rapidly expanding commercial sector. Reflecting Saigon's re-emerging commercial role in Vietnam, this city offers many more upscale hotels, restaurants, and shops that cater to its relatively sophisticated business clientele. When it comes to business and commerce, Saigon is where the action is. You should have a very good time in this vibrant city.

GETTING TO KNOW YOU

If you want to be politically correct, especially when dealing with government officials, you should refer to this city as "Ho Chi Minh City." Since most locals still refer to their city as Saigon, it's okay to talk about Saigon when in Saigon. If you want to be administratively correct, Ho Chi Minh City encompasses an area of over 2,000 square kilometers with nearly 90 percent of the area being rural. In fact, only 3 million people live in the urbanized area of Ho Chi Minh City. The remaining 4 million reside in the city's rural areas. Only one of 17 urban districts is officially called Saigon – District 1. That's where you will most likely spend most of your

Most locals refer to their city as Saigon – not Ho Chi Minh City. It's okay to talk about Saigon when in Saigon.

time and money shopping, dining, sightseeing, and sleeping. So, welcome to the real Saigon where the treasures and pleasures are readily at hand.

A FRENCH COLONIAL CITY

While Saigon has a long and tumultuous history, its modern origins are primarily French. In 1859 the French colonialists established Saigon as their colonial headquarters for the new colony of Cochin China. During the nearly 100 years of French occupation, the French did in Saigon what they normally did so well in all of their colonies – brought "French civilization" to this tropical city. You still see the remnants of this French influence in the city's architecture, arts, tree-lined streets, café culture, and bread – the ubiquitous baguette. Beautiful old colonial buildings, such as the Municipal Theater (Opera House) and the city hall and post office, as well as several old hotels, villas, and the Notre Dame Cathedral, testify to the French presence. Less successful has been the French language – it has not survived the onslaught of English as Saigon's major foreign language. Indeed, French tourists are often disappointed in discovering how little the Vietnamese retained of the French language when trying to check in at the front desk of their hotel. How soon they forget their past benefactor!

❑ A city of 7 million people, only 3 million reside in the city proper.

❑ Saigon is one of 23 districts – District 1 – where you will most likely spend most of your time and money shopping, dining, sightseeing, and sleeping.

❑ Despite the crowds and chaotic traffic, getting around Saigon is relatively easy. You will seldom get lost for more than 10 minutes!

❑ Use taxis which are very cheap (around US$1 per ride) and relatively safe, comfortable, and fast.

The fall of Saigon in 1975, which is clearly depicted in the well preserved Presidential Palace (now called the Reunification Palace) and museums, had a dramatic impact on the local economy and the livelihoods of local residents for more than a decade. However, with the advent of *doi moi* in the 1980s, Saigon has gradually recovered and is now back in the business of doing what it seems to do so well – making and spending money. Typically chaotic and always fast-paced and energetic, this is a city of great hope for Vietnam's future economic development and way of life. It remains Vietnam's most Westernized city and its great window to the global economy.

Getting Briefed, Oriented, and Connected

Most major hotels provide their guests with an 8½" x 12" flier that includes a map on one side and a list of attractions or travel and safety tips on the other side. These maps highlight most of the city's major attractions in District 1, which are within easy walking distance or a short taxi or cyclo ride.

You may also want to pick up two magazines which include maps and information – primarily listings of hotels, restaurants, entertainment, and services – on Saigon as well as Hanoi:

- **The Guide:** Published monthly as a supplement to the *Vietnam Economic Times*. Costs VND 13,000. You also can access part of *The Guide* online: www.vneconomy.com.vn

- **Timeout:** Published weekly as a supplement to the *Vietnam Investment Review*, which is produced by the Ministry of Planning and Investment.

Both can be purchased in bookstores (Fahasa, or Xuan Thu, at 185 Dong Khoi Street is the largest, with 14 other branches in the city) or from street vendors.

Several websites provide useful information on Saigon. The first four websites are especially good sources for information on various aspects of travel and shopping in Saigon:

■ **Vietnam Avenue**	vietnamavenue.com/ Saigon/index.html
■ **Groovy Saigon**	groovysaigon.com
■ **1Saigon**	1saigon.net
■ **Saigon Today**	saigontoday.net
■ **Saigon Connect**	saigonconnect.com
■ **SaigonTourist**	saigon-tourist.com
■ **Vietnam.com**	vietnam.com
■ **Vietnam Travel**	vietnam-travel.ws
■ **Things Asian**	thingsasian.com

If you want review the local news, visit **Ho Chi Minh Globe** – www.hochiminhglobe.com – which functions as a gateway to Vietnamese newspapers, including the *Saigon Times Daily*.

A CITY OF MOTORBIKES AND DISTRICTS

Saigon is literally overrun by motorbikes – a city of over 7 million people with more than 2 million noisy and polluting motorbikes that tend to rule the streets of Saigon. Be very careful when crossing streets – or you may get hit by a speeding motorbike.

Saigon is administratively divided into 23 districts – 6 rural and 17 urban. However, most visitors focus on District 1 (Saigon) and District 5 (Cholon or Chinatown). These two districts encompass Saigon's major shopping areas. When we refer to various districts in addresses, we abbreviate with a "D." For example, "District 1" becomes "D1."

For travel-shoppers, Saigon is an easy city to navigate. Most major hotels, restaurants, shops, and sites are conveniently located within easy walking distance, or a short $1.00 taxi ride, within the central commercial area. This area, also known as District 1 and Saigon, includes such noted hotels as the Renaissance, Sofitel Plaza, Majestic, Rex, Continental, Caravelle, Marriott, Legend, and Saigon Prince. It also includes such well known attractions as the History Museum, Central Post Office, Museum of the Revolution, Reunification Palace, War Remnants Museum, Fine Arts Museum of Ho Chi Minh City, and Notre Dame Cathedral. Shoppers discover hours of interesting shopping along five major thoroughfares that define this city's best shopping: Dong Khoi Street, Nguyen Hue Boulevard, Le Loi Boulevard, Le Thanh Ton Street, Pasteur Street, and the area around the Municipal Theater (Opera House).

Saigon also has two other areas worth visiting – District 3 and District 5. District 3 is located just west of District 1 and includes a few interesting shops. District 5 is known as Cholon, or Chinatown, a bustling commercial and residential area to the west of downtown Saigon. Here you'll discover a fascinating central market and several interesting temples.

Despite the crowds and chaotic traffic, getting around Saigon is relatively easy. If you stay in District 1, most restaurants, shops, and sites will be within walking district. However, you may want to frequently use taxis, which are very cheap and relatively comfortable and safe. Most rides cost between 12,000 and 20,000 dong (US$.85 to US$1.58). You'll seldom spend more than 14,000 dong (US$1.00) on a taxi ride.

Like many other cities in Vietnam, Saigon is a beehive of street-level activity. Although hot and steamy at times, with cool breezes in the late afternoon and early evening, there's never a dull moment here. From motorists, pedestrians, and motor launches to shopkeepers, sidewalk vendors, cyclo drivers, and street urchins, the city is abuzz with colorful and noisy activities. Like an orchestra without a director, Saigon muddles through its daily routines. At times disorienting, you'll never get lost in this city for more than 10 minutes – our barometer of an easily navigable city! The people are friendly and helpful, with many speaking enough English to help you cope with getting where you want to go. Armed with a basic map (your hotel front desk should have xeroxed copies for guests) and some idea of where you want to go (names and addresses in this or other books and websites), you should have no problem getting around by foot, cyclo, or taxi. While crossing the street is often challenging as you face a disorderly army of lumbering motorbikes, cyclos, bicycles, and taxis speeding through intersections, your street-level patience, running, and dodging skills will be well rewarded as you discover many wonderful shops, restaurants, and sites.

THE BASICS

Saigon is a relatively easy city to get to and around in. Armed with a map and a list of names and addresses, you should be able to easily navigate this city on foot and by taxi and/or cyclo.

ARRIVING

The first thing you notice when arriving at Tan Son Nhat Airport is the chaos. It's a busy place with numerous taxis and cyclos out front. The distance from the airport to central Saigon is seven kilometers and the trip takes from 15 to 30 minutes by taxi, depending on traffic. Since many hotels offer a complimentary shuttle service to their properties, be sure to look around the arrival hall and outside to see if your hotel has a representative available for transportation. If not, go out front and get a taxi. Taxis are metered (Airport Taxi or Vina Taxi) and they should work, although some drivers may not want to use their meter. The trip to the city center should cost around US$8 but no more than US$10.

GETTING AROUND

You can join the locals and navigate the city by bicycle, cyclo, motorbike, or bus. Cyclos are charming ways to get around the city. However, the quickest, safest, and most convenient and comfortable (air-conditioned) way to move in this city is by **taxi**. While taxis are more expensive than other modes of transportation, they are so cheap that they beg to be used by all but the most tightwad visitors. Many of the drivers speak some English, although some have difficulty with directions. (Tip: scope out your destination *before* getting in a cab and then point to your map if you want to make sure you're going in the right direction!) The flag fall at press time is US$.85 and most rides will cost no more than $1.50. You can usually catch taxis at the major hotels or call them (radio cabs) to pick you up. Over 30 taxi companies operate in Saigon. The major companies include: **Airport Taxi** (Tel. 844-6666), **Colon Taxi** (Tel. 836-3636), **Festival Taxi** (Tel. 845-4545), **Gia Dinh Taxi** (Tel. 898-9898), **Mai Linh Taxi** (Tel. 822-6666), **Vina Taxi** (Tel. 811-1111), **Saigon Taxi** (Tel. 842-4242), and **Red Taxi** (Tel. 844-6677).

You also may want to consider renting a car with driver. They are readily available through hotels or travel agencies. A car with driver for a 10-hour day should cost about US$35.

Tours and Guides

Several tour operators can be found in Saigon. Your hotel concierge or front desk can usually recommend a reputable tour company that offers a menu of half- and full-day tours or can arrange tour packages for several days in Vietnam and neighboring countries. We've been pleased with the services provided by Trails of Indochina:

❑ **Trails of Indochina:** 307/7 Nguyen Van Troi Street, Tan Binh District, Tel. 844-1005 or Fax 844-3350. Email: toi@fmail.vnn.vn. Website: trailsofindochina.com.

Alternatively, contact the following groups, which can offer a variety of individualized and group travel services:

❑ **Asian Wings Travel Co.:** 49 Hai Ba Trung, Tel. 834-3088 or Fax 934-3090.

❑ **Buffalo Tours:** 11 Hang Muoi, Tel. 828-0702 or Fax 826-9370. Email: buffalo@netnam.org.vn. Website: buffalo tours.com.

❑ **Exotissimo:** Saigon Trade Center, 37 Ton Duc Thang, D.1, Tel. 825-1727 or Fax 829-5800. Email: exohan@exotissi mo.com. Website: exotissimo.com.

❑ **Focus Travel:** 31 Nguyen Chi Thanh, Tel. 771-6820 or Fax 771-6821.

❑ **Green Peace Café Travel:** 12 Hang Hanh, Tel. 828-6505.

❑ **Mailinh Co.:** 64 Hai Ba Trung, D.1, Tel. 825-8888.

❑ **New Global Co., Ltd.:** 81 Ly Tu Trung, D.1, Tel. 842-2036 or Fax 829-6907.

❑ **Oscan Tourism:** 32 Bis Nguyen Thi Dieu, D.3, Tel. 823-1021 or Fax 823-1024.

❑ **Saigon Tourist:** 49 Le Thanh Ton, D.1, Tel. 829-8914. Website: saigon-tourist.com.

❑ **TF Travel Agent:** 60 Ngo Quyen, Tel. 843-2666 or Fax 843-2374.

❑ **Vietnam Tourism:** 234 Nam Ky Khoi Nghia, Tel. 829-0776 or Fax 829-0775. Email: <u>vnthcm@hcm.vnn.vn</u>. Website: <u>vietnamtourism.com</u>.

❑ **Vinatour:** 28 Le Thi Hong Gam, D.1, Tel. 829-7026. Email: <u>vinatour@hn.vnn.vn</u>.

You'll also find several **travelers' cafes** along Pham Ngu Lao Street in District 1, which offer a variety of inexpensive travel services, as well as Internet connections, for budget travelers.

INTERNET CONNECTIONS

Saigon has several Internet cafes where you can use the Internet by the minute (VND200) or hour (VND11,000). Within District 1, the following places offer Internet services. Some function as travelers' cafes in providing useful travel services:

❑ **C & T Cyber Café:** 47 Ngo Duc Ke, Tel. 821-2222.

❑ **Café 333:** 201 De Tham.

❑ **Emotion Café:** 26 Bui Vien, Tel. 829-4977.

❑ **Ibox Café:** 135 Hai Ba Trug, Tel. 825-6718.

❑ **Saigon Net:** 4 Nguyen Van Binh (Tel. 822-9845); 29 Thai Van Lung (Tel. 825-1256); and 220 De Tham (Tel. 837-2573).

❑ **Sinh Café:** 246 De Tham, Tel. 836-7338.

❑ **Viet Phuong Co.:** 361 Pham Ngu Lao, Tel. 836-7479.

As is the pattern in most cities, a disproportionate number of Internet cafes can be found in and around the area where backpackers congregate for inexpensive accommodations, restaurants, and cafes. In the case of Saigon, this is along both sides of De Tham Street in District 1.

SHOPPING SAIGON

Saigon offers an amazing amount of shopping for everything from fine art, jewelry, and silk garments to handicrafts, tribal artifacts, lacquerware, and pirated CDs and software. In one moment you're shopping in upscale boutiques and home decorative shops and the next moment you're navigating your way through crowded and fascinating market lanes and dusty bric-a-brac shops. Shopping in Saigon is both fun and rewarding for those who know what to buy, where to go, and how to handle pricing and shipping.

SAIGON'S SHOPPING CULTURE

While shopping in Vietnam is the most well developed in Saigon, it's still in the pre-shopping mall and department store stage. Most shopping takes place in small street shops and galleries or in large traditional markets. Shoppers are well advised to focus their shopping on a few key streets, major city markets, and museums.

Many shops will give 10 to 20% discounts – but only if you ask.

Like elsewhere in Vietnam, shopping in Saigon involves bargaining. Many shops will give 10 to 20 percent discounts but only if you ask. In markets discounts can be as much as 50 percent. Never buy art at the full asking price, even though the price appears to be fixed. Most galleries, including the very top galleries representing Vietnam's best artists, can discount art by 20 to 30 percent – and even more if the artist agrees to your offer. Whatever you do, don't be afraid to ask for 30-percent discounts – you'll be pleasantly surprised how often ostensibly "no discount" shops will agree to your offer.

10 ADDITIONAL SHOPPING RULES

Most of the 21 shopping rules we identified for Hanoi in Chapter 5 are applicable to Saigon. However, 10 additional rules apply to shopping in Saigon:

1. **If you plan to take many of your delicate purchases with you, find a packing and shipping company to safely re-pack your items using lots of bubble wrap and cardboard.** Several shops in District 1, especially along Hai Ba Trung Street, sell such packing materials. They normally sell these materials by the kilo – around 35,000 dong per 1 kilo.

2. **Use taxis to get around the city.** Cyclos and bicycles may be charming, but they are often more trouble than they are worth, especially if you have limited time and need to carry items with you. Taxis are plentiful, comfortable, and cheap in Saigon. They make navigating and shopping this city extremely convenient. The price is usually right – we seldom play more than US$1.50 for an air-conditioned taxi ride.

3. **Avoid shopping at lacquer factories that cater to tourists.** You can't miss these places – they usually have tour buses and vans parked out front and offer friendly customer service. Visit these places for the demonstration but you'll pay dearly for everything that is for sale in their showroom – up to five times more than what you can buy similar items for in the markets or along the main shopping streets. These places kick back commissions to tour guides and overcharge for mediocre-quality goods. If your tour guide tells you these places offer great shopping, don't believe him or her. Your tour guide is about to supplement his or her income by getting you to purchase in these rip-off joints.

4. **Avoid shopping at shopping emporiums designed to exploit Japanese tourists.** Like lacquer factories, these places (Miss Aodai at 21 Nguyen Trung Nan, Ward Ben Nghe, near the Sofitel Plaza Saigon Hotel, is a good example) are organized to take advantage of busloads of Japanese tourists. Signs are often in Japanese, sales people speak some Japanese, and each section of the shop is well organized with nice displays. The quality of goods is usually good but not to justify charging three to five times more than the going market rate.

5. **Look for several upscale boutiques and home decorative shops that offer tasteful designs that appeal to international visitors.** More so than anywhere else in Vietnam, Saigon has several shops that meet the standards of many shoppers who are looking for unique and quality items that will fit well into their wardrobe or home decor. Many shops, influenced by expatriates and individuals with international design talent, offer very nice quality items.

6. **Look for jewelry in Saigon.** As you may quickly discover in other areas in Vietnam, it's often difficult to

find shops selling jewelry. In Saigon you'll find numerous jewelry shops and stalls across from the huge central market, Ben Thanh, as well as along Saigon's major shopping streets.

7. **Look for unique items in Saigon.** Several shops produce beautiful model clipper ships and offer numerous collectibles not found in other places in Vietnam. Many of the modern lacquer designs are found in Saigon.

8. **While a lot of excellent quality art can be purchased in major art galleries, be sure to check out art exhibits held at Saigon's major hotels.** These exhibitions often feature the unique works of artists who are not represented by the major commercial galleries. For a schedule of upcoming art shows, be sure to visit Quynh Pham's website: www.galeriequynh.com.

9. **Make shopping one of your major fun activities in Saigon.** After visiting a few museums, which can be done in one to two days, there's not much to do in Saigon other than dine, bar-hop, and visit some outlying areas, such as the Cu Chi Tunnels, the Saigon River, and the Mekong River delta area. But if you get into Saigon's interesting shopping scene, you'll discover a whole new dimension to this city that is usually overlooked by other guidebooks that primarily look for history and culture. That's unfortunate because some of the most interesting aspects of this city is found by shopping its many shops, galleries, and markets. Shopping can become a wonderful three-day adventure.

10. **Check out the quality of all pirated and knock-off goods.** Numerous markets and shops offer pirated CDs, videos, and DVDs. While cheap, many of these Chinese-produced items are very poor quality – they skip tracks or frames. If you buy such items, be sure to try them out before making such purchases. The Russian Market is filled with such items.

WHAT TO BUY

There's plenty to shop for in Saigon, from inexpensive pirated CDs and touristy handicrafts and souvenirs to beautiful silk garments, tailored clothes, fine art, home decorative items, lacquerware, and jewelry. The market appeals to a wide range of discriminating and not-so-discriminating travelers. If you enjoy poking around in markets and street shops for inexpensive and unexpected treasures, Saigon will prove to be a great deal of shopping fun. If you're looking for quality art, antiques and collectibles, home decorative items, jewelry, and fashionable silk garments, many of Saigon's more discriminating shops will be well worth exploring.

The following product lines are readily available in Saigon and especially in the many shops, galleries, and markets found along several adjacent streets in District 1.

ART

Saigon is a excellent center for purchasing serious, fun, and trashy art. While Hanoi still is Vietnam's preeminent center for serious art and major artists, numerous galleries in Saigon represent the works of both Hanoi and Saigon artists. For a comprehensive guide to nearly 500 artists and 25 contemporary art galleries in Saigon, look for the increasingly hard-to-locate *Fine Arts World of Ho Chi Minh City*. You may be able to find this nearly 200-page directory in a few art galleries or at the **Fine Arts Museum of Ho Chi Minh City** (97A Pho Duc Chinh Street, D1, Tel. 829-4441). The guide also features several artists and includes articles on the history and the state of fine arts in Vietnam. Several leading commercial art galleries, which display the works of major Vietnamese artists, include **Ancient Gallery** (50 Mac Thi Buoi Street, D1, Tel. 822-7962); **Galerie Vinh Loi** (41 Ba Huyen Thanh Quan Street, D3, Tel. 822-2006); **Duc Minh Art Gallery** (23 Ly Tu Trong Street, D1, Tel. 823-2449); **Tu Do** (53 Ho Tung Mau, D1, Tel. 821-0966); **Dong Phuong Art Gallery** (135 Nam Ky Khoi Nghia Street, D1, Tel. 930-9716, near the entrance of the Unification Palace); **Particular Gallery** (123 Le Loi Avenue, D1, Level 3, Tel. 821-3019); **Gallery Le Xuan** (44 Dong Khoi Street, D2, Tel./Fax 822-4580, 2nd Floor); **Xuan Gallery** (32 Vo Van Tan Street, D3, Tel./Fax 930-4277); **Hong Hac Art Gallery** (9A Vo Van Tan Street, Tel. 824-3160); **101 Cativnat** (101 Dong Khoi Street, D1, Tel. 822-7643); **Galerie Lotus** (47 and 55 Dong Khoi Street, D1, Tel. 829-2695); and five art galleries attached to the lower level of the **Fine Arts Museum of Ho Chi Minh City** (97A Pho Duc Chinh Street, D1) – **Gallery Shop**, **Blue Space Contemporary Art Center** (Tel.821-3695), **Lac Hong Art Gallery** (Tel./Fax 821-3771), **Nhat Le Art Gallery** (Tel./Fax 821-6447), and **Art XX1 Gallery** (Tel./Fax 821-6447). A few major hotels, such as the Renaissance Hotel and the New World Hotel, sponsor art exhibitions.

For a schedule of upcoming exhibitions, as well as professional assistance with Saigon's art scene, including art consultation services, contact **Quynh Pham** who operates the Galerie Quynh contemporary art gallery: Tel./Fax 821-7995, Mobile 84-90-680-812, or Email: qpham@galeriequynh.com. Also, visit her website for examples of the type of serious Vietnamese contemporary art she offers at art shows as well as at her soon-to-find permanent exhibition location: www.galeriequynh.com.

While most of these galleries may appear to have fixed prices, like commercial art galleries in Hanoi, everything is negotiable, with some paintings being discounted by 30 percent or more – but only if you bargain hard for such a discount,

which may involve calling the artist for negotiating a final deal. The best discounting may take place in what appear to be the more intimidating top art galleries, which also quote the highest initial asking prices. Few galleries actually purchase art from artists, who may have similar paintings available in several galleries in both Saigon and Hanoi. Since most major artists are not represented by a single gallery and much of the art is consigned to galleries, there is very little price integrity with art. Therefore, as in the case of shopping for art in Hanoi, you are well advised in Saigon to shop around for the same artists. For example, you may be able to purchase a Cuong in one art gallery for US$400 whereas a similar Cuong in another art gallery will be priced at US$500 – and that's before you start bargaining for a 20 to 30 percent discount.

COPY PAINTINGS

Numerous special "art galleries" – better termed "copy paint shops" – also specialize in producing inexpensive copies of famous paintings, from the masters to contemporary artists, as well as portraits and commissioned paintings. Many of these shops congregate in and around **Mac Thi Buoi Street** in District 1. Just tell them what you want, and they can usually complete it in a few hours or days – the ultimate exercise in copy art. If you want a portrait of yourself, family members, your pet, your home, or your favorite photo, just bring a good photo from which a painter can copy. At the same time, if you would like to own your very own painting of Andy Warhol's classic *Marilyn Monroe*, visit the **Saigon Art Gallery** (77 Mac Thi Buoi Street, D1, Tel. 829-8778) where you will find this striking painting along with hundreds of other copies of famous paintings. Nearby **Hung Long Art Gallery** (86 Mac Thi Buoi Street, D1, Tel. 829-7887) will be happy to whip up another Andy Warhol along with hundreds of other masterpieces, portraits, and commissioned paintings – anything you want committed to canvas. While many such "galleries" produce good quality reproductions, many others look like real amateur paintings (remember the old paint-by-number days?). Observing many of these copy painters at work can be a very entertaining art shopping experience. Within District 1, you'll often see an open front shop filled with five or more copy painters working on canvases from photos of master paintings and individuals seeking inexpensive portraits of themselves, family members, their dog or cat, or their home.

❑ Numerous galleries in Saigon represent the works of both Hanoi and Saigon artists.

❑ You'll find few real antiques in Saigon – many are reproductions made to look like old pieces.

❑ Old ceramics are especially difficult to take out of Vietnam due to export restrictions on antiques.

EMBROIDERED PICTURES

The fine art of embroidering pictures is well represented in a few Saigon galleries. The work tends to be exceptionally fine and represents an old art tradition in Vietnam called picture embroidery. While much of the art appears to be very touristy, much of it also represents an exquisite art form that portrays everything from landscapes to portraits of individuals, animals (fabulous tigers), religious scenes, and still life forms. While technically a fascinating art form, the end products may or may not appeal to your tastes. Two of Saigon's major galleries and showrooms for such art are **Diem Tham Quam** (81 Dong Khoi, D1, Tel. 822-2856) and **XQ Vietnam Hand Embroidery** (26 Le Loi Boulevard, D1, Tel. 829-9866).

ANTIQUES AND COLLECTIBLES

If you like to go treasure hunting for antiques and collectibles, Saigon offers a few interesting opportunities that may yield a few surprises. Most of Saigon's antique and collectible shops are found along one narrow street in District 1 – **Le Cong Kieu** – which is located near the Fine Arts Museum (97A Pho Duc Chinh Street). Both sides of this street are lined with small antique and collectible shops offering everything from trash to treasures. Most shops are small, cramped, and dark – the perfect places to go sleuthing for unexpected treasures. Some shops offer good quality furniture, ceramics, bronzes, and home accessory pieces while other shops include zippo lighters, pens, medals, watches, opium pipes, baskets, silver, paintings, gongs, and all types of bric-a-brac.

You can easily spend a hour or two exploring the many shops along this intriguing street. However, keep in mind that there are actually few real antiques found in these shops; many ostensibly antique items, especially bronzes and ceramics, are copies or "new antiques." And if you would acquire a real

 antique, you might have difficulty taking it out of Vietnam because of government restrictions on the export of antiques, although some shops are adept at paying "handling fees" to officials or reclassifying items as "reproductions" when shipping them to ensure they leave the country trouble-free. Old ceramics are extremely difficult to take out of Vietnam. Nonetheless, you may find some attractive items in these shops.

We especially like **Binh Minh** (16 Le Cong Kieu Street, Tel. 829-8133) for ceramics, bronze figures, stone carvings, and porcelain – both old and new pieces; **Dinh Van Phuc** (18 Le Cong Kieu Street, Tel. 821-6971) for baskets, furniture, ceramics, and bronzes; and **Quang Minh** (32 Le Cong Kieu Street, Tel. 914-0442) for furniture, ceramics, and bronzes. A small **no name shop** at 27 Le Cong Kieu Street has a nice collection of bells and other small collectibles.

Aside from the shops along Le Cong Kieu Street, there is one other shop offering some attractive antiques amidst its many home decorative items: **Nguyen Freres** (2A Le Duan Boulevard, D1, Tel. 822-9654). Located directly across the street from the Sofitel Plaza Hotel, this shop also maintains a 900-square meter warehouse of old furniture and accessory pieces which is located about 15 minutes by taxi or motorbike from the shop.

LACQUERWARE

Lacquerware is widely available in Saigon's many handicraft, art, and home decorative shops. Much of the lacquerware found in the handicraft and souvenir shops along Dong Khoi Street is very inexpensive, easy to pack in your luggage, and makes nice gift items. However, lacquerware can be a tricky business if you end up in the wrong places. If you visit the local lacquer factory, which is primarily frequented by tour groups, expect to pay about five times the going rate for similar items found in shops elsewhere in Saigon. The lacquer factory pays tour guides and drivers commissions to bring tourists to their factory, which includes an interesting demonstration area plus a showroom filled with over-priced and often dreadful looking traditional lacquer furniture, screens, paintings, and accessory pieces that would not integrate well in many Western homes. If you visit this factory, take the tour and survey the showroom selections, but plan to shop elsewhere for lacquer items, which are cheaper and better designed. The salespeople argue that their high prices reflect their high quality, but we weren't convinced. The high prices represent a combination of tour guide commissions and pure greed at clipping unsuspecting tourists.

Numerous art and handicraft shops along two main shopping streets in District 1 – **Dong Khoi Street** and **Le Loi Boulevard** – offer a wide selection of inexpensive lacquer items, from chopsticks, bowls, and vases to serving trays, coasters, and napkin rings. For inexpensive souvenir lacquer items, try **Anthentique** (38 Dong Khoi Street, Tel. 822-1333) and **Saigon Souvenir** (57-69 Dong Khoi Street, Tel. 822-9419). For really nice quality, well designed, and more expensive lacquer tableware and accessory pieces, be sure to visit **Heritage** (53 Dong Khoi Street, Tel. 823-5438) and **Precious Oui** (29A Dong Khoi, Tel. 825-6817).

HOME DECORATIVE ITEMS

If you're interesting in acquiring some nicely handcrafted items to enhance your home decor, from baskets and ceramics to furniture and accessory pieces, be sure to visit these five shops: **Nguyen Freres** (2A Le Duan Boulevard, D1, Tel. 822-9654); **Indochine House** (27 Dong Du, D1, Tel. 822-7318); **Celadon Green** (29 Dong Du, D1, Tel. 823-6816); **The Home Zone** (41 Dinh Tien Hoang, at the corner of Le Duan, Tel. 822-8022); and **L & H Decoration** (22-36 Nguyen Hue Boulevard, Kiosque 7B, D1, Tel. 822-6799). Both Nguyen Freres and The Home Zone are located across the street from the Sofitel Plaza

Hotel; Indochine House and Celadon Green are located next to each other. Many of the art and handicraft shops also include attractive home decorative items.

HANDICRAFTS AND GIFTS

Saigon abounds with shops offing a wide range of handicrafts. Many of the shops along Dong Khoi Street in District 1, such as **Phat Dat** (49 Dong Khoi Street, Tel. 822-8210), **Saigon Souvenir** (57-69 Dong Khoi Street, Tel. 822-9419), **Authentique** (38 Dong Khoi Street, Tel. 822-1333), and **Le Xuan** (44 Dong Khoi Street, D2, Tel./Fax 822-4580), offer a wide range of handcrafted items, including lacquerware, tablecloths, silver, porcelain, and wood boxes. Several other shops include handicrafts, especially clothes, handbags, bags, and dolls, produced by several ethnic and tribal groups in Vietnam. We especially like **East Meets West** (24 Le Loi Boulevard, D1, Tel. 823-1553); **Sapa 1** (29 Ngo Doc De, D1, Tel. 825-8942); **Sapa 3** (223 De Tham, D1, Tel. 836-5163); and **Craft Home** (39A Ngo Duc Ke, D1, Tel. 823-7786 and 85 Pasteur, D1, Tel. 822-7955). The area around Sapa 3 – **De Tham Street** – includes several other handicraft shops that especially cater to budget travelers and backpackers that tend to congregate along this street because of its cheap accommodations, restaurants, and Internet cafes. Also, if you are near the Sofitel Plaza Hotel, visit **Tin Handicraft** (2A Le Duan Boulevard, D1, Tel. 822-9786), which is located directly across the street from the hotel and adjacent to one of our favorite home decorative, furniture, and antique shops, Nguyen Freres. **The Russian Market** (135 Nguyen Hue Boulevard, D1) also has a shop on the second floor that offers handicrafts (Phi Long Ngoc Chao) as does the nearby **shopping arcade** at 22-36 Nguyen Hue Boulevard.

JEWELRY

While you may not see many jewelry stores in Hanoi, you will find several such stores and centers in Saigon. For the largest concentration of jewelry stores offering a wide range of similar jewelry products and designs, be sure to visit the many jewelry shops and stalls across the street from the central market (Ben Thanh) in District 1. Here you'll find dozens of jewelry stores selling rings, gold bracelets, necklaces, and chains. Several of the shops also offer money exchange services. The largest concentration of jewelry shops, which actually consists of 40 jewelry stalls, is housed in a brightly lit government jewelry center with a sign on the front that reads **Phong Kiem Dinh**

Da Quy. You can't miss this center since it's directly across the street from the market as well as in the middle of several jewelry shops. Since prices here are both fixed and reasonable, you need not waste your time trying to bargain. Next door is an even larger jewelry dealers' center with 80 small counters offering similar items. Most of this jewelry is in traditional designs with a heavy concentration of jade, gold necklaces, and many small jewelry pieces. Look for such shops as **Cua Hang Trung Tom So 1** (178 Le Thanh Ton, Tel. 822-2142); **Kim Yen** (172 Le Thanh Ton, Tel. 822-8025); **Cong Ty Vang Bac Da Quy Quan 1** (166 Le Thanh Ton, Tel. 822-3509); **Xuan Hung** (176 Le Thanh Ton, Tel. 823-0211); **Bich Ngoc** (174 Le Thanh Ton, Tel. 829-1737); and **Chieu Thu** (186-188 Le Thanh Ton, Tel. 825-1839).

For more stylish and innovative jewelry, be sure the visit the following jewelry stores: **Alphana Jewelry** (159 Dong Khoi Street, D1, Tel. 829-7398); **Anpha Jewelry** (167 Dong Khoi Street, D1, Tel. 825-1918); **Vietnam National Gem and Gold Corporation** (88 Mac Thi Buoi Street, Tel. 822-2923); **Saigon Jewelry Company** (6 Nguyen Trung Truc, D1, Tel. 822-5189); and **Artistic Gemstone Enterprise** (2D Nguyen Trung Truc, D1, Tel. 822-5189).

MODEL BOATS, SHIPS, AND PLANES

While one might normally classify this product line under handicrafts, they are so unique and special in Saigon that we believe these items deserve a special heading. These are not toys or child's play. Indeed, many people collect these model boats, ships, and planes, which we also have found in a couple of shops in Bangkok, especially the model boats and ships at the Height in River City Shopping Center. Ranging in size from one to five feet in length, these models are beautiful display and collector items. Two small shops near the La Camargue Restaurant include a nice collection of such items: **Kien Dung** (18 Cao Ba Quat Street, D1, Mobile Tel. 090-651088) and **Thong** (28 Cao Ba Quat Street, D1, Tel. 822-1539).

CLOTHES, FASHION, AND ACCESSORIES

You'll find numerous shops throughout Saigon that offer a wide selection of clothes and accessories. However, much of what you see are styles, colors, and sizes most appropriate for local residents. Many of the best shops are concentrated along Dong Khoi Street and Mac Thi Buoi Street in District 1. A few shops offer some excellent quality garments and accessories appropriate for visitors in search of unique and quality items. While most of these shops have a good selection of ready-made clothes, they also do tailoring work.

Saigon's premier silk, garment, and accessory shop is the upscale **Khaisilk** (107 Dong Khoi Street, D1, Tel./ Fax 829-1146; and 98 Mac Thi Buoi Street, D1, Tel. 823-4634). If you

visit only one such shop in Saigon, as well as in Hanoi, make sure it's Khaisilk. Unlike Khaisilk in Hanoi, this branch shop is a class operation – beautiful selections and displays on three separate floors. Indeed, you may not recognize this shop if you already visited their more traditional shop in Hanoi.

If you are interested in traditional ethnic clothes, which have been beautifully restyled for Westerners, as well as the graceful Ao Dai and fashionable handbags, shoes, shawls, blouses, children's smocked dresses, and Pashminas, be sure to visit **Anh**. It currently operates three shops in Saigon:

- 69 Dong Khoi Street, D1, Tel./Fax 822-7603.
- 22-36 Nguyen Hue Boulevard, D1, Tel. 822-0324 or Fax 822-7603. Email: ethnicfolkartanh@hcm.vnn.vn.
- Tax Plaza, 135 Nguyen Hue Boulevard, D1, 1st Floor, Tel./Fax 821-3716.

Sapa (Sapa 1 at 29 Ngo Doc De, D1, Tel. 825-8942; and Sapa 3 at 223 De Tham, D1, Tel. 836-5163) also has a line of refashioned ethnic clothes from the famous Sapa region.

Also check out **Zakka** (134 Pasteur Street, D1, Tel. 824-5345) for fashionable clothes, fabrics, and accessories (handbags, shoes, ties). This small but upscale shop is especially popular with Japanese visitors. A few other clothes and accessory shops worth visiting include **Donga Silk** (89 Mac Thi Buoi Street, D1, Tel. 825-8325); **Kenly Silk** (132 Le Thanh Ton Street, D1, Tel. 829-3847); **Coconut Shop** (100 Mac Thi Buoi, D1, Tel. 823-0523); **Minhhanh** (24 Dong Khoi Street, D1, Tel. 824-5774); and **Couture House** (39A Ngo Duc Ke, D1, Tel. 823-7786 – also uses the name Craft House, Craft Home, and Craftware Shop).

TAILORING

You can get some very inexpensive tailoring done in Saigon. However, make sure you're dealing with a tailor who understands exactly what you need and who can clearly communicate with you. While tailoring is often one of the highlights of shopping in Vietnam, it also can be very disappointing if you don't communicate well your styling, fabric, and color preferences. Top clothing and accessory shops, such as **Khaisilk** and **Anh** (see above), are skilled in providing excellent tailoring services to foreigners. If you're looking for a good tailor, check with the concierge at one of the top hotels in Saigon; they usually know, based on recent feedback from their well-heeled clients, who does excellent tailoring work. One of Saigon's top tailors is **Cao Minh Tailor** (148-150 Pasteur Street, D1, Tel. 822-4298), which uses both British and Italian wools. Working from photos in fashion magazines, they can usually complete a suit in one week for about US$200. Next to Zakka is a tiny but very reputable seamstress (dressmaking) shop called **Phuc Loi** (136 Pasteur, D1, Tel. 824-3171), which produces dresses and blouses. If you bring your own fabric and pictures, this shop can complete a blouse within three to four days at a cost of only US$8!

BOOKS

Saigon boasts several bookstores but few stock English-language titles. The city's largest bookstore is **Fahasa** (Xuan Thu) at 185 Dong Khoi Street, D1, Tel. 822-4670. Also try **Bookazine** (28 Dong Khoi, D1, Tel. 829-7455), and **Viet My – Stern's Books** (4 Dinh Tien Hoang, D1, Tel. 822-9650, opposite the Sofitel Plaza Hotel). You'll also find a few used bookstores, with numerous English-language paperbacks, along the backpackers' street in District 1 – De Tham Street. **Con Meo** (243 De Tham Street), for example, has a good selection of used English-language books and CDs, many of which deal with Vietnam and Cambodia.

PIRATED MUSIC, VIDEOS, WATCHES, AND HANDBAGS

Saigon is a large market for Chinese-produced CDs, DVDs, and videos. The largest concentration of such items can be found on the ground floor of the **Russian Market** (135 Nguyen Hue Boulevard, D1). Once a popular center for Russians, who used to come here and buy cheap clothes in large quantities, today the Russian Market is a mixture of cheap clothes, handicrafts, backpacks, jewelry, and pirated CDs, DVDs, videos, and watches. Consisting of three dingy floors of shops located in a building adjacent to a corner grocery and drugstore (Nguyen Hue Boulevard and Le Loi Boulevard), the pirated items are found in several small stalls on the ground floor. Most DVDs sell for less than US$3 each (around 35,000 dong) and CDs (without case) go for as little at $1.25 each (around 15,000 dong). Be sure to bargain for everything here, since the shops are very competitive and initial asking prices are at least 20 percent above what you should be paying. However, don't get carried away here, as the quality of these items is at best marginal. Many of the CDs and DVDs have flaws causing them to skip or pause at unexpected times. At least 50 percent of our purchases here had some type of flaw. If you do decide to purchase a CD or DVD, ask to have it played so you can see if it has a flaw. If you carry a CD and/or DVD player, try your purchases out immediately to determine if you've acquired flawed copies. If you encounter a problem, the friendly and entrepreneurial vendors here will exchange the item – but do so within 48 hours of your purchase.

The knock-off watches, which are found in abundance at the Russian Market, come in familiar name brands – Rolex, Cartier, and Gucci. Expect to pay between US$10 and US$20 for these imitation watches.

The departure lounge at **Tan Son Nhat Airport** has 10 shops offering duty-free goods as well as local products. You also can buy knock-off watches (Rolex) and leather handbags (Versace). This is one of the few international airports we have ever encountered that permits such items to be sold in such a public and international arena. Indeed, there is nothing subtle about selling pirated goods in Vietnam!

DUTY-FREE

Saigon has one duty-free shop located in the central business district – **Saigon Duty Free Shop** (102 Nguyen Hue Boulevard, D1, Tel. 823-4548). It carries the usual assortment of imported brand name perfumes, liquors, tobacco products, clothes, and accessories. The shop is especially popular with Japanese tourists who tend to disproportionately patronize such duty-free shops. You'll also find a duty-free shop (DFS) in the smoky departure lounge at **Tan Son Nhat Airport**, another popular stop for Japanese tourists in search of imported name brand items.

PLACES TO AVOID

Not all shops represent good quality and value. Some may try to take advantage of unsuspecting tourists who know little about the local shopping scene, including authenticity and cost of products. For example, you should be wary of any shop that claims to be selling real antiques, especially antique porcelain. Not only is it illegal to export such items, chances are they are fakes. You may also want to pass on the **lacquer factory** that is organized to gouge tourists with high prices that may run as high as 500 percent above retail! The same is true for a shop located behind the Sofitel Plaza Hotel – **Miss Aodai** (21 Nguyen Trung Ngan, Ward Ben Nghe, D1, Tel. 822-2139). This is the ultimate clip joint – organized to fleece unsuspecting busloads of Japanese tourists who are led here by their exploitative guides and drivers who do very well in the commission department. Contrary to what many people may think, as in many other countries, this is a typical Japanese operation designed by Japanese to exploit fellow Japanese travelers who normally do not leave their group to explore a destination, much less shop on their own. The quality of the products is not bad, but this operation is close to being criminal when prices are three to five times above retail! If you're not Japanese, you may not get much service here. Signs are in Japanese and the staff speaks more Japanese than English. It's the same story we've encountered in many other countries with shops aimed at Japanese tourists. Beware of Miss Aodai – she may fleece you royally but tell it's all about "quality" – the siren of most such rip-off joints!

THE MORE YOU LOOK

Saigon is a surprising city of shops, markets, merchants, and vendors that beg to be discovered. Just walk down the city's major streets and you'll find a fascinating variety of products, services, or shop activities. Stroll along Nguyen Hue Boulevard and Le Loi Boulevard, for example, and you'll encounter numerous camera shops and sidewalk vendors with makeshift camera repair operations, although you may be reluctant to use the sidewalk repair vendors along Nguyen Hue Boulevard who seem to use a very low-tech approach to camera repair – a screwdriver! Explore the length of Dong Khoi Street and you'll probably satisfy at least 75 percent of your shopping needs. Dive into the city's major markets and you'll see a riot of colors and activities that make Saigon such an intriguing place to travel and shop.

More so than any other city in Vietnam, Saigon is undergoing rapid changes due to its newly evolving economy. Since many local residents and their families, who were ostensibly on the wrong side of history in 1975, are still restricted from entering government service, most of them are forced to become entrepreneurial, which means working for private companies or starting their own businesses. As a result, new shops are constantly opening or moving to new locations. Depending on how the Vietnamese economy and tourism shake out in the future, we expect more and more quality shops to open in Saigon. They will offer designs and selections that appeal to their growing international audience in search of quality products. Expect to see more and more shops like Khaisilk, Heritage, Anh, Ancient Gallery, Galerie Vinh Loi, Alphana Jewelry, Nyuyen Freres, and Indochine House to take route in Saigon's newly evolving shopping culture.

> *New shops are constantly opening in Saigon. Expect to see more quality shops in the near future.*

WHERE TO SHOP

Saigon is essentially a street shop and market city for shopping. Most shopping areas are relatively concentrated and can be easily walked, although a taxi comes in handy in going from one area to another.

MAJOR SHOPPING STREETS

While Saigon does have one major department store (Diamond along Nguyen Thi Minh Khai, behind Notre Dame Cathedral), most shopping takes place in shops that are found along four major streets in District 1:

- Dong Khoi Street
- Nguyen Hue Boulevard
- Le Loi Boulevard
- Pasteur Street

Several side streets within this relatively concentrated shopping area – **Mac Thi Buoi, Dong Du, Ngo Duc Ke**, and **Le Thanh Ton** – include many art, home decorative, clothing, and accessory shops. You can easily walk to all of these streets, starting with the main shopping street of **Dong Khoi** near the Renaissance Hotel. Another small shopping area is located directly across the street from the Sofitel Plaza Hotel on **Le Duan Boulevard**.

SPECIALTY STREETS

Saigon never had Hanoi's guild tradition that resulted in certain streets specializing in particular products. Nonetheless, you will find some specialization by neighborhoods. While you'll find a disproportionate number of art, handicraft, and souvenir shops along Dong Khoi Street, a few major tailors along Pasteur Street, and camera shops and repair services along Nguyen Hue Boulevard and Le Loi Boulevard, a couple of other streets tend to specialize in particular products:

❏ **Le Cong Kieu Street:** This is Saigon's "Antique Street" with dozens of small shops offering a wide range of old and new antiques. The emphasis here is definitely on furniture, ceramics, bronzes, and lots of interesting and dusty bric-a-brac.

❏ **Le Thanh Ton:** This is Saigon's traditional jewelry dealers' street which also is located across from the city's main market, Ben Thanh. You'll find more than 100 small jewelry stores, stalls, and counters offering gold rings, bracelets, chains, jade, and small items. Many of the shops also provide money exchange services.

MARKETS

If you enjoy visiting colorful, bustling, and crowded markets, Saigon and its neighboring city of Cholon have two huge markets that will satisfy your curiosity as well as offer you some great photo opportunities. **Ben Thanh Market** is Saigon's (District 1) central market. **Ben Tay Market** is Cholon's (District 5) central market. The two markets are located about 30 minutes from each other and both are well worth visiting just for the cultural experience. Chances are you will buy very little in these places since these markets are primarily oriented toward the daily shopping needs of local residents. Ben Tay Market is probably the most interesting of the two markets because of its "Chinatown" (Cholon) location and its size. Like the streets leading to this market, it's a very vibrant and chaotic market that exudes a sense of traditional commerce – haggling, shouting, narrow lanes, suppliers constantly hauling goods in and out of the market's narrow walkways. From Ben Tay Market you can conveniently explore the famous Heavenly Lady Temple as well as four other interesting temples in Cholon. Ben Thanh Market is more convenient to get to because of its District 1 location. It's also a smaller, more sedate, and orderly market. Both markets have wet (fish, meat, fruits, vegetables) and dry (clothes, household, and consumer goods) sections.

❑ **Ben Thanh Market:** Located opposite the jewelry shops and stalls on Le Thanh Ton Street, this is Saigon's central market for District 1. Relatively clean and orderly, and much smaller than Ben Tay Market in Cholon, this is an interesting market offering lots of fish, meats, vegetables, fruits, and flowers. You may find a quick 15-minute stroll through this market is all you need to get a sense of people, place, and produce. The many beautiful flowers and fruits and vegetables piled high in front of the market make for a good photo opportunity. However, the most interesting shopping for visitors is outside the market.

❑ **Ben Tay Market:** Located about five kilometers southwest of Ben Thanh Market in District 5 of Cholon – Vietnam's famous Chinatown of nearly 700,000 residents – this is the most interesting of all markets in Vietnam. It's both a wholesale and consumer market, with emphasis placed on wholesale. It has size, chaos, noise, and character. The surrounding neighborhood appears to be in an arrested form of crumbling decay, with many buildings begging to be restored to their former colonial glory. This is great street-level theater for adventuresome shoppers and travelers. Get ready to dodge lots of cars, motorbikes, bicycles, and carts as you attempt to navigate the streets on the outside of the market as well as the narrow lanes often shared by speeding motorbikes within the market. While the market is comprehendible to local shoppers, you may want to just wander through it on your own to absorb the many activities and discover how such a chaotic market functions. It's a fun place to explore for about 30 minutes but no more than an hour (redundancy quickly sets in and the trash and water under your feet soon lose their novel appeal). You'll find lots of food here, from dried shrimp and fresh fish to rice noodles. Be sure to take your camera on this adventure. You may find your most interesting people-oriented photos were taken in and around this market.

❏ **Russian Market:** Located in the heart of the central business district at 135 Nguyen Hue Boulevard (near the intersection with Le Loi Boulevard) this three-story shopping center is filled with shops and stalls selling inexpensive clothes, backpacks, luggage, and accessories as well as jewelry and knock-off watches, CDs, DVDs, videos, and handbags. The second and third floors primarily include shops selling inexpensive clothes, reminiscent of the days when the Russians came here to buy such items in large quantities. A small arts and crafts shop, **Phi Long Noc Chao**, offers a nice selection of lacquerware and chopsticks at reasonable prices. The ground floor includes several small jewelry stalls and counters as well as vendors offering counterfeit watches, knock-off handbags, and pirated CDs, DVDs, and videos. As we noted earlier, while the many Chinese-produced pirated CDs, DVDs, and videos are attractive buys at US$1 to US$3 each, the quality of these illegal reproductions is often poor if not pathetic; many cannot be played because of production flaws. You may end up with a lot of cheap trash which could also be a problem with Customs officials when you return to your country.

Saigon also has several other neighborhood wet and dry markets. But few are as interesting as the three identified here. If you visit these three markets, you'll probably have enough market experience to satisfy your curiosity throughout Vietnam and elsewhere in Southeast Asia, with the exceptions of the fabulous Weekend Market in Bangkok, the "antiques" market (Jalan Surabaya) in Jakarta, and Stanley Market in Hong Kong.

BEYOND THE CENTER

Ninety-five percent of your shopping can be done on foot within the central business district, which includes browsing four major streets which intersect with one another. Outside these major shopping streets and the three major markets of Saigon, you'll find a few special shops that can be easily reached by taxi. Most museums have small shops selling handicrafts, books, and memorabilia. The **Fine Arts Museum** at 97A Pho Duc Chinh (D1), for example, has five art galleries attached to its building. A few other galleries tend to be spread out within District 1. Some of the best galleries requiring a short taxi ride include:

❏ **Galerie Vinh Loi:** 41 Ba Huyen Thanh Quan Street, D3, Tel. 822-2006.

❑ **Xuan Gallery:** 32 Vo Van Tan Street, D3, Tel./Fax 930-4277.

❑ **Hong Hac Art Gallery:** 9A Vo Van Tan Street, Tel. 824-3160.

❑ **Duc Minh Art Gallery:** 23 Ly Tu Trong Street, D1, Tel. 823-2449.

❑ **Dong Phuong Art Gallery:** 135 Nam Ky Khoi Nghia Street, D1, Tel. 930-9716, to the right of the entrance of the Reunification Palace.

Several of the small arts, crafts, and used book and CD shops along the backpackers' street – **De Tham Street** – including **Sapa 3** (223 De Tham, D1, Tel. 836-5163), can be reached within 5 to 10 minutes by taxi from the central business district. You'll also find 10 duty-free, arts, crafts, jewelry, and knock-off watch (Rolex) and handbag (Versace) shops in the departure lounge of the international airport

---

BEST OF THE BEST

Several shops in Saigon stand out above all the others as special for international visitors in search of unique and appealing treasures. If you have limited time to shop in Saigon, you may want to focus your attention on these shops, which offer good quality and selections. While service is not a strong point of many shops – especially if they are operated by sales clerks rather than by the owners – in general the service in these shops is relatively good.

ART

❑ **Ancient Gallery:** *50 Mac Thi Buoi Street, D1, Tel. 822-7962 or Fax 822-7962. Website: www.apricot-artvietnam.com (for its parent company in Hanoi, Apricot Gallery). Open 8:30am to 8:30pm.* A relatively new gallery for Saigon (opened October 2000), the Ancient Gallery is owned and operated by Hanoi's top commercial art gallery – Apricot Gallery (see Chapter 5 on Hanoi). As such, it offers similar quality paintings as well as represents the same group of artists. If you've visited the Apricot Gallery in Hanoi, you'll immediately recognize the similarity. The gallery prides itself on presenting only Vietnam's leading artists – the ones who are most commercially successful. A very nicely appointed gallery with peaceful music playing in the background, its three floors present many of Vietnam's top artists. We're especially fans of Cuong, who works on cheesecloth rather than on a standard canvas, and Chuong, who produces bright and beautiful lacquer paintings.

❏ **Galerie Vinh Loi:** *41 Ba Huyen Thanh Quan Street, D3, Tel. 930-5006 or Fax 930-3154. Email: vinhloi.art@hcm. vnn.vn. Website: www.galerievinhloi.com.* This is one of Saigon's top galleries for representing Vietnam's most commercially successful artists. Housed in an attractive gallery outside the central business district, its two floors include very selective displays of several major artists, such as Hoang Phuong Vy, Cuong, Nguyen Thang Binh, Le Vuong, Buu Chi, Tran Luu Hau, Dao Hai Phong, Chuong, Hau, Bui Huu Hung, and Phuong. Be sure to visit their website, which includes photos of paintings and information on each artist.

❏ **Galerie Quynh:** *Tel./Fax 821-7995 or Email: qpham@galerie quynh.com. Website: www.galeriequynh.com.* At present this is not a gallery in terms of visiting a permanent physical art space, although the owner is in the process of acquiring such space for exhibiting both paintings and sculptures. The space will include a huge sculpture garden. In the meantime, please check the website for updates on this project. Vietnamese-American art specialist Quynh Pham has taken on a challenging task of representing serious contemporary art in Vietnam in the midst of what has become an extremely commercialized enterprise. Indeed, many critics of today's art scene in Vietnam say that its many commercial art galleries really don't represent today's serious art because they are too commercialized and thus primarily designed for tourists and businesses. With a critical eye on serious quality art and emerging Vietnamese artists, Galerie Quynh periodically sponsors art exhibitions in Saigon, many of which are held at major hotels. The owner, Quynh Pham, also serves as an art consultant to anyone interested in Vietnam's contemporary art scene, including visiting key artists and galleries. Her website includes the selected works of six contemporary abstract artists, articles and reviews, and a calendar of upcoming art exhibitions in both Saigon and Hanoi – an excellent resource for keeping up with Vietnam's contemporary art scene and for identifying the "best of the best" in paintings and sculpture.

❑ **Duc Minh Art Gallery:** *23 Ly Tu Trong Street, D1, Tel. 823-2449, Fax 931-6020, or Email: ducminh-art@hcm.vnn.vn.* This is one of Saigon's oldest, most reputable, and serious art galleries. Less commercial than most art galleries, it represents both master artists and young artists. While the shop has some paintings on display, it actually has a very large inventory, which you can check out by viewing their "catalog" of additional paintings. Since this gallery is planning to move to a larger space in the near future, please call before you visit to make sure the gallery has not changed locations.

❑ **Tu Do Art Gallery:** *53 Ho Tung Mau, D1, Tel. 821-0966, Fax 821-8690, or Email: tudogallery.hcm.vnn.vn. Website: www.tudogallery.com.* This is the oldest private art gallery in Vietnam, which has operated for more than 12 years. It represents a group of 25 artists who are not found in most other art galleries. Look for the works of Minh Duc, Bui Quang Anh, Siu Pham, Nguyen Thanh Son, Luu Cong Nhan, and Do Duy Tuan. Many of their works are presented on the gallery's website.

❑ **Hong Hac Art Gallery:** *9A Vo Van Tan Street, Tel. 824-3160 and Email: honghac@SaiGon.net.vn. Website: honghacgallery.8k.com.* This small but well respected and very knowledgeable gallery presents the works of 30 artists. Many are young artists whose paintings are very reasonably priced. The gallery's website includes the bios and works of 14 artists, which also can be purchased online. We especially like the long and narrow paintings of self-taught Nguyen Bao Toan depicting rural village scenes and water buffalo.

❑ **Dong Phuong Art Gallery:** *135 Nam Ky Khoi Nghia Street, D1, Tel. 930-9716 or Fax 808-5066.* Located near the entrance of the Reunification Palace, and with a sign out front saying "Orient Art," this gallery includes the works of 60 artists from Saigon and Hanoi – all who have graduated from the Fine Arts University. You'll find a good range of paintings here, with small paintings beginning at US$2! If you're interested in meeting any of the artists who live in the Saigon area, the gallery will arrange for you to meet them at their home studios, including several famous artists.

❑ **Lac Hong Art Gallery:** *97A Pho Duc Chinh Street, D1, Tel./Fax 821-3771 or Email: lachonggallery@hcmvnn.vn. Website: www.lachonggallery.com.* Attached to the Fine Arts Museum, this is a relatively new gallery. It's also located next door to four other galleries which offer similar quality works of art: **Gallery Shop**, **Blue Space Contemporary Art Center** (Tel.821-3695), **Nhat Le Art Gallery** (Tel./Fax 821-6447), and **Art XX1 Gallery** (Tel./Fax 821-6447).

❑ **Particular Gallery**: *Level 3, 123 Le Loi Avenue, D1, Tel. 821-3019, Ext. 304, Fax 829-0930, or Email: info@vietnamartist.com. Website: www.vietnamartist.com.* This small single-room gallery offers the works of three major contemporary Vietnamese artists: Nguyen Thanh Binh, Ton That Bang, and Bui Huu Hung. Most of the gallery's inventory can be viewed on their website.

❑ **Gallery Le Xuan**: *44 Dong Khoi Street, D2, Tel./Fax 822-4580, 2nd Floor.* This looks like a souvenir and Internet shop, until you go to the second floor where you will find a serious art gallery. Includes a good selection of reasonably priced paintings, including several by one of our favorites, Cuong.

ANTIQUES AND HOME DECORATIVE ITEMS

❑ **Nguyen Freres**: *2A Le Duan Boulevard, D1, Tel. 822-9654, Fax 825-1358, and Email: ngttuanh@hcm.vnn.vn.* Located directly across the street from the Sofitel Plaza Hotel, this is a delightful home decorative shop that also offers furniture and antiques. But there is more to this shop than what initially meets the eye. The shop displays a nice selection of reconditioned colonial-style furniture, including a unique collection of French art decor chairs. Includes attractive table runners, placemats, and small home decorative items. The shop also will make furniture to clients' specifications. Especially popular with expatriates and Japanese visitors. Serious buyers, including dealers, should request to visit the shop's warehouse, which is located within 15 minutes of this shop and includes a 900-square meter facility for storing, reconditioning, and making furniture. Very experienced in working with international clients and shipping abroad.

❑ **Binh Minh**: *16 Le Cong Kieu Street, D1, Tel. 829-8133 or Fax 822-3769.* This may be the closest you come to a real antique shop. Located in the heart of Saigon's antique street, the shop is jam-packed with old and new ceramics, bronze figures, brass items, stone carvings, ivory, and porcelain. Experienced in packing and shipping abroad, the shop also will make wood and brass items to order. Accepts Visa and MasterCard.

❑ **Indochine House**: *27 Dong Du, D1, Tel. 822-7318, Fax 822-7317, or Email: haiart@hcm.vnn.vn*. If you visited this shop in Hanoi, you know what to expect from this attractive branch shop. This uniquely designed two-story shop, which includes an open walkway and bridge on the second floor, specializes in quality arts, crafts, and home furnishings. Offers a tasteful selection of silk, furniture, ceramics, and a few paintings. Displays excellent quality antique furniture on the second floor.

❑ **Heritage**: *53 Dong Khoi Street, Tel. 823-5438, Fax 830-2760, or Email: heritagevn@yahoo.com*. While this may appear to be more of an upscale lacquerware shop, we view it more as a hybrid home decorative, fashion, and accessory shop. It includes beautifully designed red and black lacquer table-ware along with traditional woven baskets and stylish purses, scarves, and neck pieces. The owner, Nhung, is a popular singer who occasionally visits the shop in early evening. Prices tend to be higher than normal – two to three times more than one might expect from shopping elsewhere – but the quality and designs here are exceptional.

❑ **Precious Oui**: *29A and 27 Dong Khoi Street, Tel. 825-6817, Fax 822-6593, or Email: Quasarkhanh@reh.vnn.vn*. Includes two small but well appointed adjacent shops – **Precious Home** at 29A Dong Khoi and **Precious Lady** at 27 Dong Khoi – filled with uniquely designed lacquerware, home accessories, buffalo bone combs, silver jewelry, pillows, scarves, and chess sets.

❑ **L & H Decoration**: *22-36 Nguyen Hue Boulevard, Kiosque 7B, D1, Tel. 822-6799 or Email: miki@hcm.vnn.vn*. Located just off the pedestrian walkway (to your right if heading northeast) that links Nguyen Hue Boulevard with Dong Khoi Street, this very small but lovely shop is especially popular with Japanese visitors in search of top quality tableware, placemats, napkins, pillows, and hand fans. An exceptionally nice shop, with many creative designs and appealing colors, that stands out above most of the more touristy shops. For shoppers looking for something special – for gifts or for themselves.

❑ **Celadon Green**: *29 Dong Du, D1, Tel. 823-6816, Fax 822-6593, or Email: Quasarkhanh@hcm.vnn.vn*. Located next door to the Indochine House, this small shop offers a limited but attractive selection of ceramics, lacquer, tableware, and stone boxes. A good source for acquiring small gift items and interior accent pieces.

❏ **The Home Zone:** *41 Dinh Tien Hoang, D1 (at the corner of Le Duan and across the street from the Sofitel Plaza Hotel), Tel. 822-8022 or Fax 829-6410.* A cross between Pier 1 and Bed, Bath, and Beyond. This is a very modern and trendy home furnishings shop that includes a wide range of items for kitchens, bathrooms, and patios. Includes colorful picture frames, ceramic and porcelain dishes, stainless steel cutlery, wood garden and patio furniture, woven seagrass mats and carpets, placemats, napkins, rattan trays, and kitchen tools. Includes some imported items.

LACQUERWARE AND ACCESSORIES

❏ **Heritage:** *53 Dong Khoi Street, Tel. 823-5438, Fax 830-2760, or Email: heritagevn@yahoo.com.* Offers very nicely designed lacquer tableware for contemporary homes. Includes plates, bowls, chopsticks, boxes, and display pieces. Includes several other items, which are summarized under the previous "Antiques and Home Decorative Items" section.

❏ **Precious Oui:** *29A Dong Khoi, Tel. 825-6817, Fax 822-6593, or Email: Quasarkhanh@reh.vnn.vn.* Also known as **Precious Home** and **Precious Lady**, this small shop includes a very nice collection of quality lacquerware produced in unique designs.

HANDICRAFTS, SOUVENIRS, AND GIFTS

❏ **Le Xuan:** *44 Dong Khoi Street, D1, Tel. 829-6900.* This initially looks like another typical tourist souvenir shop offering similar selections of handicrafts as found in other shops along this busy shopping street. But there's more to this place than initial street appearances. The shop does have a good selection of souvenirs and handicrafts, such as lacquerware, chopsticks, wood boxes, silver, old watches, and tablecloths, at reasonable prices. At the same time, it includes an Internet café (in the rear) and a serious art gallery upstairs (Le Xuan Gallery). Very personable and helpful staff to assist you with your many shopping needs.

❏ **East Meets West:** *24 Le Loi Boulevard, D1, Tel. 823-1553, Fax 872-8198, or Email: le-m-hung-emw@hcm.vnn.vn.* Offers a nice selection of tribal clothes, bags, baskets, dolls, and lacquerware. Includes some woven baskets from various hill tribes.

❑ **Sapa 1 and Sapa 3:** *29 Ngo Doc De, D1, Tel. 825-8942, and 223 De Tham, D1, Tel./Fax 836-5163. Email: sapa123@hot mail.com*. Specializes in handicrafts and clothes from the popular hill tribe area of Sapa in northern Vietnam. Primary emphasis is on clothes and related textiles but also includes some woven baskets. Offers many of its own clothing designs using Sapa textiles.

❑ **Craft Home:** *39A Ngo Due Ke, D1, Tel. 823-7786 and 85 Pasteur, D1, Tel. 822-7955. Email: Crafthome@netnam2.org. vn*. This is a combination craft and fashion shop. Includes fashionable handicrafts, purses, and fabrics.

❑ **Kien Dung:** *18 Cao Ba Quat Street, D1, Mobile Tel. 090-651088*. If you collect or admire model clipper ships, boats, and planes, this shop offers a nice collection of such hand-crafted items. Look for a similar shop nearby that offers its own unique collection of such handcrafted items: **Thong** (28 Cao Ba Quat Street, D1, Tel. 822-1539).

JEWELRY

❑ **Alphana Jewelry:** *159 Dong Khoi Street, D1, Tel. 829-7398. Email: alphana@netnam2.org.vn*. Located across the street from the Caravelle Hotel, this busy shop offers an excellent selection of quality jewelry that especially appeals to the design tastes of international visitors. No wonder since they design their jewelry from major catalogs of international jewelers. All jewelry is made at their jewelry workshop in Saigon.

❑ **Anpha Jewelry:** *167 Dong Khoi Street, D1, Tel. 825-1918, Fax 829-1996, or Email: anphajewel@vol.vnn.vn*. Located on the corner of Dong Khoi Street and Le Loi Boulevard, this small but busy shop offers a good range of nicely designed jewelry using rubies, sapphires, jade, amethyst, peridot, blue topaz, and aquamarine. Also sells loose stones. Designs and prices appear to be good.

❑ **Saigon Jewelry Shopping Center:** *66T Le Loi Boulevard, D1, Tel. 823-1139*. Reputable professional gem and jewelry dealer offering quality selections. Includes certified gem report with purchases. Also includes the following companies: **SJC Gold and Gem Laboratory** (4-6 Nguyen Trung Truc, D1, Tel. 829-4060); **Artistic Gemstone Enterprise** (2D Nguyen Trung Truc, D1, Tel. 822-5189); and **Saigon Jewelry Enterprise** (418 Nguyen Thi Minh Khai, D3, Tel. 832-2511).

CLOTHES AND ACCESSORIES

❑ **Khaisilk:** *107 Dong Khoi Street, D1, Tel./Fax 829-1146; and 98 Mac Thi Buoi Street, D1, Tel. 823-4634. Email: khaisilksg@ hcm.fpt.vn.* One of those "must visit" shops in Saigon. This is Vietnam's premier silk, clothing, and accessory boutique. While you may have visited Khaisilk's main shop in Hanoi, you'll hardly recognize it here in Saigon since it's truly a first-class operation designed to appeal to international visitors in search of quality fabrics, garments, and accessories. Beautifully laid out on three floors, the shop oozes with class. Offers excellent quality fabrics along with nicely designed dresses, blouses, and shirts. Also includes a good selection of handbags, scarves, and shoes. Be sure to go to the third floor, which includes robes, pillows, pajamas, and gorgeous silks. The shop does tailoring work in case you cannot find your size, colors, and styles. A great place to shop for yourself as well as find gifts.

❑ **Anh:** *22-36 Nguyen Hue Boulevard, D1, Tel.822-0324, Fax 822-7603, or Email: ethnicfolkartanh@hcm.vnn.vn. Tax Plaza, 135 Nguyen Hue Boulevard, D1, 1st Floor, Tel./Fax 821-3716; or 69 Dong Khoi Street, D1, Tel./Fax 822-7603.* If you are interested in acquiring fashionable clothes and accessories with a traditional ethnic flair, Anh is the place to visit. Its three shops include an attractive selection of restyled ethnic clothes and accessories. It includes a nice collection of Ao Dai as well as numerous blouses, handbags, shoes, shawls, children's smocked dresses, and Pashminas.

❑ **Zakka**: *134 Pasteur Street, D1, Tel. 824-5345; and 22-36 Nguyen Hue Boulevard.* A small but very fashionable boutique offering a nice selection of clothes, fabrics, and accessories (handbags, shoes, ties). The main shop at 134 Pasteur Street is especially popular with Japanese visitors. The second shop in the pedestrian mall at 22-36 Nguyen Hue Boulevard primarily offers clothes and shoes.

❑ **Donga Silk:** *89 Mac Thi Buoi Street, D1, Tel. 825-8325.* Located across the street from Khaisilk's newly renovated

Mac Thi Buoi Street shop, the relatively new boutique offers a nice selection of clothes, scarves, neckties, handbags, and silk yardage. Includes inexpensive children's smocked dresses, which go for as little as US$16. Does both traditional and Western-style tailoring work.

❑ **Sapa 1 and Sapa 3:** *29 Ngo Doc De, D1, Tel. 825-8942, and 223 De Tham, D1, Tel./Fax 836-5163. Email: sapa123@hot mail.com.* Offers a line of refashioned ethnic clothes from the Sapa region. Also see description above under "Handicrafts, Souvenirs, and Gifts."

TAILORING

❑ **Cao Minh Tailor:** *148-150 Pasteur Street, D1, Tel. 822-4298 or Fax 873-8261.* This is one of Saigon's best tailors, who is used to producing top quality suits for both men and women. Offers a good selection of both British and Italian wools. A suit normally takes one week to produce and costs approximately US$200, depending on the fabric selection. Bring your own photos of the suit style you wish to have made or choose photos from the shop's many fashion magazines.

❑ **Phuc Loi:** *136 Pasteur, D1, Tel.824-3171.* Located next to Zakka boutique, this tiny seamstress stop is known for making excellent quality dresses and blouses. The shop includes its own selection of fabrics but will also work from a customer's fabric. Be sure to bring a photo or an actual garment you want copied – the more details the better. It usually takes three to four days to complete a blouse, which costs about US$8 if you bring your own fabric. Limited English spoken.

EMBROIDERED PICTURES

❑ **Diem Tham Quam:** *81 Dong Khoi, D1, Tel. 822-2856 and Fax 822-7240.* Also known as the **Dalat XQ Silk Embroidery Company**, this expansive three-story gallery includes hundreds of finely embroidered and fascinating pictures depicting Vietnam, its people, and its many legends. Some pictures are embroidered on both sides. The beautiful tiger pictures are especially striking. While many of the pictures may be too ethnic for your home decor and art tastes, at least visit this gallery to appreciate its unique and intricate art work. Its home base is in the resort city of Da Lat (56-58

Hoa Binh, Tel. 063-83-0042) where it has a large studio and workshop.

❑ **XQ Vietnam Hand Embroidery:** *26 Le Loi Boulevard, D1, Tel. 829-9866.* Located near the handicraft shop East Meets West, this two-story gallery includes numerous examples of embroidered pictures.

ACCOMMODATIONS

Saigon responded to its economic boom in the 1990s with the construction of numerous four- and five-star hotels. Today, it offers a wonderful selection of fine hotels as well as several which have yet to be opened because of the economic downturn during the past four years: Marriott, Westin, Holiday Inn, and Hyatt. Some may never open or they may be sold to other property owners. The newest five-star property, The Legend, opened in October 2001. Given the city's over-capacity of four- and five-star hotels, these properties are especially good values since their rooms are now deeply discounted. For example, five-star hotels with published (rack) room rates of over US$200 often go for US$60 to US$80 a night. The Marriott chain with its Renaissance, New World, and Marriott properties, tends to dominate five-star accommodations with nearly 60 percent of such rooms in Saigon.

Several websites provide quick access to Saigon's major hotels. Most also offer special discounted room rates for making reservations through their websites:

■ Asia Hotels	asia-hotels.com
■ Asia Travel Tips	asiatraveltips.com
■ Hotels Travel	hotelstravel.com/vietnam.html
■ Hotels Vietnam	hotelsvietnam.com
■ Saigon Hotels	saigon-hotels.net
■ Vietnam Rooms	vietnamrooms.com

At present, you should have no problem arriving in Saigon and finding a hotel room. Again, the best values are with the city's many fine five-star hotels, which are more than willing to offer substantial discounts even if you arrive without a reservation.

Saigon offers lots of hotels considered five-star or luxury by international standards. Some are wonderful new hotels whereas others are older properties that have been renovated – some renovations were carried out better than others! As is the case in Hanoi, no doubt additional hotels are constantly being added. The Marriott was partially completed when we were in Saigon, with the expectation that after many delays it would open by the summer of 2001. However, as we go to press it is still "under construction." Our personal favorites in Saigon are the Renaissance Riverside Hotel Saigon and the Sofitel Plaza Saigon. The Renaissance Riverside has a superb location, the facilities are first-rate, and the staff is really dedicated to assisting its guests. On top of that, ask for a room with a river view and you can be fully entertained by watching the ferries load and unload their passengers at the docks below. The Sofitel Plaza also offers comfortable rooms, excellent restaurants and a staff dedicated to meeting the needs of each guest.

Saigon's best hotels, with easy access to the city's major shopping and sightseeing attractions, include the following properties:

❑ **Renaissance Riverside Hotel Saigon:** *8-15 Ton Duc Thang Street, District 1, Ho Chi Minh City, Vietnam, Tel. (848) 822-0033, Fax (848) 823-5666. Website: www.renaissancehotels. com/sign.br. Email: rsvn.rrhs@hem.vnn.vn.* Five-star luxury property located in the heart of Saigon's business district within easy walking distance to major shops and shopping streets, views over the Saigon River or city, and a staff dedicated to guest services – sums up the major strengths of the Renaissance Riverside Hotel which opened in October 1999. Winner of the 2000 Premier Travel Award for Excellence awarded by AsiaTravelTips.com, this hotel highly impressed us. The lobby is welcoming with its cream colored walls that make the space lighter – both day and night – than many hotels in the city. The front desk staff welcomes guests with a smile and their professional, yet friendly service is at the guests' disposal day and night. Sixty percent of the guestrooms overlook the busy Saigon River where one can become mesmerized watching the throngs of people on foot, bicycles, or motor scooters piling on and off the ferry boats. The hotel's 349 guestrooms and suites on 21 floors are elegantly furnished and equipped with all the expected amenities and include two handicap-friendly rooms. More spacious than most hotel guestrooms in the city, the desk is large enough to really work on; the lighting is good both for working at the desk or reading in bed; a bedside touch control panel operates lighting, radio and television – which also has remote control. The fully equipped mini-bar includes tea and coffee making facilities. Travelers who chose Renaissance Club rooms located on the 18th to 21st floors will find tastefully appointed rooms, a private lounge with a spectacular river view where a daily continental breakfast is served along with all-day refreshments and snacks, evening cocktails and hors d'oeuvres and offering a selection of newspapers. *Kabin*, a Chinese restaurant, serves cuisines from the Canton and Szechuan provinces as well as an assortment of regional dim sum at lunch time. The *Riverside Café* serves Eastern and Western cuisines and provides a selection of buffet and a la carte dishes for breakfast, lunch, and dinner. The *Lobby Lounge* and *Poolside Terrace* offer light dining selections. The pool, set in a landscaped terrace garden located on the 22nd floor, provides a bird's-eye view of the city and river below. The adjoining health club features the latest fitness equipment as well as steam, sauna, and massage facilities. It is one of the best fitness facilities we have encountered. Business Center; Health and Fitness Center; Meeting and Banquet Facilities.

❑ **Sofitel Plaza Saigon:** *17 Le Duan Boulevard, District 1, Ho Chi Minh City, Vietnam, Tel. (848) 824-1555, Fax (848) 824-1666. Email: sofitelsgn@hcmc.netnam.vn.* Located in the heart of Ho Chi Minh City within walking distance of several tourist attractions and the main business district, guests are immediately welcomed by a very efficient and friendly staff. The lobby, which makes overly generous use of marble, is accented by two large columns clad with geometric cut spirals of dark wood. The 229 guestrooms are nicely furnished and decorated in soothing earth tones. Rooms are equipped with full five-star amenities including tea and coffee making facilities. Bathrooms are compact. Non-smoking floors and rooms for the disabled are available. The Sofitel Executive Club offers additional services including complimentary breakfast, private check-in/out, complimentary time use of a computer and printer, and late check-out. *Café Rivoli* offers a buffet lunch and dinner as well as an international a la carte menu. *Aromasia*, an Asian specialty restaurant, tempts diners with a range of flavors from Vietnam, Thailand, Japan, Indonesia, Malaysia, India, and China. The *L'Elysee Bar* serves a buffet lunch and afternoon tea or a selection of drinks and healthful snacks on a terrace overlooking the boulevard. Business Center; Clark Hatch Fitness Center; Conference and Banquet Facilities.

❑ **The Legend Hotel:** *2A-4A Ton Duc Thang Street, District 1, Ho Chi Minh City, Tel. (848) 823-3333 or Fax (848) 823-2333. Website: www.legendhotelsaigon.com. Email: sales@legend hotelsaigon.com.* This is Saigon's newest five-star hotel, which opened October 2001. Centrally located along the Saigon River, this well-appointed property includes 282 rooms and six restaurants and bars. The *Atrium Café* serves Continental and Southeast Asian dishes, and the *Crystal Jade Palace* offers Cantonese cuisine. It also includes a Japanese restaurant. Business Center; Fitness Center; an outdoor swimming pool; Conference and Banquet Facilities.

❑ **Caravelle Hotel:** *19 Lam Son Square, District 1, Ho Chi Ming City, Vietnam, Tel. (848) 823-4999, Fax (848) 824-3999. Website: www.caravellehotel.com. Email: hotel@caravellehotel.vnn. vn.* Centrally located opposite the city Opera House, the Caravelle is in the heart of the commercial, shopping and entertainment areas of the city. Voted the best luxury hotel by the *Vietnam Economic Times*, whether in the original 10-story Caravelle Hotel or in the contemporary 24-story tower, the 335 well appointed guestrooms, which include 8 suites and 24 serviced apartments, welcome the guest. In addition to expected amenities – including tea and coffee making facilities – compact disc players and VCRs are available on request. Nonsmoking floors and rooms are available as are specially equipped rooms for the disabled. Signature Floors provide additional services and amenities. Wining and dining venues provide a range of culinary choices. *Port Orient* offers an a la carte menu and international specialty buffets; *Asian Reflections* creates dishes with the exotic flavors of Asia infused with the West; the *Lobby Lounge*, *Pool Bar*, and *Saigon Saigon Bar* provide beverages and light snacks. Business Center; Health and Fitness Center; Conference and Banquet Facilities.

❑ **New World Hotel Saigon:** *76 Le Lai Street, District 1, Ho Chi Minh City, Vietnam, Tel. (848) 822-8888, Fax (848) 823-0710. Email: nwhs@hcm.vnn.vn.* Located in the heart of the business and commercial district of the city, each of the New World Hotel Saigon's 498 guestrooms – including 28 suites and 32 business units – is well equipped with the full array of five-star amenities. Executive floors offer additional services and amenities. The *Dynasty* restaurant is considered by some to be the city's best Chinese restaurant. Dim sum is a special treat. The *Parkview Coffee Shop* offers a la carte or buffet which includes Western and Asian specialties. In the *Lobby Lounge*, enjoy a cool drink, afternoon tea or cocktail to the music of the resident pianist. The *Poolside Bar* offers a spa menu, fresh juices, cool cocktails and homemade ice cream. The *Saxophone Bar* offers a game of pool or games on

TV while one enjoys a beverage and a chat with friends. Business Center; Health Club; Conference and Banquet Facilities.

❑ **Omni Saigon Hotel:** *251 Nguyen Van Troi Street, Phu Nhuan District, Ho Chi Minh City, Vietnam, Tel. (848) 844-9222, Fax (848) 844-9198. Email: omnires@marcopolohotels. com.* Located on the fringe of the center of town, the Omni Saigon offers 240 well appointed guestrooms, suites, and serviced apartments. All amenities expected of a five-star hotel are provided. An upgrade to the Continental Club offers additional luxury and services, including views from the private Club floor lounge situated on the top floor; complimentary buffet breakfast as well as tea and coffee with cookies served throughout the day and drink and snacks served in the evening. *Lotus Court* presents fine Cantonese cuisine; *Café Saigon* presents varied dinner theme buffets; *Nishimura Japanese Restaurant* offers a wide variety of Japanese cuisine, including sushi and teppanyaki; *OJ's Café* offers juices and California-style sandwiches – menu for those with a concern for healthful yet tasty foods; the *R & R Pub and Lounge* serves light meals. Business Center; Health and Fitness Center; Conference and Banquet Facilities.

❑ **Saigon Prince Hotel:** *63 Nguyen Hue Boulevard, District 1, Ho Chi Minh City, Vietnam, Tel. (848) 822-2999, Fax (848) 824-1888. Email: saigon-princehtl@hcm.vnn.vn.* Located in the heart of the city within easy walking distance of the major shopping areas, the Saigon Prince offers easy access to businesses as well. Heavily frequented by Japanese tourists, the 203 guestrooms and suites offer comfortable furnishings and the expected amenities. At the 24-hour *Chatterbox Restaurant* you can savor Vietnamese cuisine or sample from Singaporean, Malaysian, Indonesian, or Western favorites. *Zendokoro Ichiyu* serves one of the best Japanese cuisines in the city. Business Center; Health Club (no swimming pool but includes a plunge pool); Conference and Banquet Facilities. Managed by Duxton Hotels International.

❑ **Hotel Majestic:** *1 Dong Khoi Street, Ho Chi Minh City, Vietnam, Tel. (848) 829-5514, Fax (848) 829-5510. Email: majestic.s.hotel@bdvn.vnd.net.* Located in the heart of the city convenient to shopping, business, and entertainment venues, one of the great old colonial hotels, Hotel Majestic was opened in 1925. The exterior retains its original French colonial architecture, and the interior has been renovated locally by Saigon Tourist. This four-star facility offers 122 guestrooms including 30 suites with expected amenities. *Cyclo Café* offers international cuisine; *Serenade Restaurant* located on the top floor, offers an a la carte Western menu; the *Merry Pool Bar* serves beverages and light snacks; the *Breeze Skybar* offers Vietnamese specialties, fresh seafood, barbecue and an a la carte menu. Business Center; Health Facilities; Conference and Banquet Facilities.

❑ **Rex Hotel:** *141 Nguyen Hue Boulevard, Ho Chi Minh City, Vietnam, Tel. (848) 829-2185, Fax (848) 829-6536. Website: www.rexhotelvietnam.com. Email: rexhotel@sgtourist.com.vn.* Located in the city center, the Rex Hotel served as a base for the American press corps during the Vietnam War. The public areas exhibit an eclectic mix of Chinese furniture and statues that is a bit overwhelming and some tastes might describe as garish. 227 guestrooms with amenities. *Apricot* serves Vietnamese, French and Chinese selections; *Rex Royal Court* offers Vietnamese meals; and *The Rooftop Garden* offers international – primarily Vietnamese, French and Chinese – menus round the clock. You may want to visit *The Rooftop Garden* for a drink to experience both a sense of history and the view of the central city below. Business Center; Fitness Center; Conference and Banquet Facilities.

❑ **Hotel Equatorial:** *242 Tran Binh Trong Street, District 5, Ho Chi Minh City, Vietnam, Tel. (848) 839-7777, Fax (848) 839-0011. Website: www.equatorial.com. Email: info@hcmequatorial.com.* Located in the Cholon (Chinatown) District, about 15 minutes from downtown, the staff of the Equatorial tries to make up for the slight distances guests must travel to reach many central locations, by providing excellent service to them. The location is very convenient to the airport. The 333 guestrooms and suites provide all the expected amenities. *Café California* offers a range of international food, while *Kampachi Japanese Restaurant* and *Golden Phoenix Chinese Restaurant* offer those respective national cuisines. There is a *Coffee Bar* and a *Poolside Swim-up Bar* for beverages and light snacks. Business Center; Fitness Center; Conference and Banquet Facilities.

❑ **Novotel Garden Plaza Saigon:** *309B-311 Nguyen Van Troi, Tan Binh District, Ho Chi Minh City, Vietnam, Tel. (848) 842-1111, Fax (848) 842-4370. Email: rsvn-gpparkroyal@hcm.vnn.vn.* Novotel Garden Plaza Saigon is located near the fringe of the town center just a short drive from the international airport. The 155 guestrooms and suites provide the expected amenities. The Orchid Club Floors offer additional services and amenities. The *Garden Restaurant* offers both Asian and Western cuisine while the *Blue Lotus Fun Pub* and *Lobby Lounge* offer snacks and beverages. Business Center; Fitness Center; Conference and Banquet Facilities.

RESTAURANTS

Dining in Saigon is often a real treat with great food, entertainment, and ambience. Saigon has a excellent selection of restaurants, from elegant Vietnamese and French restaurants to small French bistros and delightful Thai, Cambodian, and Indian restaurants. While most of the top Vietnamese and French restaurants are found outside hotels, most five-star hotels offer excellent Continental, Chinese, and Japanese restaurants.

Most people tend to dine early in Saigon – from 6pm to 9pm. Several restaurants include live musical entertainment. All restaurants listed here are found in District 1, unless otherwise designated.

VIETNAMESE

❏ **Mandarin:** *11A Ngo Van Nam, Tel. 822-9783.* You really need reservations, although begging can help, to get into this very popular and elegant restaurant. Serves outstanding dishes, from spring rolls to noodles. Nothing disappoints, including the fine service. Open for lunch and dinner.

❏ **Lemongrass:** *4 Nguyen Thiep Street, Tel. 822-0496.* This small but popular restaurant is a favorite of many tourists and expatriates. Offers a good sampling of Vietnamese cuisine from its tempting menu – just pick something and it will probably be excellent. Includes traditional music played by two musicians. Open for lunch and dinner.

❏ **Blue Ginger:** *37 Nam Ky Khoi Nghia Street, Tel. 829-8676.* Offers elegant dining, an excellent selection of Vietnamese dishes, and good service – the perfect combination for dining out in Saigon. Includes a nightly (7:30pm) traditional musical performance.

❏ **Vietnamese House:** *93 Dong Khoi Street, Tel. 829-1623.* Centrally located, this popular restaurant serves excellent spring rolls, beef rolls, sauteed prawns with snow peas, soft shell crabs, and many noodle dishes. The second floor dining room is less crowded and hectic than the first floor and includes traditional musical entertainment. Good food but service can be slow. Open for lunch and dinner.

❑ **Hoi An:** *11 Le Thanh Ton Street, District 1, Tel. 823-7694.* Another popular upscale Vietnamese restaurant which belongs to the owners of the Mandarin.

❑ **Cool Saigon:** *20 Dong Khoi Street, District 1, Tel. 829-1364.* Offers trendy new Vietnamese cuisine.

❑ **Ancient Town:** *211 Ter Dien Bien Phu, District 3, Tel. 829-9625.* Popular with the expat press community, this restaurant offers an expansive menu of both traditional and Nouvelle Vietnamese cuisine.

FRENCH

❑ **Camargue:** *16 Cao Ba Quat, Tel. 824-3148.* This restaurant looks, feels, and tastes just right. Indeed, it doesn't get much better than this wonderful restaurant with its great ambience and fine dishes. We had our best dining experience in all of Vietnam here. Housed in a charming old French colonial villa, and offering both indoor and outdoor dining options, this is one of Saigon's most romantic restaurants, especially when dining outside. The food is outstanding and the service is excellent. Try the bean soup, crab, Chateaubriand, and cream brulee (three types). The fish and duck dishes are superb. Includes a popular bar and billiards room. The interesting photos on the walls are for sale. Make this one of your first restaurant choices since you may want to return again before you leave Saigon! Dinner only.

❑ **Augustin:** *10 Nguyen Thiep Street, Tel. 829-2941.* Centrally located (next door to Lemongrass, between Dong Khoi Street and Nguyen Hue Boulevard), this small, crowded, and inexpensive bistro consistently produces excellent French cuisine. Good wine selections. Open for lunch (except Sunday) and dinner.

❑ **Le Caprice:** *Landmark Building, 5B Ton Duc Thang Street, 15th Floor, Tel. 822-8337.* Offers a nice view of the Saigon River from the top floor of the Landmark Building. Serves excellent French cuisine in an elegant setting. Lunch and dinner.

❑ **La Villa:** *11 Thai Van Lung Street, Tel. 822-3240.* This elegant restaurant, located in a French villa, offers excellent French, Continental, and Thai cuisine.

❑ **Restaurant Bibi:** *8A/8D2 Thai Van Lung (Don Dat) Street, Tel. 829-5783.* Delightful small bistro serving excellent French and Mediterranean cuisine.

❑ **Le Beaulieu:** *Sofitel Plaza Saigon, 17 Le Duan Boulevard, Tel. 842-1555.* During the day, this restaurant functions as Café Rivoli for breakfast and lunch. In the evening it becomes a delightful French restaurant, Le Beaulieu. Serves a massive buffet of pizza, prawns, crabs, fish, cheeses, and desserts. Can also order a la carte.

OTHER

❑ **Angkor Encore:** *5 Nguyen Thiep, Tel. 822-6278.* This is a pleasant surprise, located directly across the street from the popular Vietnamese Lemongrass Restaurant. Try the banana flower salad, rice noodle with chicken, stir-fried deer, and curried shrimp. The affable and enthusiastic owner, Daniel Hung, a photographer and survivor of the Killing Fields, makes the rounds of the tables to make sure patrons understand this unique cuisine and select the best dishes. A terrific restaurant to acquaint yourself with Khmer cuisine, if your next stop is Cambodia! Adds 4% for using a credit card.

❑ **Marine Club Restaurant:** *17A4 Le Thanh Ton Street, Tel. 829-2249.* Popular with expats, this international restaurant is one of Saigon's "in" spots. Includes a wood-burning pizza oven and entertaining piano bar. Will even deliver their gourmet pizzas.

❑ **'A' The Russian Restaurant:** *361/8 Nguyen Dinh Chieu Street, District 3, Tel. 835-9190.* A surprisingly good Russian and Central Asian restaurant with lots of character. Serves excellent dishes, such as beef Stroganoff, kebabs, dumplings, and caviar. Lots of liquor flows here along with a loud nightly crowd.

❑ **Moonfish Café:** *6 Dong Khoi Street, District 1, Tel. 823-8822.* Welcome to Vietnamese-California nouvelle cuisine. Large centrally located trendy café with a modern setting.

❑ **Chao Thai:** *16 Pai Van Lung Street, District 1, Tel. 824-1457.* Saigon's best and most upscale Thai restaurant serving lots of spicy dishes. Located in a charming old villa.

❑ **Ashoka:** *17/10 Le Thanh Ton, District 1, Tel. 823-1372.* Serves excellent North Indian dishes in an attractive setting.

❑ **Ohan Restaurant:** *71-73 Pasteur Street, District 1, Tel. 824-4896.* Excellent Japanese restaurant, which is especially popular with Japanese business people.

SEEING THE SITES

While there is not a great deal to do within Saigon, the city does have a few interesting museums and sites to visit, which may or may not appeal to you. Most can be covered within two days. However, be forewarned that many of these places may be underwhelming and disappointing because of their heavy dose of stereotypical, amateur propaganda. Indeed, you may be hard-pressed to find a serious, professional museum that goes beyond a one-sided political story designed to glorify the communist revolution in Vietnam – an ongoing attempt to further educate the Saigonese, and the rest of the world, of the virtues of Ho Chi Minh and his struggling and victorious revolutionaries. As such, you may not want to linger long in some of these places – 30 minutes in some museums is just about right! Some of the most interesting sites lie outside the city, which may take an additional two days to visit.

> *Museums are often underwhelming and disappointing propaganda venues.*

MUSEUMS

❑ **Museum of History (Bao Tang Lich Su):** *Nguyen Binh Khiem, D1. Open Tuesday-Sunday, 8-11:30am and 1-4:30pm.* Housed in a pagoda-style building near the entrance of the Botanic Gardens (Thao Cam Vien), this museum displays artifacts from the Stone Age through the Cham and Khmer periods and into the Vietnamese dynastic period. Includes a section on minority cultures. Offers an interesting collection of Dong Son bronze drums, Buddhas, jewelry, ceramics, inlaid furniture, and imperial garments and accessories.

❑ **Ho Chi Minh Museum (Khu Luu Niem Bac Ho):** *1 Nguyen Tat Than Street, D4, Tel. 839-1060. Open 7:30-11:30am and 1:30-4:30pm.* Housed in the interesting old (1863 circa) French colonial customs building – itself an object for viewing – this museum is devoted to presenting the history and memorabilia of Vietnam's great hero.

❑ **War Remnants Museum (Nha Trung Bay Toi Ac Chien Tranh):** *38 Vo Van Tan, D3. Open 7:30-11:45am and 1:30-4:45pm.* Housed in the former U.S. Information Service building, this museum takes the honors for bad taste and excessive propaganda. The government is still having trouble naming this rather offensive anti-American museum – it used to be called the "Museum of American War Crimes." The focus is almost solely on the war evils of America – nothing on the role of the South Vietnamese army or the Viet Cong. Many visitors feel it's the ultimate tacky propaganda museum. It probably turns off more tourists than it educates. It's unfortunate since this could be a very good museum if placed in the hands of professionals. Nonetheless, you'll probably end up here, as it is Saigon's most popular museum for tourists. It comes complete with aging American planes, tanks, and artillery at the entrance and photos, maps, diagrams, models of death and destruction, and deformed fetuses in jars. Includes examples of infamous tiger cages. The only tasteful section of this museum is the interesting photo gallery, which includes many photos of the war taken by international journalists. The government really needs to further reassess this museum, since it most likely is having unintended consequences with tourists who know propaganda when they see it in such a blatant form. But old communist habits are probably hard to break.

❑ **Fine Arts Museum of Ho Chi Minh City (Bao Tang My Thuat):** *97A Pho Duc Chinh, D1, Tel. 821-0001. Open 7:30am to 4:30pm.* This is a real mixed gallery. If you spend most of your time on the first floor, you get the impression that this is primarily the museum of propaganda art. The first floor includes numerous paintings with revolutionary and war themes, a mixture of amateur and professional art. It also includes an interesting children's art section. The second floor is devoted to paintings (look for *Uncle Ho Fishing in Viet Bac Barracks*), bronzes, ceramics, and an unusual display of revolutionary artists' equipment (the life of artists often on-the-run in combat). The really good stuff for serious ancient art lovers is on the third floor – Champa stone carvings (many more interesting pieces than found in the Cham Museum in Danang). But the most interesting parts of this museum are the five art galleries attached to the building (to the right and rear), which sell the works of many talented Vietnamese artists. See the above shopping sections on "Art." Our recommendation: spend 30 minutes in the museum – primarily on the third floor – and 90 minutes in the five art galleries. You may find some attractive art to purchase from these shops.

❑ **Reunification Palace (Hoi Truong Thong Nhat):** *106 Nguyen Du Street, D1, Tel. 823-3652. Open 7:30-10:30am and 1-4pm. Admission fee: 10,000 dong.* This is the former presidential palace of the South Vietnamese government – the famous place where the tanks of the National Liberation Front crashed the front gates in 1975 to symbolize the final collapse (or liberation) of Saigon. The palace is a major attraction for both local and international tourists, including many school children who swamp the corridors and rooms. Visitors primarily tour the many rooms to view 1960s furniture and equipment – cabinet, assembly, dining, war command, bar and dance floor, and residential quarters. The words "tacky" and "kitsch" often come to mind as one tours this compound. The building also includes a helicopter pad with a helicopter. The second floor includes a souvenir shop as well as a good view of the city, boulevard, and nearby park. The war command rooms in the basement are some of the most interesting rooms, especially the ones filled with aging communication equipment, which truly look is if they belong to a bygone era. It's an interesting building and compound to visit because of its historical significance.

❑ **Museum of the Revolution (Tao Tang Cach Mang):** *65 Ly Tu Trong Street, D1, Tel. 829-9741. Open Tuesday-Sunday, 8am-4:30pm.* Housed in the beautiful old Gia Long Palace (1886 circa), this museum is devoted to chronicling the communist struggle and revolution in Vietnam vis-a-vis the French and Americans. Includes lots of photos, maps, artefacts, documents, weapons, and dioramas. Soviet tanks, a U.S. helicopter, and antiaircraft guns can be found in the garden area outside the building.

CHURCHES AND PAGODAS

❑ **Notre Dame Cathedral (Nha Tho Duc Ba):** Centrally located in a square at the north end of Dong Khoi Street, and across from the grand Central Post Office, this impressive red brick French built (1877-1880) neo-Romanesque cathedral almost looks out of place in Saigon. Nonetheless, it's an impressive building which is heavily used. Worshipers overflow into the streets during the 9:30a ● Sunday mass. If you are Catholic and want to attend mass, other masses also are held at 5:30am, 7:30am, and 5pm on Sundays.

❏ **Emperor Jade Pagoda (Chua Ngoc Hoang** or **Phuoc Hai Tu):** *73 Mai Thi Luu Street, D1.* Built in 1909 by the Cantonese community, this is Saigon's most colorful, distinctive, and detailed Chinese pagoda with numerous statues and carvings reflecting both Buddhism and Taoism.

❏ **Cholon Pagodas:** Some of Saigon's best pagodas can be found in Cholon. Most at one time served as congregational halls for the various Chinese communities in Cholon, especially the Cantonese, Fukienese, Fujian, and Chaozhou. The major pagodas are found along Nguyen Trai Street and Tran Hung Dao Boulevard. You may want to hire a cyclo to take you to a few of these places:

- **Quan Am Pagoda:** 12 Lao Tu Street.
- **Ha Chuong Hoi Quan Pagoda:** 802 Nguyen Trai.
- **Thien Hau Pagoda:** 710 Nguyen Trai.
- **Nghia An Hoi Quan Pagoda:** 678 Nguyen Trai.
- **Tam Son Hoi Quan Pagoda:** 118 Trieu Quang Phuc Street.

❏ **Saigon Pagodas:** While Saigon has more than 150 pagodas, unless you are really into pagodas (after visiting three or four you'll get the idea), you may want to visit a few of these major pagodas in addition to the Emperor Jade Pagoda:

- **Ong Bon Pagoda:** 264 Hai Thuong Lai Ong Boulevard.
- **Phung Son Tu Pagoda:** 338 Nguyen Cong Tru Street.
- **Dai Giac Pagoda:** 112 Nguyen Van Troi.
- **Vinh Nghiem Pagoda:** Nguyen Van Troi.
- **Xa Loi Pagoda:** 89 Ba Huyen Quan Thanh Street.
- **Giac Lam Pagoda:** 118 Lac Long Quan Street.

OTHER CITY ATTRACTIONS

❑ **Central Post Office (Buu Dien Truing Tam):** *Intersection of Hai Thuong Lai Ong Boulevard and Chau Van Liem Boulevard (opposite Notre Dame Cathedral). Open 7:30am to 7:30pm.* We don't normally find post offices to be interesting attractions. However, this one is an exception. It has been beautifully restored to its former colonial glory. Constructed by the French (1886-1891), this architectural masterpiece functions as an all-purpose post office, shipping, and communication center. You can buy stamps, postcards, magazines, and newspapers here as well as make international phone calls, send faxes, mail letters, and ship packages through the local postal system, and use FedEx and Airborne Express for arranging international air shipments (each has windows). Great to look at but not very efficiently run when it comes to actually using the postal services – expect long lines and questionable procedures from the overstaffed postal bureaucracy.

❑ **Municipal Theater (Nha Hat Thanh Pho):** *Intersection of Le Loi Boulevard and Dong Khoi Street, Tel. 829-1249.* Frequently referred to as the Opera House and National Theater. The beautiful old colonial landmark building was constructed in 1899 as the city's opera house. It subsequently served as the National Assembly for the South Vietnam government. After 1975 it once again became the Municipal Theater where local musical, dance, and gymnastics performances take place. It occasionally hosts an international operatic performance.

❑ **Saigon River:** *District 1, between Nguyen Hue Boulevard and Dong Khoi Street.* There's lots of fascinating river activity, especially boats and ferries, around the docks at the end of Dong Khoi Street. If you are fortunate enough to be staying at a high-rise hotel with a room overlooking the river, you'll enjoy viewing the river and pedestrian traffic, especially the loading and unloading of the crowded ferries that taxi back and forth from the river banks. If you're interested in taking an interesting day trip along the Saigon River by a converted diesel-operated rice barge or stay overnight on a house boat, contact the **Mekong Star**. They operate a small fleet of boats that tour the river. The day tour includes stops at an ancient temple, a ceramics village and factory, and the interesting market town of Binh Duong. Passengers relax on the upper deck viewing the river scenes, drinking, and dining (take a hat and sunscreen for a sunny day as well as lots of film – a great photo opportunity). It's a relaxing way to spend a day along the river. While you can stay overnight on the boats, we recommend taking a day trip, which is ideally suited for many visitors who are able to see and do a great deal along the river during an eight-hour period. The Mekong Star also offers similar trips to the Mekong Delta and occasionally takes boats as far as Phnom Penh in Cambodia. While by no means luxurious, the charming rustic accommodations are more than adequate for visitors who are used to the basics of travel. The crew and service are very responsive to the needs of guests. For more information of these unique river tours, visit the Mekong Star's website (www.mekongstar.com) or contact them as follows:

In the USA:

Mekong Star
621 Georgia Avenue
Palo Alto, CA 94603
Tel. 800-546-7890
Fax 650-813-1101
info@mekongstar.com

In Vietnam:

TanNam Hai Co.
58 Mac Dinh Chi
Ho Chi Minh City
Tel. 848-823-6379
Fax 848-829-7526
tnhco@bdvn.vnn

❏ **Zoo and Botanical Garden (Thao Cam Vien):** *Intersection of Nguyen Binh Khiem Street and Le Duan Boulevard.* A good place for strolling and feeling sorry for the poorly maintained animals. The gardens were originally developed in 1864 and have gone through various periods of neglect and rehabilitation. Popular with local children. You may want to put this one on your list of *"I have absolutely nothing more to do in Saigon – maybe this is better than what I read!"* Probably not, but it will kill an hour or two and make you appreciate your zoos and gardens back home.

OUTSIDE SAIGON

❏ **Cu Chi Tunnels:** *65 kilometers northwest of Saigon by way of Highway 22.* This is one of the most popular and educational sites to visit outside Saigon. Except for the aging and scratchy propaganda film you view before visiting the complex and tunnels, this trip is well worth taking. It gives you an up-close view of what life (largely underground) was really like for the Vietcong during the American War, and why they were so tenacious, and eventually victorious, in the face of superior firepower. The Cu Chi Tunnels are a network of nearly 250 kilometers of underground tunnels where thousands of Vietcong lived and worked during the American War. It consists of numerous rooms, narrow passages, trap doors, field hospitals, and command posts. The area open to the public is only a sampling of the vast and complex network that lies beneath the ground. Tour guides accompanied by a local representative explain the various tunnels and rooms as well as put simulated mines in the pathways and offer booby trap demonstrations. You can even crawl through one of the hot and narrow tunnels, which is still a challenge for a large person or someone with claustrophobia. Many visitors come here on a guided tour, which can be arranged through most travel agencies and tourist cafes in Saigon. Most such day tours include a visit to the nearby Cao Dai Holy See in Tay Ninh. You'll find several shops near the exit of the Cu Chi Tunnels complex selling lacquerware, toys, souvenirs, and fermented bottled snakes.

❑ **Cao Dai Temple:** *95 kilometers northwest of Saigon by way of Highway 22.* Located in the town of Tay Ninh, this is the center for Caodaism, the controversial religion which was founded in 1926, that combines elements of Christianity with Buddhism, Confucianism, Taoism, Islam, and Vietnamese spirit worship. Approximately 3 million Vietnamese practice Caodaism. Once very political and militaristic, this religious sect now primarily focuses on its religious activities. Most visitors come here to visit the Disneyland-like Cao Dai Temple and observe the impressive daily services that take place at 6am, 12noon, 6pm, and midnight and last one hour (you can observe from the balcony and take pictures). The most impressive services take place at 12noon. Most tour groups include the Cao Dai Temple in a day trip to the nearby Cu Chi Tunnels (60 kilometers from Tay Ninh).

❑ **Mekong Delta:** Saigon is a good base for exploring various sections of the nearby Mekong Delta, a flat and often flooded region of ricefields, rivers, and canals which is home to nearly 15 million people. You can easily arrange a tour of the Mekong Delta through a travel agency or take a hydrofoil from downtown Saigon. You also might want to consider taking a two-day trip of the Mekong Delta on the **Mekong Star** riverboat. (see above discussion of the Saigon River and the Mekong Star, www.mekongstar.com) The best time to visit this area is between October and May, the ostensible dry season. While you can spend several days exploring the many cities, towns, and villages in this area, many visitors take a day tour by boat to visit a couple of major places and sample the local cuisine – fish, fruit, and rice dishes. The city of **My Tho**, for example, is only two hours (70 kilometers) from Saigon and is a good place to stop for lunch and visit the nearby **Island of the Coconut Monk** and **Tan Long Island**. There's not much else to see and do in this rather worn port city of 150,000 residents. Farther southwest (108 kilometers from My Tho) is the friendly and pleasant city of **Can Tho**, which serves as the capital of the Mekong Delta.

❏ **Angkor Wat:** This fabulous Hindu temple complex in neighboring Cambodia – a "must see" for anyone visiting Vietnam – is much more than just a side trip from Saigon, although it can be easily arranged as such. We examine Angkok Wat, as well as Phnom Penh, as a separate destination in the next chapter on Cambodia.

ENJOYING YOUR STAY

Many visitors to Saigon quickly run out of things to do after spending a couple of days sightseeing within the city. However, travel-shoppers can find a lot to do to fill up at least four days in Saigon. If you venture outside the city to visit the Cu Chi Tunnels, the Cao Dai Temple, and the Mekong Delta, you can easily spend more time in the Saigon area.

Saigon is gradually acquiring a lively nightlife centering on bars, clubs, and discos.

There's not a great deal to do in Saigon during the evening other than dining, drinking, dancing, and shopping. The city is gradually acquiring a lively nightlife, which tends to center on bars, clubs, and discos that are popular with expatriates and include jazz, blues, and country music. Saigon also has dozens of hostess bars noted for their charming young ladies who primarily get compliant Japanese, Korean, Taiwanese, Hong Kong, and Singapore businessmen to buy overpriced drinks in exchange for conversation, karaoke singing, and companionship. For a quick rundown on what's happening in Saigon, check out the listings in the weekly "Ongoing" section of *Timeout* (a supplement to the *Vietnam Investment Review*). It will include dining specials and promotions, who is playing at which bars, and special exhibitions and live performances. Also check with your hotel concierge. Trendy bars, discos, and clubs are constantly opening and closing in Saigon.

Some of the most interesting street entertainment takes place along Dong Khoi Street on **Sunday evenings**. The street and sidewalks are nearly wall-to-wall with young people and motorbikes cruising the area to see what's going on and parading their latest fashions. It's one huge "townie" parade, which many visitors find fascinating if not at times overwhelming with too many people. If you enjoy people-watching and purposeless crowds, Sunday night along Dong Khoi Street is the city's cheapest form of entertainment.

Aside from Dong Khoi Street on Sunday evenings, some of Saigon's liveliest evening entertainment establishments, which are primarily bars with food and music, include the following places:

❑ **Apocalypse Now:** 2C Thi Sach Street, District 1, Tel. 824-1463.

❑ **Blue Gecko:** 31 Ly Tu Trong Street, District 1, Tel. 824-3483.

❑ **Blue Ginger:** 37 Nam Ky Khoi Nghia, District 1, Tel. 829-8676.

❑ **Buffalo Blues:** 72A Nguyen Du Street, District 1, Tel. 822-2874.

❑ **Catwalk:** New World Hotel, 76 Le Lai Street, District 1, Tel. 824-3760.

❑ **Hard Rock:** 22 Mac Thi Buoi, District 1, Tel. 822-1023.

❑ **L'Elysee Bar:** Sofitel Plaza Saigon Hotel, 17 Le Duan Boulevard, District 1, Tel. 824-1555.

❑ **Marine Club:** 17A4 Le Thanh Ton, District 1, Tel. 829-2249.

❑ **Maya:** 6 Cao Ba Quat Street, District 1.

❑ **Q Bar:** Municipal Theater, 7 Cong Truong Lam Son, District 1, Tel. 823-5424.

❏ **Queen Bee:** 104-106 Nguyen Hue, District 1, Tel. 829-1836.

❏ **Saigon-Saigon Bar:** Caravelle Hotel, 19 Larn Son Square, District 1, Tel. 823-4999.

❏ **Underground:** Basement, Lucky Plaza, 69 Dong Khoi Street, District 1, Tel. 829-9079. Website: www.under groundsaigon.bizland.com.

❏ **Vasco's Bar:** 16 Cao Ba Quat, District 1, Tel. 824-3149.

❏ **Wild Horse Saloon:** 8A1/D1 Thai Van Lung (Don Dat) Street, District 1, Tel. 825-1901.

Some of Saigon's most popular **music clubs** and **disco coffee bars** include:

❏ **Café Saigon:** 212A Tran Hung Dao Street, District 1, Tel. 839-4749.

❏ **CAT Cyber Café:** 47 Ngo Duc Ke Street, Tel. 821-2222.

❏ **Feeling:** 112 Nguyen Hue Boulevard, District 1, Tel. 822-5693.

❏ **Modestos:** Me Linh Point Tower, Ho Huan Nghiep Street, District 1, Tel. 823-7868.

❏ **Nhac tre n.1:** 1 Le Thanh Ton Street, District 1, Tel. 822-9044.

❏ **Old Olympic:** 97 Nguyen Thi Minh Khai Street, District 1, Tel. 835-6757.

❏ **The Cave:** 102 Nam Ky Khoi Nghia Street, District 1, Tel. 822-3014.

Saigon's disco scene tends to get started around 11pm and ends around 2am. Some of the most popular **discos** include:

❏ **Club Monaco:** 651 Tran Hung Dao, District 5, Tel. 835-1723.

❏ **Hazard:** Corner of Hai Ba Trung and Hguyen Thi Minh Kai, District 1.

❑ **Metropolis:** 30 Nguyen Cu Street, District 1, Tel. 837-4828.

❑ **Spaceship Club:** Trung Tam Thuong Mai and Giai Tri Commercial and Entertainment Center, 34 Ton Duc Thang, District 1.

❑ **Speed:** 79 Tran Hung Dao Avenue, District 1, Tel. 821-2716.

A CITY AND COUNTRY OF SURPRISES

After a few days in Saigon, you'll most likely discover what many other visitors quickly learn about this place. This is a very energetic and entrepreneurial city. It's full of surprises for those who have the time and curiosity to explore its many treasures and pleasures. What's especially exciting about this place is its serendipitous and rapidly changing nature. On the one hand, it's Saigon, a city noted for its entrepreneurism. While it lives in the shadow and under the controlling scrutiny of Hanoi, Saigon manages to throw a great deal of sunshine on Vietnam as a whole. Vietnam may not yet be ready for "prime time," but Saigon is moving this fascinating country into what appears to be an irreversible direction of greater economic growth attendant with its increasing involvement with the global economy. Hanoi may be more charming than Saigon, but Saigon is moving Vietnam into prime time.

7

Cambodia

I F YOU'VE NEVER BEEN TO CAMBODIA, PLAN TO include it as a side trip when visiting Vietnam. It's so easy to get to, and adding a four- to seven-day extension to your Vietnam adventure is all you need to get a good sampling of Cambodia's highlights, including the incredible Angkor Wat temple complex.

Many short-term visitors to Cambodia head directly for Angkor Wat to spend a few days exploring the many temple complexes near the staging town of Siem Reap. In fact, a few international airlines now fly directly from Saigon, Bangkok, and Sukhothai to Siem Reap and thus eliminate the need to stop in Phnom Penh along the way. However, we recommend spending at least a couple of days in Phnom Penh before going on to Siem Reap. Phnom Penh's wonderful National Museum, least two days of exploration in preparation for Cambodia's major tourist attractions in Siem Reap.

GETTING TO KNOW YOU

After nearly three decades of horrendous political, economic, and social upheaval – including one of the world's worst cases of genocide (more than 1.5 million people out of a total population of 7 million exterminated by the fanatical Khmer Rouge through a combination of execution, starvation, and disease) – Cambodia has gradually come back to life. It has been a tough road to travel for a country that most outsiders seemed to want to forget. It's a country struggling to reclaim its place as one of Southeast Asia's most beautiful, peaceful, and prosperous countries. It's also a place in which tourism will increasingly play a role in the country's future development. Surprising to many visitors, its people are very friendly and spontaneous, despite the many heart-wrenching stories each has to tell about the death and destruction wrought upon them and their family and friends during the killing years of 1975-1979.

Plan to spend a couple of days in Phnom Penh before going on to Siem Reap.

DISCOVERING CAMBODIA

Any way you look at it, Cambodia is a very poor Third World country. At the same time, it's a very young, beautiful, friendly, and intriguing place that is rich in history, architecture, and culture. Everywhere you go, you see young people, which is indicative of the country's high mortality rate during the 1970s and its high birth rate during the 1980s and 1990s. While much of the country is neither easy nor comfortable to get around – rugged roads and limited accommodations – Cambodia's two major destinations are exceptions to this general rule. Phnom Penh and Siem Reap (Angkor Wat) boast world-class hotels and many good restaurants and entertainment venues.

GETTING THERE

Both Phnom Penh and Siem Reap can be easily reached by plane from Saigon and Bangkok. A few airlines fly directly to

Phnom Penh from Saigon, Bangkok, Kuala Lumpur, Singapore, Hong Kong, and Guangzhou: Royal Air Cambodge (from all six cities), Lao Aviation (from Vientiane), Vietnam Airlines (from Saigon), Thai Airways International (from Bangkok), Dragonair (from Hong Kong), Malaysian Airlines (from Kuala Lumpur), and Silk Air (from Singapore). Bangkok Airways has daily flights from Bangkok to Siem Reap. Bangkok has the best and least expensive connections to Cambodia. The international airports in Phnom Penh and Siem Reap charge a US$20 and US$10 departure tax respectively. Domestic airport departure taxes for Phnom Penh and Siem Reap are US$10 and US$4 respectively. These departure taxes are payable in U.S. dollars.

You also can reach Phnom Penh and Siem Reap by road from Vietnam and Thailand, but these can be very long and difficult trips recommended only for those who don't mind killing a lot of time on some very challenging roads. Adventuresome travelers may want to take a boat from Saigon via the Mekong River to Phnom Penh or a boat from Phnom Penh to Siem Reap via Tonle Sap Lake. Flying is really the most sensible way for most visitors to reach both Phnom Penh and Siem Reap.

WHEN TO GO

The best time to visit Cambodia is November to February. Similar to Thailand and Vietnam, these are relatively dry and mild months for travel in Cambodia. While this also is the peak tourist season, in comparison to Thailand and Vietnam, few people visit Cambodia, with the exception of Angkor Wat. Visiting Cambodia at other times of the year can be miserably hot and humid. March to May can be very hot – our least favorite time for most of mainland Southeast Asia. June to September is the rainy season, although the rains are often intermittent.

ENTRY REQUIREMENTS

A visa and valid passport are required for entry into Cambodia. You can acquire a visa upon arrival at the international airports in Phnom Penh and Siem Reap. A tourist visa costs US$20 (cash) and requires two passport-size photos. You can also acquire your visa at a Cambodian embassy or consulate prior to arrival and thus avoid waiting in line (10 to 30 minutes) at the airport to complete the visa application process. Tourist visas are good for 90 days.

GETTING AROUND

You'll find plenty of inexpensive taxis at the airports as well as in the cities to take you around. While you can rent a self-drive car, it's much more convenient to hire a car and driver to take you around. It will probably cost you the same as renting a self-drive car. For only US$25 to US$35, you can hire a car and driver for a 12-hour day. Taxi drivers will be happy to serve as your driver for the day, or you can arrange for a car and driver through your hotel or a travel agency. Less convenient, cheaper, and perhaps more charming modes of transportation are motorcycle taxis, cyclos, buses, motorcycle rentals, and bicycle rentals. Unless you have a lot of time to kill, go with the more expensive and convenient car and driver. You'll especially appreciate a car and driver when shopping.

CURRENCY AND MONEY

Cambodia's currency unit is called the Riel (R). It's available in banknotes in the following denominations: 100, 200, 500, 1,000, 5,000, and 10,000. The current exchange rate is about 4,000R to US$1. Many major hotels, restaurants, and shops state their prices and U.S. dollars and prefer U.S. dollars to the local currency. Many places will accept credit cards, but they may want to add five percent to the total in order to offset their credit card commission charges. Major banks and hotels will cash traveler's checks. Banks are usually open from 8:30am to 3:30pm, Monday through Friday and on Saturday morning. Local money changers (unofficial) may give you a better exchange rate for U.S. dollars, but it's really not necessary to exchange a great deal of money since U.S. dollars are very acceptable wherever you travel in and around Phnom Penh and Siem Reap.

❏ Phnom Penh and Siem Reap both boast world-class hotels and good restaurants.

❏ The best time to visit Cambodia are the dry and mild months of November to February.

❏ You can acquire a visa upon arrival at the international airports – passport, two photos, and US$20 cash.

❏ It's most convenient – and relatively inexpensive – to hire a car and driver to get around in Cambodia.

❏ Many places prefer U.S. dollars to the local currency, the Riel (R).

TRAVEL AND TOUR AGENCIES

While you can easily visit Phnom Penh and Siem Reap on your own, you may want to arrange for a car, driver, and guide through a tour agency. Most agencies can provide personalized services to meet your individual needs in both Phnom Penh and Siem Reap. Contact the following groups for such assistance:

❑ **Hanuman Tourism-Voyages:** No. 123, Norodom Boulevard, Sangkat Tonle Basak, Khan Chamkar Mon, Phnom Penh, Cambodia. P.O. Box 2321. Tel. (855-23) 218-396 or 218-396. Fax (855-23) 218-398 or 210-418. Email: hanu man@bigpond.com.kh. Website: hanumantourism.com. In Siem Reap, contact their local branch office: Hanumanalaya: No. 0143, Mondol 3, Khum Slokram, Siem Reap Province, Cambodia. Tel. (855-63) 380-328. Fax (855-63) 380-328. This tour agency also operates one of Cambodia's best antiques and arts shops – Hanuman Antiques and Arts (see below).

❑ **Ravy Tours:** 53A, Street 63 (Prah Trasak Phaem) Boeung Reing, Phnom Penh. Tel./Fax (855-23) 215-618 or (855-12) 904-914. Email: ravyvoyages@bigpond.com.kh.

❑ **VLK Royal Tourism:** 195Eo, Monivong Boulevard, Phnom Penh, Cambodia. Tel. (855-23) 884-999, 884-488, 723-331, 725-061; Fax (855-23) 723-168. Siem Reap Office: Tel. (855-12) 867-403; Fax (855-63) 963-556. Email: vlktravel @camnet.com.kh. Website: vlktravelcom.

❑ **Intra Co.:** 2-3, Street 118 Phnom Penh, Cambodia. Tel. (855-23) 428-596, 427-153, 360-409. Fax (855-23) 218-578. Email: intra@bigpond.com.kh.

❑ **Amary Co., Ltd.:** 305 AB, Mao Tse Toung Street, Phnom Penh, Cambodia. Tel./Fax (855-23) 216-226, 216-202. Email: amary@bigpond.com.kh.

❑ **Avia Angkor Travel Co., Ltd.:** 192Eo, Monivong Boulevard, Phnom Penh, Cambodia. Tel. (855-23) 212-567, 219-0670. Fax (855-23) 426-311. Email: avia.angkor.travel@ camnet.com.kh. Website: www.camnet.com.kh/ata.travel.

❑ **Eureka Travel:** Shop 2, 158 Sihanouk Boulevard, Lucky Complex, Phnom Penh, Cambodia. Tel. (855-12) 842-964 or (855-23) 218-938. Fax (855-23) 218-939. Email: eureka. travel@bigpond.com.kh.

❑ **World Express Tours Co., Ltd.:** 148Eo, Street 169, Phnom Penh, Cambodia. Tel. (855-23) 884-574, 884-787, or (855-12) 846-840. Fax (855-23) 884-787. Email: <u>world express@bigpond.com.kh</u>.

❑ **Transpeed Travel:** No. 19, Street 106, Phnom Penh, Cambodia. Tel. (855-12) 811-919, 811-212. Fax: 855-23) 723-999 or 722-533. Email: <u>info@transpeedholiday.com</u>. Website: <u>transpeedholiday.com</u>.

❑ **Delmex S.A.R.L. & Phoenix Tours:** No. 206Eo, Kampuchea Krom Street, Phnom Penh, Cambodia. Tel./Fax: (855-23) 426-770, 880-411. Email: <u>Delmex@camnet.com. kh</u>.

For information on 29 additional travel agents and tour operators in Cambodia, including some website and email links, check out this gateway travel site:

<u>www.canbypublications.com/miscpages/travagents.htm</u>

ONLINE INFORMATION

For useful online information relating to travel in Cambodia, with special reference to Phnom Penh and Siem Reap, visit Kenneth Cramer's very informative website:

Canby Publications   <u>www.canbypublications.com</u>

This company also publishes popular monthly visitors' guides to Phnom Penh, Siem Reap, and Sihanoukville, which are available once you arrive in each of these cities (check with your hotel front desk or concierge).

> *The Phnom Penh Visitors Guide*
> *The Siem Reap Visitors Guide*
> *The Sihanoukville Visitors Guide*

Each 30- to 40-page guide is filled with maps, ads, travel tips, and recommended hotels, restaurants, sightseeing, and entertainment.

For useful links to information on Cambodia, check out this Cambodia-related travel site:

Cambodia-Travel   <u>cambodia-travel.ws/links.htm</u>

Also explore these websites for information on Cambodia:

Cambodia Indochina   cambodia.indochina-services.com
Cambodia Travel   cambodiatravel.com
Go Cambodia   gocambodia.com/travel
Visit-Mekong   visit-mekong.com/cambodia

SAFETY AND PRECAUTIONS

Cambodia is a relatively safe place to travel to these days. The travel advisories of five or 10 years ago, when the Khmer Rouge were sometimes a threat to tourists in parts of Cambodia, are no longer relevant. Your major precautions pertain to the water (drink only bottled water), traffic (be careful crossing streets and roads or driving yourself), possible robberies (watch your valuables and don't walk around at night in Phnom Penh), and malaria (only in certain areas of the country, but not Phnom Penh or Siem Reap).

LANGUAGE AND STREET GUIDES

While English and other foreign languages are not widely spoken in Cambodia, nonetheless, you should have few problems getting around Phnom Penh and Siem Reap with English. Many people, who are disproportionately young, speak some basic English or you will quickly find someone who does. In general, the Khmer are a very friendly and hospitable people You'll find many of the charming children and young people who function as street vendors and volunteer guides speak some English and are eager for you to buy something from them or use their guide services (some will attach themselves to you with the expectation of receiving a small tip at the end of their tour). If you are sightseeing on your own, you may want to occasionally hire them as a guide. This is often their own means of income that also assists their poor families. Tip them US$1-2 for their 15- to 45-minute services.

❑ Several Internet travel sites, such as www.canbypublications.com, can help you prepare for your trip to Cambodia.

❑ Cambodia is a relatively safe place to travel to these days.

❑ Many people in Phnom Penh and Siem Reap speak some basic English or you will quickly find someone who does.

SHOPPING CAMBODIA

While Cambodia is by no means a shopper's paradise, it does offer many unique and interesting items for travel-shoppers.

Expect to find many of the following items in the street shops, markets, museums, and rehabilitation centers in Phnom Penh and Siem Reap:

❑ **Antiques:** A few shops in Phnom Penh specialize in antique furniture, Buddhas, lacquerware, silver boxes, inlaid mother of pearl boxes, betel nut boxes, lime containers, bronze bells, and numerous small collectibles. Be sure to patronize reputable shops and be especially cautious when buying antiques from market vendors. Many items that may look like antiques are actually "new antiques" – copies of the real thing. Several markets are crammed with ostensible antiques that look awfully new and should be sold as handicrafts.

❑ **Art:** Several shops near the National Museum in Phnom Penh (Street 178) offer a wide range of inexpensive paintings produced by local students from the School of Fine Arts. Most look amateurish and many paintings are simply dreadful. The best quality art can be found in a few shops at the major five-star hotels.

❑ **Textiles:** Cambodia is famous for its handwoven ikat silk textiles which are produced in numerous villages. The most famous silk weaving village is **Koh Dach**, which is located northeast of Phnom Penh along the Mekong River (take a boat). Several boutiques and vendor stalls in the markets as well as several handicraft, home decorative, and antique shops and workshops offer a good range of textiles. Many handicap, skills training, and income generating project centers have workshops and showrooms in and around both Phnom Penh and Siem Reap offer a wide range of textile products.

❑ **Silver:** The largest concentration of silver shops is found along Samdech Sothearos Road, just north of the Royal Palace, in Phnom Penh. They offer a variety of silver items, from hammered decorative animal boxes and small handbags to bracelets, plates, and jewelry. Much of this silver is sold by weight and is 70-80 percent pure silver. Market stalls within the major markets of Phnom Penh and Siem Reap also include similar silver items.

❑ **Gems and jewelry:** Cambodia mines rubies, sapphires, and emeralds in the western part of the country. Several shops, especially in Phnom Penh's Central Market and Russian Market, offer loose stones of varying quality. Since the quality and authenticity of these stones are not guaranteed, make sure you know the difference between real and fake stones as well as the quality of cuts, which may be rough. Several shops also offer a wide range of quality jewelry, from the fabulous offerings of Lotus at the Hotel Le Royale in Phnom Penh to inexpensive gold and silver jewelry in the various markets of Phnom Penh and Siem Reap.

❑ **Reproduction sculptures:** Since Cambodia is often synonymous with the stone sculptures of Angkor Wat and other ancient temple complexes, no wonder local entrepreneurs have created a thriving reproduction sculpture business. Starting with the shop near the entrance of the National Museum in Phnom Penh, you'll see many good reproductions of famous stone sculptures, with a decided preference for heads. Most are relatively inexpensive, although somewhat heavy to include in your suitcase! Don't be fooled by anyone who tries to sell you an old stone sculpture from one of the temple complexes. Chances are they are expensive reproductions. The real stuff is either in the National Museum in Phnom Penh or was long ago sold to some German, French, English, or American museum or is in a private collection or shop in Bangkok, Hong Kong, Japan, or London.

❑ **Handicrafts:** Numerous shops, rehabilitation centers, and markets brim with a wide assortment of handcrafted items. These include woven baskets, wood carvings, gongs, lacquerware, ceramics, stuffed animals, picture frames, handbags, wallets, bells, woven trays, placemats, coconut crafts, and musical instruments.

❑ **Pirated music, software, and watches:** Cambodia is a shopper's paradise for pirated music and software produced in China. Many of these items are found in the markets, especially the Russian Market in Phnom Penh where you will find numerous stalls offering thousands of pirated music CDs, DVDs, software, videos, and watches. Software that might cost US$200 for an original copy goes for as little as US$2 in these markets. Knock-off watches normally go for US$8 to US$18. Like most pirated items, the quality of such purchases is not guaranteed. In general, we found the quality of such items to be better in Cambodia than in Vietnam.

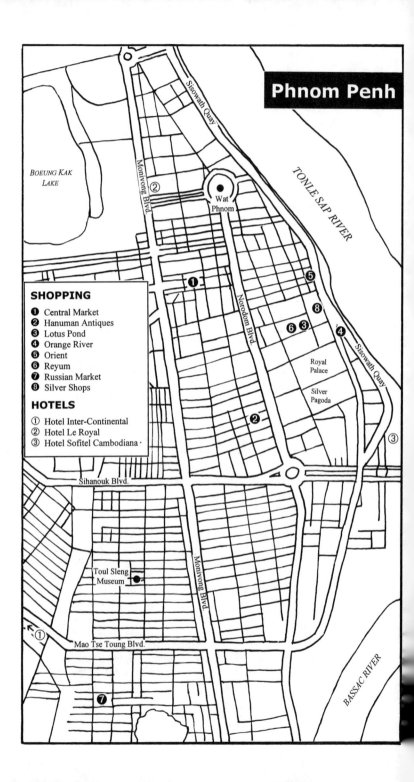

SURPRISING PHNOM PENH

There's just enough to see and do in Phnom Penh, including shopping, to justify two days in this interesting gateway city and capital of Cambodia – one day each for intense sightseeing and shopping. Three or four days would be better, especially for exploring areas outside the city. Located at the confluence of the Tonle Sap, Mekong, and Bassac rivers as well as on the southern tip of Southeast Asia's largest lake, Tonle Sap, Phnom Penh has come a long way since it was literally emptied, within 48 hours, of its 2 million inhabitants by the fanatical and brutal Khmer Rouge in April 1975. With new five-star hotels, international restaurants, discos, banks, travel agencies, and shops, Phnom Penh continues to take on the air of a newly developing city. It's a surprise to many visitors who still have an image of its difficult past. Many symbols of this city, society, and culture survived the nightmare that swept through here more than two decades ago: the National Museum, Royal Palace, and Silver Pagoda. The city also offers many shopping and dining delights.

❑ There's just enough to do in Phnom Penh to justify a two-day visit here. Three days would be even better.

❑ The international airport is a 20-minute, US$7 ride to most hotels in the city.

❑ Phnom Penh is a relatively easy city to navigate with a map and car.

❑ There's not a great deal to do in this city after seeing the major sights, except for shopping!

THE BASICS

Assuming you arrive in Phnom Penh by air, the small but modern international airport is about 20 minutes from the city center by taxi. As you leave the arrival hall, you may want to exchange some money (US$100 is plenty) at the airport bank window. But count your money carefully at the window, in front of the cashier who may have difficulty giving you the right amount of cash. Overwhelmed with so many small banknotes (Riels), you can easily walk away but later discover you were shorted a few thousand Riels, which may be intentional. Indeed, on our last trip we were shorted 12,000R (US$3) when exchanging a US$100 bill. We were not the only ones in line to experience this little problem.

You'll find an airport-controlled taxi stand, with many worn vehicles, just outside the arrival hall. A 10-kilometer ride from the airport to your hotel in the city costs a flat US$7, regardless of the number of passengers or bags.

THE CITY STREETS

While you can get around the city by bus or cyclo, we recommend taking taxis or hiring a car with driver, which is relatively inexpensive. Armed with a good map and recommended place names, you should be able to get around the city with ease by car.

You'll quickly discover that Phnom Penh is a relatively easy city to navigate. Laid out in a grid plan, with parallel and perpendicular streets, most hotels, restaurants, shops, markets,

and sights are confined to a four square-kilometer area that runs from the Tonle Sap River in east (Sisowath Quay is the main north/south street fronting on the river) to Monivong Boulevard on the west to Street 90 (just north of Wat Phnom) in the north to Mao Tse Toung Boulevard in the south. Depending on traffic and the condition of some streets, which may be torn up, you can reach most places within 10 to 20 minutes by car.

Phnom Penh is a city of cars and motorbikes. Traffic flows relatively well, except for one section along the main street running along the river, Sisowath Quay – between Streets 130 and 184.

Be prepared to encounter beggars at several sites frequented by tourists, especially near the National Museum, Royal Palace, Wat Phnom, Toul Sleng Genocide Museum, and the Russian Market. Many of the beggars, victims of land mines and missing one or more limbs, are on crutches or in wheelchairs. The men normally extend their caps for money. You'll also find many old women begging. Be forewarned that giving to one beggar will most likely result in drawing a very large crowd of other eager, and surprisingly fast moving, beggars! Our advice: carry lots of very small bills (500R and 1000R) to accommodate several people in such spontaneous crowds. Unlike beggars in many other countries, most beggars in Phnom Penh are very friendly and appreciative, but at times they can become real pests. If you really want to help such people, consider shopping at several rehabilitation and skills training centers (see below) that are organized to assist many of Cambodia's physically handicapped and economically disadvantaged peoples. You'll be supporting worthwhile causes and programs that are operated by nonprofit groups (NGOs). Indeed, shopping is one of the most worthwhile things you can do in Cambodia to help the disadvantaged!

SHOPPING PHNOM PENH

Shopping is one of the real highlights of Phnom Penh. Indeed, you'll quickly discover there is not a great deal to do in this city after seeing the major sights, which are few in number and can be quickly covered in one day.

Most of Phnom Penh's shopping is confined to two major city markets and several street shops, which are found along a few shopping streets near major sightseeing attractions. You'll find it's more convenient to combine sightseeing with shopping because of the close proximity of each. For example, if you're vis-iting the National Museum and Royal Palace, you'll want to ex-plore several of the arts and crafts shops immediately along the north side of the National Museum, along **Street 178**, and the many silver shops just north of the Royal Palace along **Sam-dech Sothearos Street**. If you are visiting Toul Sleng Genocide Museum, you'll want to head south for 12 blocks where you will come to the popular **Rus-sian Market** at the intersections of streets 450 and 155. You'll need transportation to get to these places.

When shopping in the markets and in most shops, expect to bargain. Most places will discount from 10 to 40 percent, depending on your bargaining skills. A few shops have fixed prices. Tourist shops often have inflated prices where you should drive a hard bargain. For example, we found a similar US$3 silver animal in a shop along Sothearos Street that was being sold for US$8 in a gem and jewelry store visited by many tour groups. Our rule of thumb is that if a shop looks like a tour group stop, where tour guides most likely will get commissions on their clients' purchases, try to bargain for at least a 50-per-cent discount.

MARKETS

Phnom Penh has two major covered markets worth visiting. As with most such markets, you are expected to bargain hard for everything.

❑ **Russian Market (Psah Toul Tom Poung):** *Intersection of Street 444 and Street 155 in the southern part of the city (six blocks south of Mao Tse Toung Boulevard).* This is our favorite market in Cambodia. It's dark and somewhat dumpy, but it's lots of shopping fun, a favorite shopping stop for most tourists in Phnom Penh. The market is jam-packed with small stalls offering similar types of items – silver, jewelry, loose stones, gongs, lacquer boxes, silk and cotton fabric, clothes, T-shirts, lime containers, floor mats, hats, luggage, shoes, beauty items, and ceramics from Vietnam. Several stalls offer "antiques" which look very new, although you may find a few genuine antiques among the many offerings. Some of the most popular stalls offer hundreds of Chinese-produced pirated CDs, software, and DVDs that go for US$2 each, if you bargain. You'll also find many knock-off watches. Except for the many deformed beggars that pester shoppers, this is a fun place to pick up some great bargains on cheap items. Expect to spend at least an hour browsing through the many stalls. Everything here is cash and carry.

❑ **Central Market (Psah Thmei):** *Intersection of Kampuchea Krom Boulevard (Street 128) and Street 61.* Also known as the New Market, this huge yellow art deco-style building was completed in 1937. It's the city's central market for everything from produce and household goods to clothes and handicrafts. The east side of the market, facing Street 53, is of special interest to tourists who cruise through the small stalls in search of T-shirts, handicrafts, books, maps, and postcards. Like many such markets found elsewhere, this busy and congested market is a cultural experience. You may or may not find much to buy here.

STREET SHOPS

A few streets have a high concentration of shops of interest to tourists. Two major such streets intersect near the Royal Palace and National Museum. You are well advised to just walk these two streets which also have popular restaurants nearby.

❑ **Street 178:** *Runs east to west on the north side of the National Museum.* This is primarily a one-block section, between Street 53 and Street 61, famous for its "painting galleries." In fact, you'll find about 10 art galleries and souvenir shops along this street. Done by amateur artists from the museum, many of the paintings are dreadful – colorful gaudy scenes of Angkor Wat, villages, dancers, and nudes. The galleries also include soapstone and wood carvings which aren't much better in terms of artistic merit. You'll also find several ceramics, jewelry, and handicraft shops near the art galleries. In particular, look for **Lotus Pond** (57, Street 178, Tel. 855-23-210-374) for uniquely designed silk fabric and home decorative items; **Reyum** (47, Street 178, Tel. 855-23-217-149) for a nice collection of ceramics; and **Museum Jewellery** (45, Street 178, Tel. 855-23-812-131) for silver, jewelry, loose stones, paintings; and knock-off watches.

❑ **Silver Shops of Samdech Sothearos Street:** *Runs north of the Royal Palace near the intersection of Street 178.* Here you'll find more than 10 traditional silver shops offering a wide range of similar silver products: hammered animal boxes, purses, trays, bracelets, and chains. Some shops also include ceramics, loose stones, jade, and jewelry. Very little English spoken at these shops. The initial asking prices are generally good here. Since there are so many shops selling similar items, be sure to shop around and compare prices before making any purchases. Look for the following shops: **Chhor Vy** (24Eo), **Pich Channy** (22Eo), **Kosal Rachna** (20Eo), **Te Meng Huor** (14Eo), **Angkor Thom Handicraft** (12Eo), **Kheng Peo Silver Shop** (21Eo), and **Peng-Hor** (31Eo).

HOTEL SHOPS

The major five-star hotels have a few quality shops in their lobby areas or shopping arcades. The major ones include:

❑ **Hotel Le Royal:** *Street 92 off Monivong, Phnom Penh, Cambodia. Tel. (855-23) 981-888.* In addition to the signature shop for wine and pastries, the small shopping arcade includes the Bangkok-based **Lotus** for fabulous jewelry and accessories and **Happy Cambodia Painting Gallery** for colorful paintings by French-Canadian Stephane Delapree.

❑ **Hotel Cambodiana:** *313 Sisowath Quay, Phnom Penh, Cambodia. Tel. (855-23) 426-288.* The shopping in the lobby area includes another **Happy Cambodia Painting Gallery** for paintings; **Minosa Silk Shop** for nice silk fabric, clothes, and bags; **Master Diamond Jewelry** for jewelry from Hong Kong and Bangkok; and **Champa** for very nice reproduction stone statues, lacquer, baskets, silver, and clothes.

❑ **Hotel Inter-Continental:** *296 Mao Tse Tung, Phnom Penh, Cambodia. Tel. (855-23) 424-888.* Look for **Khmer Potteries Art** for pottery and crafts; **Khmer Village** for handicrafts, silverware, silk and sculpture; and **Paloma Gallery** for paintings.

REHABILITATION AND SKILLS TRAINING CENTERS

As you will quickly see throughout Cambodia, this country has many physically handicapped, disadvantaged youth, and poor village communities. Some people are victims of land mines while others have disabilities due to diseases such as polio or HIV/AIDS. And still others have few income-generating opportunities. The government lacks the necessary resources to serve as a safety net for such people. As a result, several NGOs operate rehabilitation and skills training centers for the handicapped and underprivileged, who produce a wide range of arts, crafts, and garments. These items are sold through rehabilitation and training center workshops and showrooms. Don't expect to find great shopping at these places, although you may be surprised to find some very interesting handcrafted items that make great gifts items. For examples of what you might encounter when taking this shopping route, start by viewing online several nice handicrafts produced by villagers associated with the income-generating Song Khem ("Hope") Collection: www.songkhem. org. Above all, visit these places with the idea of contributing to some worthwhile nonprofit causes that are trying to improve the lives of many people who might otherwise be out on the streets begging. This is the type of shopping that makes lasting contributions to the lives of others. If you don't find anything to buy, you might want to leave a cash contribution in support of their efforts. Doing so will probably make you feel good about what you are doing for others.

❑ **Rehab Craft Cambodia:** *373 Sisowath Quay, Phnom Penh, Cambodia, Tel. (855-23) 880-574. Email: rec@camnet.com.kh. Website: camnet.com.kh/rehabcraft. Also has a presence in the airport departure lounge along with Apsara.* Offers T-shirts, small stuffed animals, coconut crafts (chopsticks, spoons, stirrers), key chains, shawls, picture frames, eyeglass cases, and silk purses and wallets.

❏ **Tabitha Cambodia:** *25, Road 294, Phnom Penh, Cambodia. Tel./Fax (855-23) 721-037. Email: tabitha@forum.org.kh.* Produces handicrafts.

❏ **Hagar Crafts:** *Near Wat Phnom, across from the entrance to the Sharaton Hotel, Phnom Penh, Cambodia. Tel. (855-23) 217-478 or Fax (855-23) 217-477. Email: hagar@camnet.com.kh.* Project supports disadvantaged women and children. Offers hand-woven products.

❏ **NCDP Retail Outlet:** *3, Norodom Boulevard, Phnom Penh, Cambodia. Tel. (855-23) 210-140. Email: ncdpretail@forum. org.kh.* Handcrafted items produced by the disabled.

❏ **Rajana:** *Next to the Russian Market, corner of Streets 450 and 155, Phnom Penh, Cambodia. Tel. (855-23) 364-795. Email: 012818130@mobitel.com.kh.* Offers silk paintings, drawings, silver, jewelry, cards, drawings, iron work, bamboo crafts, and hill tribe crafts produced by young people.

❏ **Seedling of Hope:** *1419 Chak Angkre Krom, Phnom Penh, Cambodia. Tel. (855-23) 216-002. Email: b_dmaher@bigpond. com.kh.* Offers quilts and blankets produced by individuals ill with HIV/AIDS.

❏ **Song Khem Collection:** *118, Street 113/330 (opposite the Toul Sleng Genocide Museum), Phnom Penh, Cambodia. Tel. (855-12) 897-469. Email: songkhem@camnet.com.kh. Website: www.songkhem.org.* Sponsored by the Girls' Brigade in Singapore, this income generating project for villagers offers a variety of arts and crafts – handwoven fabrics, greeting cards, silk bags, coconut products, wooden lampshades, signs, and picture frames. View their products online.

❏ **Wat Than:** *180, Norodom Boulevard, Phnom Penh, Cambodia. Tel. (855-23) 216-321 or Fax (855-23) 311-731.* This workshop and showroom of the Maryknoll skills training center for landmine victims and the polio-disabled offers a variety of silk handicrafts.

BEST OF THE BEST IN SHOPPING

If you have limited time in Phnom Penh, you may want to go directly to these shops, which we found to be some of the best in Cambodia:

❑ **Hanuman Antiques and Arts:** *Villa No. 34, Street 222, Khan Daun Penh, Phnom Penh, Cambodia. Tel. (855-23) 211-915 or 724-022. Fax (855-23) 211-916 or 427-865. Email: hanuman@bigpond.com.kh.* This is one of our favorite shops in all of Cambodia. It's the only real Khmer antique shop in Phnom Penh. Housed in the residence of the owner – who also operates the Hanuman Tourism-Voyages (see above) and who lost all of her family except for two daughters in the genocide of the 1970s – this tasteful shop includes two floors of top quality antiques, home decorative items, silk fabric, jewelry, and loose precious stones. The antiques and home decorative items are primarily found on the first floor, although a few of these items are also displayed on the second floor. Nicely displaced in cabinets and on shelves are old ceramics, silver boxes, Buddhas, lacquerware, bells, and betel nut boxes. While most of the antiques are from Cambodia, a few items are from Thailand and Burma, which adds nice color to what are basically very dark Khmer items. The silk shop, along with the jewelry and stones, are on the second floor.

❑ **Orient:** *245 Sisowath Quay, Phnom Penh, Cambodia. Tel. (855-23) 215-308 or Fax (855-23) 215-108. Email: orient@ bigpond.com.kh. Open 10am to 7pm; closed Sunday.* Facing the Tonle Sap River, this is a wonderful Chinese antique furniture and accessory shop, which also includes some Burmese lacquerware. Owned and operated by the family of the very talented Bangkok-based French jeweler Yves Bernardeau (Yves Joaillier in Bangkok's Charn Issara Tower), whose wife is Cambodian and whose sons mind the store, this is a real class operation. Look for two floors of beautifully restored Tibetan chests, Chinese tables and chairs, baskets, lacquerware, boxes, and other accessory pieces for home decorating and collecting. The shop will arrange shipping, which can be expensive. There's no problem in exporting these items from Cambodia.

❑ **Lotus:** *Hotel Le Royal. Street 92 off Monivong, Phnom Penh, Cambodia. Tel. (855-23) 981-888.* If you like jewelry and unique accessory pieces, get ready to drool. If you've visited Lotus shops in Bangkok, Chiang Mai, Phuket, Singapore, Bali, Lombok, Langkawi, New Delhi, or Siem Reap, you know what you can expect here – the very best in jewelry and accessory pieces. Lotus pieces are simply gorgeous and very expensive. From diamond-studded necklaces and Judith Lieberman-style handbags, Lotus is Thailand's answer to

Tiffany's and Cartier, but with a very Asian twist. This shop almost seems out of place in Phnom Penh – before its time – but the rich and famous who stay at the Hotel Le Royale will have some wonderful things to shop for at Lotus. After this shop, there's a steep drop-off in quality jewelry available in Cambodia. It's like going from Tiffany's to K-mart! For a sampling of what they offer in their many shops, visit the Lotus website (www.lotusartsdevivre.com) or email them in Bangkok: lotus@lotusartsdevivre.com. If you've never been to a Lotus shop, this is as good a time and place to get acquainted with this unique company.

❑ **Lotus Pond:** *57, Street 178 (near the National Museum and the No Problem Café). Tel. (855-23) 426-782 or Fax (855-23) 426-798. Email: lotuspond@bigpond.com.kh.* A combination home decorative, craft, antique, and furniture shop, Lotus Pond designs and produces its own silk fabrics and craft items. Look for nicely designed and excellent quality silver animals and bracelets, placemats, bedding, Buddhas, wood and stone carvings, and coconut craft items, such as spoons and forks. They also produce their own line of traditional furniture. Everything here is made in Cambodia – except the delightful manager, Khun Sompen, who is Thai! Lotus Pond was responsible for decorating the Khmer Pavillion in Germany in 2000. They also do craft training and plan to open a craft museum in the future.

❑ **Orange River:** *361, Sisowath Quay, next to FCCC. Phnom Penh, Cambodia. Tel. (855-23) 210-142, ext. 15. Email: orange @cafeasia.net.* This small, colorful, and attractive home decor and fabric shop, which faces the Tonle Sap River, is especially popular with expatriates. Owned and operated by a Canadian expatriate, it offers a nice selection of tableware, placemats, table runners, silver animals, candles, pillows, hand fans, picture frames, purses, floor mats, bedspreads, scarves, and fabrics.

❑ **Reyum:** *47, Street 178, Phnom Penh, Cambodia. Tel. (855-23) 217-149.* This popular art and crafts shop includes a nice selection of locally produced ceramics – bowls, cups, soap dishes, and small animals. Regularly hosts excellent traditional and contemporary art exhibitions.

❑ **Lucky Jewelry:** *No. 9 E. St., 188, Opposite Dusit Hotel, Phnom Penh, Cambodia. Also New Grand Market Bth., #109. Tel. (855-23) 911-629 or Fax (855-23) 722-174.* Offers a wide selection of loose precious stones (rubies, sapphires, diamonds) and jewelry as well as many handicrafts popular with tourists. Jewelry designs tend to be very traditional. Not all stones may be from Cambodia. Includes antique bronzes, carvings, jade, textiles, and souvenirs. A popular tourist shop near the Central Market. Check out the competition before bargaining in this shop – so you have a better idea of the value of what you're buying.

ACCOMMODATIONS

Phnom Penh offers a good range of hotels at both the luxury and budget ends of the spectrum. Within the past five years more and more four- and five-star properties have been built in Phnom Penh in anticipation of more business people and tourists visiting the area. Most hotels add a 10-percent VAT tax and a 10-percent service charge to your bill as well as include breakfast with their rates. For information on individual hotels, including online reservations and special discounts, visit the following websites:

▪ Asia Hotels	asia-hotels.com.hl/Cambodia.asp
▪ Asia Hotels Net	asiahotelsnet.com/cambodia
▪ Cambodiahotels.com	cambodiahotels.com
▪ Cambodiahotels.net	cambodiahotels.net
▪ Cambodia-Hotels	cambodia-hotels.com
▪ Cambodia-Hotels.net	cambodia-hotels.net
▪ Cambodia Hotels Travel Guide	cambodia-hotel-travel.com
▪ Cambodia-Travel.org	cambodia-travel.org
▪ Hotel Accommodations	hotel-accommodations.com
▪ TravelNow.com	travelnow.com

Phnom Penh's premier five-star hotel is the Hotel Le Royale, which is operated by the Singapore-based Raffles International Resort group. Two other five-star hotels also provide good accommodations:

❑ **Hotel Le Royal:** *92 Rukhak Vithei Daun Penh, Sangkat Wat Phnom, Phnom Penh, Kingdom of Cambodia, Tel. (855-23) 981-888, Fax (855-23) 981-168. Website: www.raffles-intl.com. Email: raffles.hir.ghda@bigpond.com.kh.* Originally opened in 1929, in buildings that blend Khmer art deco and French colonial architecture, Hotel Le Royal was carefully and expertly restored and refurbished by Raffles International.

The grand historic hotel, reopened in 1997, today fulfills all the requirements of a modern world-class hotel in facilities and amenities, while imparting Old World charm and a sense of history through a style and decor that is elegant, yet comfortable. Located in the heart of Phnom Penh, with easy access to the city's attractions such as the Royal Palace, Central Market, Russian Market, and National Museum, Hotel Le Royal's 208 guestrooms and suites are beautifully appointed with art deco style furnishings and Cambodian objects of art. Guestrooms are spread over three interconnecting low-rise wings set around the garden courtyard and swimming pools. Personality Suites take their direction from famous persons who have a close link with the hotel and are named after Jacqueline Kennedy, Somerset Maugham, Charles de Gaulle, and Andre Malraux. Memorabilia and original artifacts are placed in these suites. The Raffles Suite and Le Royal Suite are luxuriously appointed. Studio Suites, for longer-staying guests, are fitted with in-room stereo systems, especially designed work stations and full pantry facilities. *Le Royal*, the signature restaurant, offers traditional Khmer cuisine as well as Continental specialties. *Café Monivong* offers a Western or Asian buffet and an a la carte menu is available as well. The *Empress Room* serves Chinese and Japanese favorites. The *Conservatory, Writers Bar, Verandah, Elephant Bar,* and *Poolside Terrace* serve beverages and light snacks. Business Center; Health/Fitness Center; Sugar Palm Club for young residents ages 4-14; Conference and Banquet Facilities. This hotel also provides useful shopping tips in the form of recommended shops. It operates a recommended retailer program that includes a list of shops the hotel recommends as ones offering good quality, reasonable prices, and the highest standard of service. Ask the concierge for a copy of their "Recommended Retailer" program brochure, which includes a map that plots recommended shops offering antiques and furniture, silk, silver, jewelry, handicrafts, and ceramics.

❑ **Hotel Inter-Continental Phnom Penh:** *Regency Square, 296 Mao Tsé Toung, Phnom Penh 3, Kingdom of Cambodia, Tel. (855-23) 424-888, Fax (855-23) 424-885. Email: phnompenh @interconti.com. Website: interconti.com/cambodia/phnom_penh/ hotel_phnic.html.* A new high rise with a Khmer-styled entryway and located convenient to major sites of interest to the visitor. The 325 guestrooms and 29 suites offer amenities expected in a five-star hotel. Club Inter-Continental Floors offer additional services and amenities including complimentary continental breakfasts. *Xiang Palace* serves Cantonese cuisine; *Regency Café* features an international menu in an informal setting. The *Lobby Lounge* and *Pool Terrace Bar* offer beverages and light snacks. Business Center; Health/Fitness Facilities; Conference and Banquet Facilities.

❏ **Hotel Sofitel Cambodiana:** *313 Sisowath Quay, Phnom Penh, Kingdom of Cambodia, Tel. (855-23) 426-288, Fax (855-23) 426-392 or toll free in U.S. and Canada (800) 221-4542.* Situated overlooking the Mekong River, until recently the Sofitel Cambodiana was the only luxury hotel in Phnom Penh. The 267 guestrooms and suites along with marble baths offer the expected amenities. Some areas of the hotel now appear a bit worn and ready for refurbishment. The *Mekong* offers informal all-day dining with a full buffet spread. Dine on French cuisine at *L'Amboise* or Cantonese and Szechuan cuisine at the *Dragon Court Chinese Restaurant*. Outdoor casual dining is available at the *Riverside Pool Terrace*. Business Center; Health/Fitness Facilities; Conference and Banquet Facilities.

RESTAURANTS

Phnom Penh offers a good range of Asian and international restaurants. Some of the best restaurants are found in the major hotels as well as along the river at Sisowath Quay. For up-to-date information on restaurants in Phnom Penh, refer to Kenneth Cramer's monthly *The Phnom Penh Visitors Guide* or check out his recent online reviews of restaurants by going to: www.canbypublications.com/phnompenh/ppintro.htm.

❏ **Restaurant Le Royal:** *Hotel Le Royal, 92 Rukhak Vithei Daun Penh, Sangkat Wat Phnom, Phnom Penh, Kingdom of Cambodia, Tel. 981-888.* This is Phnom Penh's premier fine dining restaurant which also specializes in traditional Khmer cuisine. The beautifully appointed dining room, with high ceilings and sumptuous art and furnishings, provides an elegant setting for enjoying outstanding Khmer dishes. Excellent service. You'll probably want to dine here more than once.

❏ **Xiang Palace:** *Hotel Inter-Continental Phnom Penh, Regency Square, 296 Mao Tsé Toung, Phnom Penh 3, Kingdom of Cambodia, Tel. 424-888.* This Cantonese restaurant offers the finest Chinese dining in the city. Also open for dim sum lunch.

❑ **Foreign Correspondents Club of Cambodia (FCCC):** *363, Sisowath Quay, Tel. 724-014. Open 7am - midnight.* Nice ambience. Housed in a beautiful old colonial building facing the river. Serves excellent food, especially crab with peppercorns. Happy hour, 5-7pm. Popular with expatriates.

❑ **Garden Center:** *23, Street 57 (between Street 310 and 322), Tel. 363-002. Open 7am - 7pm.* This international restaurant is especially popular with expatriates. Nice garden setting.

❑ **Pon Lok:** *319-323, Sisowath Quay, Tel. 212-025. Open 10am - 10pm.* Pleasant riverfront setting for this popular Asian and Khmer restaurant. Try the crab with peppercorns and fish fried with ginger.

❑ **Topaz:** *102, Sothearos, Tel. 211-054. Open 6:30am - 2pm and 6-11pm.* Popular French and Thai restaurant.

❑ **Wilhelm Tell:** *90, Street 90 (behind the Hotel Le Royal), Tel. 430-650. Open 11am - 10:30pm.* Serves good Swiss and German dishes to a local crowd. Includes a beer garden.

❑ **Riverhouse:** *6, Street 110 (intersection with Sisowath Quay), Tel. 212-302. Open 10:30am - 11pm.* Nice riverside setting for both indoor and outdoor dining. Serves both Thai and Mediterranean dishes.

❑ **Nouveau Pho de Paris:** *26Eo, Monivong (close to Street 154). Tel. 723-076. Open 7am - midnight.* Popular Asian restaurant serving excellent Vietnamese, Chinese, and Khmer dishes.

SEEING THE SITES

Phnom Penh offers a few major sightseeing opportunities that should be on your "must see" lists of things to do. In a country still writing its post-1975 history, be forewarned that your sightseeing adventures will most likely be a mixture of pretty and not-so-pretty sights. In one long day you will get a very interesting education into the history and culture of Cambodia.

❑ **National Museum:** *Street 13, between Streets 178 and 184 and next to the Royal Palace). Entrance fee: US$2. Closed Mondays and 11am - 2pm daily. No cameras.* This is a marvelous museum housed in a grand old Khmer-style building, which was designed by the French and constructed from 1917 to 1920. It has gradually come back to life after being neglected in the 1970s and 1980s. The museum includes four major galleries along with four lovely lotus ponds at the open center courtyard. The ancient bronze drums and sandstone statues are especially impressive. While many exhibits are labeled in French and/or English, you are well advised to hire a French or English speaking guide at the entrance (US$2 an hour or US$10 for a group) to explain the many exhibits as you pass through the various rooms. However, you may find your guide does not speak very good French or English, and he or she may want to take a great deal of time going into all kinds of esoteric details about every piece in the museum! If you don't take charge of the situation and let your guide know you don't have all day for this museum, you could end up languishing here trying to listen to historical details that neither interest nor enlighten you. One hour in this museum should be sufficient to get a good overview of ancient to contemporary Khmer history. The museum gift shop at the entrance to the museum sells several inexpensive (US$15 - US$60) miniature sandstone replicas of the stone statuary viewed in the museum.

❑ **Royal Palace and the Silver Pagoda:** *Sothearos Street, between Streets 240 and 184. Entrance fee: US$3. Extras: US$3 for a camera and US$5 for a video camera. Closed 11:30am - 2pm.* You may want hire a guide (US$5) near the entrance to take you through the grounds of this fabulous place. Also, pay the camera fees, since this whole complex provides some wonderful photo opportunities. It may take you longer than you anticipate to go through this complex of buildings and grounds, but two hours should be sufficient. Consisting of two sections – the Royal Palace and the Silver Pagoda – the carefully manicured grounds as well as the colorful and exotic royal and religious buildings are simply magical. The Throne Hall is especially impressive. The royal chapel called the Silver Pagoda is an impressive temple whose floor is made up of 5,000 one-kilometer square silver tiles. It also includes several Buddha statues, including a small crystal Buddha in the center and a life-size gold Buddha inlaid with more than 9,000 precious stones. The current king (Norodom Sihanouk) still resides on these grounds, and the grounds are usually closed when he is in residence (check before you visit to make sure you can get in). As you head toward the exit, you find souvenir shops offering silver, lacquerware, ceramics, loose stones, jewelry, and clothes.

❑ **Wat Phnom:** *Street 96 and Norodom Boulevard. Entrance fee: US$1.* The temple (wat) at the top of this hill is as interesting as the view of the city from the hill. The wat was supposedly constructed in 1372, at the exact spot where Phnom Penh was founded. You'll find lots of people streaming up the hill to the wat as well as around the base of the hill. Elephant rides to nowhere are offered near the entrance to the hill. This also is a popular place for young budding artists to try their hand at painting Wat Phnom from the base of the hill.

❑ **Toul Sleng Genocide Museum:** *Intersection of Street 113 and Street 350. Entrance fee: US$2. Open daily 7-11:30am and 2-5pm.* This may be the most unforgettable experience in Cambodia. If you want a stark reminder of man's inhumanity to man, visit this sobering museum to the genocide committed by the Khmer Rouge after 1975. Eliminating more than 1.5 million Cambodians, the Khmer Rouge systematically murdered thousands of people who were first processed through this school, which was converted into a notorious prison. The museum documents the who, what, when, where, and how – complete with cells, torture rooms, photos of the condemned, and the skulls of the dead – of the genocide, which most countries neglected as they tried to forget the American War in Vietnam. This is a very sobering museum, one that elicits similar emotions to those experienced in any Jewish holocaust museum. You may or may not want to visit the famous Killing Fields next (15 kilometers southwest of Phnom Penh), a site that is linked to this prison. Most of the victims in the photo were either executed at this school or were taken to the Killing Fields where they were brutally murdered and tossed into shallow graves.

❑ **Choeung Ek Memorial (The Killing Fields):** *15 kilometers southeast of Phnom Penh.* This is another sobering site that further reinforces the genocide of the Khmer Rouge. Now a memorial to the thousands of people who were executed here and buried in mass graves by the Khmer Rouge from 1975 to 1979, the site is logical extension to any visit to Toul Sleng Genocide Museum.

ENJOYING YOUR STAY

There are many other things to see and do around Phnom Penh. If you enjoy seeing **temples**, you may want to visit several of the city's most popular pagodas: Wat Botum, Wat Langka, Wat Neak Kravorn, and Wat Ounalom.

One of the most pleasant experiences in Phnom Penh is to take a one- to two-hour lunch or dinner **river cruise**. The small cruise boats are docked just north of 178 Street and cost US$10 an hour.

Many visitors with little time to visit Cambodia's countryside opt to take the day-long **Mekong Island Tour**. It departs at 9:30am and returns at 3pm. Organized for tourists, this cultural tour includes observing village handicraft production and a show. The cost, including lunch, is US$32 per person. You can make reservations through the Hotel Sofitel Cambodiana or directly through the ticket office: 13Eo, Street 240, Tel. 841-610.

Phnom Penh's nightlife primarily consists of dining out and/or visiting bars and nightclubs. Both the **Hotel Le Royal** and **Hotel Inter-Continental** have bars with live music. Several pubs along the waterfront are popular in the evening. Popular discos and bars, such as **Heart of Darkness** (26, Street 51), **Casa Nightclub** (in Sharaton Hotel at Wat Phnom), **Manhattan Club** (Street 84, just east on Monivong), **Walkabout** (Streets 174 and 51, near Heart of Darkness), **Nexus** (36, Sihanouk), and **The Zoo** (36, Street 214), stay open until early in the morning, with some closing around 4:30am. Check with your hotel concierge on the latest hot spots or review the current and usually reliable listings for nightlife in *The Phnom Penh Visitors Guide* and at www.canbypublications.com.

SIEM REAP AND ANGKOR WAT

For many visitors, the main reason for going to Cambodia is Angkor Wat, a fabulous ancient stone Khmer temple complex located about 10 kilometers north of the small provincial town of Siem Reap. Built between the 9th and 14th centuries as the capital of the Khmer Empire, it is one of the great wonders of the world, on par with the Pyramids of Giza in Egypt, Machu Pichu in Peru, Temples of Pagan in Burma, the Aztec and Mayan ruins in Central America, and the Taj Mahal in India.

Rediscovered as a lost city in the jungles of Cambodia in 1860 by French naturalist Henri Mouhot, Angkor Wat and several other temple complexes in the surrounding area subsequently become highly valued by a combination of archeologists, historians, tour groups, travelers, art dealers, collectors, and looters. Today Angkor Wat is a showcase of crumbling elegance and arrested decay. Several sections have been lovingly

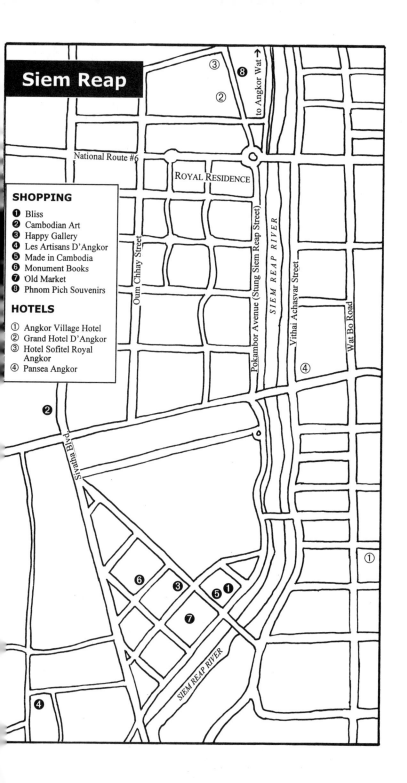

Siem Reap

SHOPPING

❶ Bliss
❷ Cambodian Art
❸ Happy Gallery
❹ Les Artisans D'Angkor
❺ Made in Cambodia
❻ Monument Books
❼ Old Market
❽ Phnom Pich Souvenirs

HOTELS

① Angkor Village Hotel
② Grand Hotel D'Angkor
③ Hotel Sofitel Royal Angkor
④ Pansea Angkor

National Route #6

ROYAL RESIDENCE

Oum Chhay Street

Pokambor Avenue (Stung Siem Reap Street)

SIEM REAP RIVER

Vithai Achasvar Street

Wat Bo Road

Sivatha Blvd.

to Angkor Wat ↑

SIEM REAP RIVER

restored while others reveal much of the natural state the ruins were found in more than 140 years ago. All of the ruins show signs of extensive looting, from decapitated statues and missing lintels to stolen Buddha heads and bas-reliefs. The looting continues even today as demand for Khmer artifacts remains high in the antique shops of Bangkok and elsewhere in the world.

THE BASICS

PLANNING YOUR TIME

One of the major challenges in planning a trip to Angkor Wat is deciding on how much time to spend there. We think three full days are plenty for seeing the major temple complexes and for enjoying Siem Reap and Toule Sap Lake. This is a place for sightseeing and enjoying the pool – and for some basic shopping, which will probably take no more than two hours to complete. There's not a great deal to do at night other than relax from a long hot day of temple hopping. The sightseeing is spread out over a much larger area than what most visitors initially anticipate. Spending less than three days in Siem Reap is really pushing your trip here, although two full and exhausting days will give you a good overview of the ancient city and temple complexes. And more than three days may become excessively redundant and boring – unless you are a real ancient temple and cultural enthusiast who wants to explore a lot more ruins, rocks, and cultural shows than most visitors.

> *Angkor Wat is a showcase of crumbling elegance and arrested decay.*

GETTING THERE

Getting to Angkor Wat is relatively easy. The nearby town of Siem Reap is regularly serviced by both international and domestic airlines. The short flight from Phnom Penh via three carriers (President Airlines, Royal Air Cambodge, and Phnom Penh Airways) takes between 30 to 45 minutes. You can also reach Siem Reap by a rough road. The nearly 300-kilometer road trip will take seven to 10 hours. Alternatively, you can take a five- to seven-hour ferry boat trip from Phnom Penh to Siem Reap via Tonle Sap Lake.

SETTLING IN AND GETTING AROUND

Once you arrive in Siem Reap, you'll be in a relatively small but very sprawling city. Situated along both sides of the Siem Reap River, this is a very laid back and quiet town noted for its old market and numerous small restaurants and hotels catering to the growing tourist trade. Within the past three years the town has acquired several new luxury hotels and resorts (Grand Hotel D'Angkor, Hotel Sofitel Royal Angkor, and Pansea Angkor) that are quickly transforming the image of this area from essentially a backpacker's paradise and adventure traveler's destination to one appealing to all classes and tastes of travelers. Indeed, you'll often find yourself touring the temple complexes and shopping in the old market shoulder to shoulder with a combination of $400 and $5 a day travelers who arrive by air-conditioned tour buses, taxis, motorbikes, and bicycles. Siem Reap is definitely going upscale with its emphasis on attracting more and more upscale travelers who enjoy the finer things in travel life. Even the new entrance fees to the temple complexes (US$20 to US$60 for a one- to seven-day pass) reflect this new emphasis.

Given the spread-out nature of Siem Reap and the many nearby temple complexes, you are well advised to rent a car and driver to tour the area. Many visitors opt for renting a motorbike, which is fine for touring Siem Reap and Angkor Wat in good weather conditions, but a car and driver is really nice for touring the larger area, especially in attempting the torturous one-hour road trip to the popular temple complex at Banteay Srei, which is only 25 kilometers northeast of Angkor Wat. You can easily rent a car and driver for US$25 to US$35 a day through your hotel or a local travel agency. However, you may also need to hire an English-speaking guide since many drivers do not speak English. If you want a guide to explain Bantaey Srei, you must take him with you. It is not possible to hire one at the complex. We had excellent service from a driver who also spoke basic English and thus eliminated the need to also hire a guide: Pich Samol (Charb Meas Association, Phom Watbo, Khum Sala Komroek, Siem Reap, Tel. 855-12- 836-501 or Fax 855-63-964-323). Some visitors opt for renting a bicycle, which is a charming way of getting around the streets of Siem Reap. But it can be a long and hot peddle to Angkor Wat and beyond!

The following travel agencies can assist you with local transportation and tour services. Many of them function as branch offices of travel agencies headquartered in Phnom Penh, although a few, such as Diethelm, have head offices in Siem Reap and branch offices in Phnom Penh. In fact, you can make all arrangements for Siem Reap and Angkor Wat through most travel agencies in Phnom Penh. Once in Siem Reap, check out these travel agencies for assistance with transportation and tours:

❑ **Hanumanalaya:** No. 0143, Mondol 3, Khum Slokram, Siem Reap, Cambodia. Tel. (855-63) 380-328. Fax (855-63) 380-328. Email: hanuman@bigpond.com.kh. Website: hanu mantourism.com. This is the branch office of Hanuman (see above) in Phnom Penh.

❑ **Neak Krorkorm Travel & Tours:** No. 003, Old Market, Siam Reap, Cambodia. Tel. (855-12) 890-156 or Fax (855-63) 964-805. Email: nktours@cmintel.com.

❑ **Apsara Tours Co., Ltd.:** No. 081, opposite the Siem Reap Hospital, Siem Reap, Cambodia. Tel. (855-63) 380-198 or Fax (855-63) 963-992. Email: apsaratours-rep@camnet. com.kh. Head office in Phnom Penh.

❑ **Diethelm Travel:** House No. 4, Route No. 5, Siem Reap, Cambodia. Tel. (855-63) 963-524 or Fax (855-63) 963-6694. Email: diethelmsr@bigpond.com.kh. Branch office in Phnom Penh.

❑ **Apex Cambodia Travel Service:** No. 18, Route No. 6, Siem Reap, Cambodia. Tel. (855-63) 963-994 or Fax (855-63) 963-994. Head office in Phnom Penh.

❑ **Asian Trails:** No. 273, Route No. 6, Siem Reap, Cambodia. Tel. (855-63) 964-595 or Fax (855-63) 964-591. Email: asiantrails@bigpond.com.kh. Head office in Phnom Penh.

RESOURCES ON SIEM REAP

History and cultural buffs will find a great deal written on Angkor Wat. However, travelers often find few resources – other than some budget travel guides which go into excruciating details on the esoteric history of each temple – that provide useful information on Siem Reap and the surrounding area. One of the best resources is Kenneth Cramer's no-nonsense monthly guide to Siem Reap: *The Siem Reap Visitors Guide*. Much of the print information can be found on the Siem Reap section of his useful website:

Canby Publications   www.canbypublications.com

SHOPPING IN AND AROUND SIEM REAP

You can easily shop Siem Reap within a couple of hours. One of your first stops should be the **Old Market** in downtown Siem Reap. This is actually a relatively new market, built six years ago. Located along the west bank of the Siem Reap River in the center of town with cafes, restaurants, bars, travel agencies, and other shops nearby, this covered market encompasses two blocks separated by a street. The market is filled with lots of handicraft and souvenir shops as well as includes a separate jewelry section, which has over 30 jewelry stalls. The handicraft shops offer the standard range of handcrafted items – fabrics, carvings, jewelry, silver boxes, bags, placemats, ceramics, T-shirts, clothes, and accessories. Similar to other markets, be sure to bargain for everything here, with discounts running from 10 to 50 percent. You'll also find a CD shop on the left side of the market. It offers a good range of pirated music, video, and software CDs, although prices here are about 25 to 50 percent higher here than in Phnom Penh's Russian Market (what goes for US$2.00 in the Russian Market sells for US$2.50 to US$3.00 here). Most shops gladly take, actually prefer, US dollars. This area closes around 9pm.

For upscale shopping, visit a few of the hotel shops at Siem Reap's two major five-star hotels and resorts – Grand Hotel D'Angkor and Hotel Sofitel Royal Angkor. **Lotus** (see Phnom Penh), for example, has a small shop at the swank Grand Hotel D'Angkor.

A few other shops worth visiting within Siem Reap include **Bliss** (24, Pokambor Street, near the Old Market) for beaded and embroidered cushions and accessories, Eurasian clothing, silks, and exotic housewares; **Happy Gallery** (near the Old Market) for paintings by Stephane Delapree; **Angkor Souvenir** (Tel. 015-637-364) and **Cambodia Art** (Tel. 885-63-964-902) – both near the Grand Hotel along Sivatha Boulevard – and **Phnom Pich Souvenirs** (near both the Grand Hotel D'Angkor and Hotel Sofitel Royal Angkor, Tel. 885-63-380-303) for arts and crafts.

Similar to Phnom Penh, you'll also find a few handicapped

production centers, which have workshops and showrooms. One of the major such places is on the right-hand side of the road on the way to Banteay Srei – the Canadian sponsored **Santeay Srei Souvenir Shop**. It includes a large selection of handcrafted carvings, clothes, fabrics, woven trays, placemats, coconut crafts, paintings, instruments, silver, and replicas of artifacts from Angkor Wat. The building to the right is part of the **Cambodian Handicraft Association**, which assists victims of land mines and polio. Its 10 resident disabled workers produce colorful handbags, fabrics, and jewelry cases which are for sale in this combination workshop/showroom. **Made in Cambodia**, which includes both Hagar Crafts and Rehab Craft Cambodia (see Phnom Penh), is a handicraft shop opposite the Old Market (Tel. 855-63-964-374), which offers handwoven silk, leather, coconut, and wood products.

Other workshops and training centers worth visiting include **Les Artisan D'Angkor – Chantiers Ecoles** (just off Sivatha, southwest of the Old Market, Tel. 885-63-964-097, Fax 855-63-380-187, Email: artcefp@rep.forum.org.kh) for a nice selection of wood and stone carvings, lacquerware, furniture, and silk textiles, handbags, and accessories; **Les Artisans D'Angkor Silk Worm Breeding Center** (Route 6, 15 kilometers west of Siem Reap) for silk weaving and products for sale; and **House of Peace** (at Wat Preah Ann Kowsay) for handcrafted leather shadow puppets.

When visiting the various temple complexes, you will encounter numerous **vendor stalls** offering a wide range of over-priced souvenirs, from T-shirts and pirated CDs (the US$3 video on Angkor Wat is great!) to musical instruments and miniature replicas of temple figures. The most popular purchases at these stalls are cold drinks, which are often a welcomed sight after a long hot walk to another temple. Be sure to bargain for everything, including the canned soft drinks and bottled water. Expect to get 20 to 50 percent discounts when bargaining in these highly touristed vendor stalls.

ACCOMMODATIONS

Siem Reap offers a large selection of inexpensive guesthouses and hotels for budget travelers that range in cost from US$4 to US$25 a night. You'll also find a few two- and three-star hotels that cost from US$30 to US$60 a night. Accommodations in these places tend to be very basic. While Siem Reap has very few four-star hotels, it has recently acquired several five-star hotels and resorts. These properties offer wonderful amenities for those who are looking for the best of the best and don't mind paying US$150 a night or more. Siem Reap's best properties include the following:

❑ **Grand Hotel D'Angkor:** *1 Vithei Charles de Gaulle, Khum Svay Dang Kum, Siem Reap, Kingdom of Cambodia, Tel. (855-63) 963-888, Fax (855-63) 963-168. Email: grand@bigpond. com.kh. Website: www.raffles.com.* Grand Hotel d'Angkor was first opened in 1932 and provided accommodation for travelers visiting the Angkor temple complex. Restored and refurbished to luxury standard by Raffles International, it reopened in 1997. The renovated main building is complemented by new wings of the same architectural design. Today the Grand Hotel d'Angkor welcomes guests with all the amenities of a luxury hotel. Located on the edge of town, 8 kilometers from the gateway to Angkor, each of the hotel's 131 guestrooms and suites are decorated with art deco country style furnishings and Cambodian objects of art. Bathrooms feature a separate shower cubicle. Though the facilities are grand, at full occupancy the public areas can feel a bit crowded. Dine on traditional Khmer cuisine or contemporary Continental cuisine at *Le Grand.* In the casual atmosphere of *Café d'Angkor* experience local Khmer or international favorites. For special occasions, the *Performance House*, an outdoor venue adjacent to the hotel, offers Khmer buffets and barbecues together with Cambodian cultural performances. The *Conservatory, Poolside Terrace, Elephant Bar,* and *Travellers' Bar* offer beverages and light snacks. Business Center; Health/Fitness Facilities; Sugar Palm Club for residents ages 4-14; Meeting Facilities for small groups.

❑ **Hotel Sofitel Royal Angkor:** *Vithei Charles de Gaulle, Khum Svay Dang Kum, Siem Reap, Kingdom of Cambodia, Tel. (855-63) 964-600, Fax (855-63) 964-610.* Opened in late 2000, the five-star Sofitel Royal Angkor is the nearest hotel (by a slight margin) to the historic Angkor Wat complex. Convenient to traditional markets and local areas of interest, set amidst landscaped gardens and around a large free-form swimming pool, the Royal Angkor is really a resort hotel. As a result of the spacious grounds and buildings, guests never feel cramped around the pool or in any of the public areas. The 239 spacious and stylishly appointed guest rooms, including 20 suites, with an elegant combination of French and Khmer style, are equipped with expected amenities. Not all the restaurants were open at the time of our visit in early 2001, but they should be up and running by the time you visit. Enjoy contemporary Western and Asian cuisine in a traditional Khmer atmosphere in *The Citidel*. At *Leaf on the Stone*, a Japanese Teppenyaki bar watch your meal freshly cooked in front of your eyes. *Mouhot's Dream* offers a fusion cuisine of Oriental and Western flavors served in a French art deco setting. *Wayfarer's* and *Explorer's Tales* offer beverages and light snacks. Business Center; Health/Fitness Center; Conference and Banquet Facilities.

❑ **Pansea Angkor:** *River Road, Siem Reap, Kingdom of Cambodia. Tel. (855-63) 963-390 or Fax (855-630) 963-391. Website: www.pansea.com/wat.html. Email: angkor@pansea.com.* This is Siem Reap's newest five-star property, which opened in September 2001. Located on the river in the center of town, this Khmer-style boutique hotel includes 55 rooms which are furnished in bamboo, wood, stone, and cotton. Includes king-sized or twin beds, large en-suite bathroom with free-form bath and shower, air-conditioning, IDD, satellite television, mini bar, safe, swimming pool, restaurant, and bar. Restaurant serves contemporary Mediterranean cuisine and selected Asian dishes. Includes two boutiques in lobby.

For a relatively comprehensive listing of accommodations in Siem Reap, visit Kenneth Cramer's website:

www.canbypublications.com/siemreap/srhotels.htm

Use the same online reservation systems previously identified for Cambodia and Phnom Penh for booking hotels in Siem Reap. Most of these reservation systems primarily include the very top four- and five-star hotels, and they often include special online discounts.

RESTAURANTS

Siem Reap has numerous small and inexpensive restaurants, cafes, and bars that primarily cater to budget travelers. Many of these places are found near the Old Market. Some of best and safest dining will be found in the major hotels. Among the many places to dine in Siem Reap are:

❑ **The Citidel:** *Hotel Sofitel Royal Angkor, Vithei Charles de Gaulle, Khum Svay Dang Kum, Siem Reap. Tel. 964-600. Open 6:30am - 10pm.* This is our favorite restaurant in Siem Reap. Serves excellent buffet breakfasts, lunches, and dinners. The dinner buffet is a real extravaganza with a wide range of international cuisines, including local dishes.

❑ **Restaurant Le Grand:** *Grand Hotel d'Angkor, 1 Vithei Charles de Gaulle, Khum Svay Dang Kum, Siem Reap. Tel. 963-888. Open for dinner only: 6:30-10:30pm.* This small but well appointed fine dining restaurant serves traditional Khmer cuisine. During high season you need to be a hotel guest in order to dine here.

❑ **Lotus Restaurant:** *Opposite the Old Market. Tel. 964-381. Open 7am - 10pm.* Serves excellent Western food at reasonable prices. Both indoor and outdoor dining.

❑ **Sampheap:** *On east side of river, across from the Royal Residence. Tel. 015-635-619. Open for lunch and dinner.* Offers an expansive menu of Khmer, Chinese, and Continental dishes. Popular with both tourists and locals.

❑ **Bayon:** *98, Wat Bo Road. Tel. 012-855-219. Open 6am - 9:30pm.* This popular restaurant serves good local dishes.

❑ **Chao Praya:** *64, Angkor Wat Street. Tel. 964-666.* Offers buffet-style dining with a wide choice of cuisines: European, Chinese, Thai, Japanese, Mongolian BBQ, and seafood.

❑ **La Noria:** *East side of river, across the river from the Grand Hotel d'Angkor. Tel. 964-242. Open 6am - 10pm.* Nice riverfront setting for this pleasant Khmer and French restaurant.

❑ **Sawasdee:** *25, Wat Bo Road, just north of Route 5. Tel. 380-199. Open 11am - 10pm.* The nice garden setting is the stage for excellent Thai dishes. One of several popular Thai restaurants in Siem Reap.

❑ **Lucky Café:** *Near the Old Market on Pokambor Avneue. Tel. 012-857-526. Open 7:30am - 10pm.* Popular for its good pizzas and sandwiches. Indoor and outdoor dining along a busy street.

SEEING THE TEMPLE SITES

While there is more to Siem Reap than just the many temples north of town, temples are what most visitors come to see in Siem Reap and what you'll always remember as the great highlight of visiting Cambodia. The main temple complex, starting with the impressive Angkor Wat and Angkor Thom, is about 10 kilometers north of the city. As you arrive at the ticket gates (essentially non-functioning toll booths), you need to decide how many days you plan to visit this huge temple complex. Tickets can be purchased as follows:

1 day	US$20.00
3 days	US$40.00 (plus two passport-size photos)
7 days	US$60.00 (plus two passport-size photos)

If you only plan to visit for two days, which is plenty for most visitors, purchase the daily US$20.00 ticket, which does not require the photos. But if you are really into the history and culture of this area and want to visit everywhere, you are probably better off with a seven-day ticket, although chances are you will quit temple trekking after the fourth day. Once you purchase your ticket, be sure to hold onto it. You'll need to show it as an admission pass to numerous sites.

Be sure to wear a good pair of walking shoes, sunglasses, and a hat or cap for doing a great deal of walking on sunny days. Also, take lots of film with you since this whole area is a photographer's paradise. You may want to take some bottled water, although there are plenty of vendor stands along the way that have an ample supply of drinks for overcoming any signs of dehydration. However, drinks along the way tend to be expensive if you pay the asking price. Indeed, those US$1.00 cans of Coca Cola should only cost $.50 – but only if you bargain with the vendors. Like everything else you might buy along this well-traveled tourist trail, bargain, bargain, bargain. You'll meet many kids along the way who will want to sell you something or become your personal guide. Most are delightful little entrepreneurs while a few may become pests.

Angkor Wat really consists of several temple complexes of which Angkor Wat is only one, albeit the most impressive and best restored. If you need a guidebook and/or map on this temple complex, you may want to visit **Monument Books** (502, Khum Svay Dong Kum, Tel. 012-882-034), which is located at the Old Market. They have a good selection of guides and maps to the temples. If you need an English-speaking guide, check with your hotel, contact a travel agency, or visit the **Khmer Angkor Tour Guide Association** at the Tourist Office (Tel. 964-347), which is located across the street from the Grand Hotel D'Angkor. Guides usually cost from US$20 to US$25 a day.

Your temple options are numerous. The following are "must see" temples that can easily take a full day to visit:

- Angkor Wat
- Angkor Thom (includes The Bayon)
- Phnom Bakheng

If your first day at these three temple complexes whets your appetite for visiting more temples, consider going to several additional sites on the second day. However, depending on how much time you spend in each place, several of these sites also could be visited on your first day since they are within one- to three-kilometers of each other:

- Banteay Kdei
- Baphuon
- East Mebon
- Neak Pean
- Preah Khan
- Pre Rup
- Ta Keo
- Ta Prohm
- Ta Som
- Thommanon

On a third day, you may want to take a trip beyond the immediate temple complex. One of the finest examples of classical Khmer art is **Banteay Srei**. A surprisingly small but very intricate temple complex, it's the highlight temple for many visitors who make the arduous 25-kilometer trip from Angkor Wat to Banteay Srei. The road is terrible – pot holes, ruts, rocks, dust, and slow construction work. It may take two or more hours to travel what initially appears to be such a short distance – at least until the road improvements are completed. Welcome to the countryside where transportation is often a real challenge!

Other Things to See and Do

In addition to visiting the area's many temples, you may want to consider doing some of the following things while in the Siem Reap area:

❏ **Tonle Sap Lake and Fishing Villages:** *15 kilometers south of Siem Reap.* This is one of the best kept sightseeing secrets in the area. For US$5 per person, you can enjoy a 1½ hour cruise through a fascinating river and lake culture of house and fishing boats. It's a very educational trip as you observe daily life on the water, from children swimming and women washing clothes to families living on houseboats, fishing, and conducting commerce on the water. Many of the fishermen are Vietnamese. You'll see many large boats coming in from Tonle Sap Lake to unload and pick up cargo. Take loads of film since this trip is a great place to get photos of daily Cambodian life along the water.

❑ **Helicopter Tours:** For a panoramic view of the many stone temples and structures in this area, take a helicopter tour. It's available through **Helicopters Cambodia Ltd.**, which is located at No. 105 in front of the Provincial Hospital: Tel. (855-15) 839-565. Email: <u>Helicopter.cam@bigpopnid.com.</u> <u>kh</u>. Their head office is in Phnom Penh: 10, Street 310, Phnom Penh, Cambodia. Tel./Fax (855-16) 814-254.

❑ **Cultural Shows:** Several hotels and restaurants offer evening cultural shows, which you can elect to see with or without dinner. Most of these colorful shows include traditional music and dance and shadow puppets. Most shows start between 7 and 8pm but may be canceled if too few people sign up. Be sure to make reservations well in advance and check before you go to make sure the show is still going. The two most popular shows, which are held in lovely settings, include:

■ **Grand Hotel D'Angkor:** Tel. 963-888. Held alongside the river at the hotel's outdoor Performance Hall.

■ **Apsara Theatre:** Tel. 963-561. Held in the beautiful wood pavilion across the street from the lovely Angkor Village Hotel.

Two other cultural shows include a classical dance show at the **Koulen Restaurant** (Tel. 964-324) and a shadow puppet show at the **Na Noria Hotel** (Tel. 964-242) on Wednesday evenings.

❑ **Nightlife:** In addition to dining and attending a cultural show, Siem Reap has a few bars and discos for late night entertainment. Depending on your age and inclination, you may or may not want to carouse around town at night visiting these nightspots. Many of them have loud music, cheap beer, and taxi-dancers. For something more sophisticated, the piano bars at both the Grand Hotel D'Angkor (**The Conservatory**) and the Hotel Sofitel Royal Angkor (**Explorer's Tales**) are delightful places to relax after a long day of temple hopping. Also check out the Grand's **Celebrity Bar** and **Travellers Bar** and the Sofitel's **Wayfarer's** English pub-style bar. Keep in mind that the Old Market, which has several restaurants, cafes, and bars nearby, stays open until 9pm, just in case shopping for souvenirs, dining, and drinking appeal to you. Popular bars and nightclubs, which usually open around 7pm and draw the budget crowd, include:

- **Zanzy Bar:** Sivatha Boulevard, opposite the Bakheng Night Club.

- **Bakheng Night Club:** Sivatha Boulevard. Disco with taxi-dancers.

- **Liquid:** 293-294, Pokambar Avenue near the Old Market.

- **The Ankor What?** Near old market.

- **Vimean Akas:** East side of the river near the bridge. Live disco music and taxi-dancers.

Index

HANOI

HOI AN AND CENTRAL VIETNAM

SAIGON

CAMBODIA

The Authors

WINSTON CHURCHILL PUT IT BEST – *"My needs are very simple – I simply want the best of everything."* Indeed, his attitude on life is well and alive amongst many of today's travelers. With limited time, careful budgeting, and a sense of adventure, many people seek both quality and value as they search for the best of the best.

Ron and Caryl Krannich, Ph.Ds, discovered this fact of travel life 18 years ago when they were living and working in Thailand as consultants with the Office of the Prime Minister. Former university professors and specialists on Southeast Asia, they discovered what they really loved to do – shop for quality arts, antiques, and home decorative items – was not well represented in most travel guides that primarily focused on sightseeing, hotels, and restaurants. While some guidebooks included a small section on shopping, they only listed types of products and names and addresses of a few shops, many of questionable quality. And budget guides simply avoided quality shopping altogether, as if shopping was a travel sin!

The Krannichs knew there was much more to travel than what was represented in most travel guides. Avid collectors of Asian, South Pacific, Middle Eastern, and Latin American arts, antiques, and home decorative items, they learned long ago that one of the best ways to experience another culture and meet its talented artists and craftspeople was by shopping for local products. Not only would they learn a great deal about the culture and society, they also acquired some wonderful products, met many interesting and talented individuals, and helped support the continuing development of local arts and crafts.

But they quickly learned shopping in many countries was very different from shopping in North America and Europe. In the West, merchants nicely display items, identify prices, and periodically run sales. At the same time, shoppers in the West can easily do comparative shopping, watch for sales, and trust quality and delivery; they even have consumer protection! Americans and Europeans in other parts of the world face a shopping culture based on different principles. Like a fish out of water, they make many mistakes: don't know how to bargain, avoid purchasing large items because they don't understand shipping, and are frequent victims of scams and rip-offs, especially in the case of gems and jewelry. To shop a country right, travelers need to know how to find quality products, bargain for the best prices, avoid scams, and ship their purchases with ease. What they most need is a combination travel and how-to book that focuses on the best of the best.

In 1987 the Krannichs inaugurated their first shopping guide to Asia – *Shopping in Exotic Places* – a guide to quality shopping in Hong Kong, South Korea, Thailand, Indonesia, and Singapore. Receiving rave reviews from leading travel publications and professionals, the book quickly found an enthusiastic audience amongst other avid travel-shoppers. It broke new ground as a combination travel and how-to book. No longer would shopping be confined to just naming products and identifying names and addresses of shops. It also included advice on how to pack for a shopping trip (take two suitcases, one filled with bubble-wrap), comparative shopping, bargaining skills, and shopping rules. Shopping was serious stuff requiring serious treatment of the subject by individuals who understood what they were doing. The Krannichs subsequently expanded the series to include separate volumes on Hong Kong, Thailand, Indonesia, Singapore and Malaysia, Australia and Papua New Guinea, the South Pacific, and the Caribbean.

Beginning in 1996, the series took on a new look as well as an expanded focus. Known as the Impact Guides and appropriately titled *The Treasures and Pleasures of . . . Best of the Best*, new editions covered Hong Kong, Thailand, Indonesia, Singapore, Malaysia, Paris and the French Riviera, and the Caribbean. In 1997 and 1999 new volumes appeared on Italy,

Hong Kong, and China. New volumes for 2000 and 2001 covered India, Australia, Thailand, Hong Kong, Singapore and Bali, Egypt, and, Rio and São Paulo.

The Impact Guides now serve as the major content for the new travel-shopping website appropriately called *i*ShopAround TheWorld:

www.ishoparoundtheworld.com

While the primary focus remains shopping for quality products, the books and website also include useful information on the best hotels, restaurants, and sightseeing. As the authors note, *"Our users are discerning travelers who seek the best of the best. They are looking for a very special travel experience which is not well represented in other travel guides."*

The Krannichs passion for traveling and shopping is well represented in their home which is uniquely designed around their Asian, South Pacific, Middle East, North African, and Latin American art collections and which has been featured on CNN and in the *New York Times*. *"We're fortunate in being able to create a living environment which pulls together so many wonderful travel memories and quality products,"* say the Krannichs. *"We learned long ago to seek out quality products and buy the best we could afford at the time. Quality lasts and is appreciated for years to come. Many of our readers share our passion for quality shopping abroad."* Their books also are popular with designers, antique dealers, and importers who use them to source products and suppliers.

While the Impact Guides keep the Krannichs busy traveling to exotic places, their travel series is an avocation rather than a vocation. The Krannichs also are noted authors of more than 35 career books (see page vi), some of which deal with how to find international and travel jobs. The Krannichs also operate one of the world's largest career resource centers. Their works are available in most bookstores or through the publisher's online bookstore: www.impactpublications.com.

If you have any questions or comments for the authors, please direct them to the publisher:

Ron and Caryl Krannich
IMPACT PUBLICATIONS
9104 Manassas Drive, Suite N
Manassas Park, VA 20111-5211 USA
Fax 703-335-9486
Email: krannich@impactpublications.com

Feedback and
Recommendations

WE WELCOME FEEDBACK AND RECOMMEN-
dations from our readers and users. If you have
encountered a particular shop or travel experience, either good or bad, that you feel should be
included in future editions of this book or on
www.ishoparoundtheworld.com, please send your comments by
email, fax, or mail to:

Ron and Caryl Krannich
IMPACT PUBLICATIONS
9104 Manassas Drive, Suite N
Manassas Park, VA 20111-5211 USA
Fax 703-335-9486
Email: krannich@impactpublications.com

_____

_____

_____

_____

_____

_____

_____

_____

More Treasures
and Pleasures

THE FOLLOWING TRAVEL GUIDES CAN BE OR-dered directly from the publisher. Complete the following form (or list the titles), include your name and address, enclose payment, and send your order to:

IMPACT PUBLICATIONS
9104 Manassas Drive, Suite N
Manassas Park, VA 20111-5211 (USA)
Tel. 1-800-361-1055 (orders only)
703-361-7300 (information) Fax 703-335-9486
Email: info@impactpublications.com
Online bookstores: www.impactpublications.com or
www.ishoparoundtheworld.com

All prices are in U.S. dollars. Orders from individuals should be prepaid by check, moneyorder, or credit card (Visa, Master-Card, American Express, and Discover). We accept credit card orders by telephone, fax, email, and online. If your order must be shipped outside the United States, please include an additional US$1.50 per title for surface mail or the appropriate air mail rate for books weighting 24 ounces each. Orders usually ship within 48 hours. For more information on the authors, travel resources, and international shopping, visit www.impact publications.com and www.ishoparoundtheworld.com.

Qty.	TITLES	Price	TOTAL
__	Air Traveler's Survival Guide	$14.95	_____
__	The Traveling Woman	$14.95	_____
__	Travel Planning on the Internet	$19.95	_____
__	Treasures and Pleasures of Australia	$17.95	_____
__	Treasures and Pleasures of the Caribbean	$16.95	_____
__	Treasures and Pleasures of China	$14.95	_____
__	Treasures and Pleasures of Egypt	$16.95	_____
__	Treasures and Pleasures of Hong Kong	$16.95	_____
__	Treasures and Pleasures of India	$16.95	_____

__ Treasures and Pleasures of Indonesia	$14.95	_____
__ Treasures and Pleasures of Italy	$14.95	_____
__ Treasures and Pleasures of Mexico	$16.95	_____
__ Treasures and Pleasures of Morocco	$16.95	_____
__ Treasures and Pleasures of Paris		
and the French Riviera	$14.95	_____
__ Treasures and Pleasures of the Philippines	$16.95	_____
__ Treasures and Pleasures of Rio/São Paulo	$13.95	_____
__ Treasures and Pleasures of Singapore/Bali	$16.95	_____
__ Treasures and Pleasures of Southern Africa	$16.95	_____
__ Treasures and Pleasures of Thailand	$16.95	_____
__ Treasures and Pleasures of Turkey	$16.95	_____
__ Treasures and Pleasures of Vietnam	$16.95	_____

SUBTOTAL ------------- $ _____

■ Virginia residents add 4.5% sales tax $ _____

■ Shipping/handling ($5.00 for the first
   title and $2.00 for each additional book) $ _____

■ Additional amount if shipping outside U.S. $ _____

TOTAL ENCLOSED ---------- $ _____

SHIP TO:

Name _____

Address _____

_____

_____

Phone Number: _____

PAYMENT METHOD:

❑ I enclose check/moneyorder for $ _____
   made payable to IMPACT PUBLICATIONS.

❑ Please charge $ _____ to my credit card:

❑ Visa ❑ MasterCard ❑ American Express ❑ Discover

Card # _____

Expiration date: _____/_____

Signature _____